KEEPERS
OF THE
WISDOM

KAREN CASEY is the author of several popular Hazelden meditation books, including *Each Day a New Beginning, The Promise of a New Day* (with Martha Vanceburg), *A Woman's Spirit, A Life of My Own*, and *Daily Meditations for Practicing the Course.*

KEEPERS OF THE WISDOM

*Reflections from
Lives Well Lived*

KAREN CASEY

HAZELDEN®

Hazelden
Center City, Minnesota 55012-0176
1-800-328-9000 (Toll Free U.S., Canada, and the Virgin Islands)
1-651-213-4000 (Outside the U.S. and Canada)
http://www.hazelden.org (World Wide Web site on Internet)

16 15 14   10 9 8 7 6 5

Library of Congress Cataloging-In-Publication Data
Casey, Karen.
    Keepers of the wisdom : reflections from lives well lived /
Karen Casey.
        p.   cm.
    Includes index.
    ISBN-13: 978-1-56838-117-6   ISBN-10: 1-56838-117-4
    1. Meditations.   2. Devotional calendars.   I. Title.
BI.624.2.C37   1996
158'.12—dc20   96-24023
                                                      CIP

Book design by Will H. Powers
Cover design by Johanna Winters
Typesetting by Stanton Publication Services, Inc.

Editor's note
Hazelden Educational Materials offers a variety of information on
chemical dependency and related areas. Our publications do not
necessarily represent Hazelden's programs, nor do they officially
speak for any Twelve Step organization.

DEDICATION

Patrick Butler was a spiritual mentor to me and thousands of people, mostly men and women who had never even met him. Because of his personal efforts on behalf of alcoholics and other addicts over many decades, tens of thousands of men and women embarked on a spiritual journey that changed their lives forever. He was far too humble to readily acknowledge this, but it's the truth, nonetheless.

Pat was a St. Paul, Minnesota, husband, father, and businessman. He was also the son and brother of alcoholics. His own recovery from alcoholism in 1951 didn't come easy, but he did recover and he realized the value of "time out" in a sober setting. When that particular setting just north of St. Paul hit hard times financially, Pat, along with his family, undertook the task of getting it fiscally sound. He was soon committing his own fortune to the Hazelden Foundation, and it has been a strong force ever since. That was nearly fifty years ago. Thousands of individuals owe their lives to Pat and his family.

My own evolution as a recovering woman and writer is owing in great part to Pat's inspiration. He showed so many of us the joy of living, thinking, laughing, and daring to take on new challenges. Even in his late eighties, he still made the trip to Hazelden every week from his home nearly forty-five mile away. He always had time for a chat with a patient, an employee or a visitor to the institution that fulfilled his mission on behal of the suffering alcoholic.

When I began interviewing people for *Keepers of the Wisdon* I realized that perhaps the wisest individual I'd ever known ha already passed on. His memory was always with me as I spok with others, which is why I have dedicated this book to him. Pa was my model for the truly gifted, passionate soul. He had a awesome appreciation for the many details of life. His vitalit and spirit surely still live.

ACKNOWLEDGMENTS

It's not easy to convey the inspiration, hope, love, and knowledge of the people I interviewed for this book. They revealed how life really works when taken a bit at a time. Because of my debt of gratitude to all of them, I publicly thank them now for opening their homes, their hearts, their very lives to us.

Jim and **Marie Burns**, thank you for your ever-so-gentle spirits. As you so eloquently said, Jim, life is about giving and receiving only love. You two embody that to the fullest. To **Edith Huey Bartholomew** and husband, **Harry**, thanks for bringing your energy for life, for art, for nature, and for one another into our world. **Janice Clark**, we were overwhelmed by your many talents as writer, painter, sculptor, and community organizer, and your enthusiasm for all of them. You still found time to tell great stories and laugh a lot. **Alpha English**, Joe and I felt as though we had been touched by an angel during our visit with you. Your gentle way, the depth of your humility, your inspired vision about life and its many possibilities have changed the future for everyone who has ever encountered you. We thank you for all of them and for ourselves, too. **Tom Harding**, the photograph you gave us hangs in my Minneapolis study. Joe and I won't soon forget your wonderful hideaway, where you pass the hours in serious contemplation and work. **Monty Cralley**, you can't imagine how many times you come to our minds. We fondly remember the trip to your lovely cabin, the warmth with which you told us your story, the love that emanated each time you mentioned *Ann*. The book you gave me has been turned to many times. The picture you let us choose has been framed and hung on our dining room wall.

Alice Merryman, how grateful I am that I kept ringing your phone. Your talent at the easel and your dexterity in caning and dollmaking are a testament to the rewards of growing old. You prove that it can be the best time of one's life.

Eva Wines, how fortunate that your art teacher never tried to change your natural talent, and how fortunate for the rest of us that you turned to painting as a way to increase the joy in your life as the years moved along. **Maria Regnier Krimmel**, it wasn't only your beautiful silver work and your luscious flower gardens that amazed us, but your culinary talents also. All those people who think that living beyond ninety quells the spirit should have the good fortune to meet you!

Violet Hensley, your fiddling was such a treat, including the affectionate "tap" on the head you gave each of us with the bow as you played and danced around the kitchen. Perhaps by now you have passed on the art of carving fiddles to one of your grandkids. **Dana Steward**, your wonderful book, *A Fine Age*, began this entire process for my husband and me. As I've said more than once, our lives have been changed forever. That you opened the door for us to a group of wonderful men and women has meant far more than my words can express. Somehow, I know you know exactly what I mean. **Helen Casey**, I know that you have been a role model for other men and women for many years. Your undying desire to try something new shows others that life is not over until it's over! What an inspiration you are.

Clara Glenn, even though you have passed on now, I suspect your spirit is peeking over my shoulder. You were a feminist probably before the word was defined. Your passion for being in the world of ideas showed other women another path to travel. All of us pay homage to you. **Abby** and **Sandy Warman**, how tenderly you both travel life's path, symbolizing what love and respect can initiate in a marriage. The care with which you nurture yourselves shows others the rewards that can come from thoughtful contemplation. **Fran Coyne**, I remember our interview well. You were my first "interviewee." I really didn't know then where this idea would take me, but what a fascinating ride it has been. Because you were so inspiring about the wonderful possibilities that await one in old age, I vowed to continue my research. Thank you for jump-starting the process.

Jim and **Ruth Casey**, I am grateful that we shared so many hours of loving conversation. The wisdom I gleaned is woven throughout this book. You each represent the rewards of an inquiring mind. (Jim, I don't doubt for a minute that you are still present in my life, though only in spirit. I think of you often.) **Louise** and **Pat Jerome**, you are surely no ordinary couple. You are eager to experience the new and to tell others about it. Your obvious friendship with each other teaches everyone who meets you what couplehood can be.

Bud and **Beverly Sherman**, I thank you for opening your hearts and sharing some of the pain that can accompany changing life circumstances. We aren't always ready for the changes when they come, but you model well what people can do when they dare to move on anyway. **Catherine Paul**, what a treat to interview you as a successfully retired woman, my aunt, and a role model for all people who want to move through retirement with style and aplomb. **JoAnn Reed**, I thank you as a sister for demonstrating that the aging process does not have to slow us down. That you have mastered the computer, begun to write children's books, and taught yourself to crochet and play golf in these last few years proves that life is always full of possibility. **Thelma Elliott**, who would ever have thought when I was causing you all kinds of grief while growing up, that I'd one day make you a part of a book I authored? Having you for a mother has helped me grow in so many ways, and watching you take on new challenges into your eighties has inspired me to try new pursuits regardless of my inexperience. I can't adequately express how lucky I feel that you're my mother.

Joe Casey, thank you for being my "way shower" on this path of creative pursuits. You never fail to see the possible in any situation. You are undaunted by challenges that would have stopped the ordinary person. With patience, great interest, undiminished emotional support, and a sense of humor that helped to change my perspective when the need was there, you have walked me through another book, just as you are walking me through an exciting life. Having you as a partner makes every endeavor I pursue seem achieveable.

There are many other people to thank as well. Their names will no doubt be recognizable to you throughout these pages. I culled many books and articles for their wisdom about living and dying, about passion and pity, about hope and fear. I have tried to pass on to you what they taught me about taking each day and making it count.

Had my father lived long enough to see me through this book, I'd have gathered his wisdom, too. He had much of it to share. I'm sure he'd have begun by saying that nothing is worth doing if it's not done to the best of one's ability. That's how he lived his life. That's what he tried to teach me, too. It has taken me a long time to wear his advice well, but this book is a testament to what I have learned.

INTRODUCTION

Researching and writing this book significantly changed my life — as a maturing woman, writer, wife, friend, daughter, sister, aunt, and step-mother. Every area of my life has been influenced by the people I met as I researched it.

I am a fifty-seven-year-old woman, but I was greatly interested in the lives of men and women twenty or thirty or more years older than myself. I knew I wanted to grow old with the same passion, vitality, and spirit that some whom I'd observed over the years apparently had. My husband, Joe, suggested that the best way to find out how to do what they had done was to ask them their "secrets." Thus my journey began.

I chose to interview men and women from many parts of the country, people who had filled many roles and done myriad kinds of work in their lives. Since my husband had been forced into early retirement because of a health challenge, he participated in my journey to seek the knowledge and wisdom that ultimately surfaces here. What a wonderful experience gathering this information was for us. We'd never attempted to truly share one another's hobbies and interests before. Writing has been my interest for many years. His has been building cars and radio-controlled planes, furniture, and cabins. We've always appreciated one another's talents, but we hadn't "crossed over" until this project. What a surprise was in store for us.

Being in the company of so many excellent souls who willingly shared their most personal opinions and observations on life, made Joe and I feel privileged. The interviews were extremely intimate. They felt like holy encounters, in fact. Each person we interviewed was full of love and the desire to share with future readers, like yourself, the recollections that brought joy and meaning to his or her life. All of these men and women wanted to be heard by others. They all wanted to do their part to make someone else's journey more rewarding. And from everyone came the message that having a purpose beyond one's self promised a daily reward which made getting up each day worth it. No man or woman seemed to feel that the purpose had to be extraordinary, but it had to have at its core some greater good, something beyond one's selfish desire. Dozens of people can't be wrong.

KEEPERS
OF THE
WISDOM

JANUARY

JANUARY 1

Life is not what you did.
It's what you are doing.

JIM BURNS

Today awaits our attention and involvement. We can sit and merely ponder the possibilities for action, thinking away the entire day. We could get involved in a volunteer effort; we always said we would when time allowed. We could reorganize the basement, the kitchen, the garage. Our lives allow for spontaneous pursuits now. Or we can keep our focus small, taking each hour as it comes and reaching out to at least one other person in every sixty-minute span of time, doing nothing major, simply expressing our aliveness.

Maybe it's a phone call that keeps us connected to the human community. Or perhaps it's writing a long overdue letter. Offering a hello and a smile to a neighbor or a fellow shopper quite specifically strengthens our connection to the human community. It's not what we do that's so important. Rather, it's making at least one human contact with another living soul that will benefit all of our lives today.

Being too busy to let others know
how much they matter to me isn't a problem any longer.
Every day offers me opportunities to connect with others.

JANUARY 2

I always have something I'm thinking about
right in front of me. That way my life stays interesting.

JAMES CASEY

Jim's situation was a bit more complicated than life may be for many of us. His ability to get around was limited because of serious health problems; however, what was true for him is still true for all of us. We need active minds. We will maintain our interest in life if we stay engaged in the world of events external to us. We have to make the effort to do this. Those of us who are lucky don't consider it much effort at all. We relish being involved with ideas and other people, but some of us may have to cultivate this process.

Some days we may wake up feeling depressed because of the circumstances of our lives. That's not unusual. Much has changed for us in the last few years. Our careers are likely over; many of our friends have died. We may have lost our spouses, too. Many days feel pretty lonely. We need things to think about besides our conditions. It's good to remember that many people are far worse off than we are. Let's not be glad about that but rather grateful that we are as comfortable as we are.

If life looks bleak today, make the decision to try something new. Perhaps a young person in the neighborhood lacks an adult role model. Might you seek him or her out? The neighbor next door seems to attract bad luck. Possibly you could extend a helping hand. There's so much to think about, really. Let's not underestimate our remaining value to others.

Today is the first day of the rest of my life. I have heard that thousands of times, but I'll take it to heart today.

JANUARY 3

The freedom from responsibility
is what I appreciate most now. I never had enough time.

RUTH CASEY

Most of us share Ruth's complaint about the past. Whether because of our jobs or the children or other family members who relied on us, we seldom had enough time to do justice to everyone else's needs, let alone our own. Of course, our own needs generally got ignored. Now we can address them fully, but do we even know how?

It takes practice to limit our focus to just ourselves, doesn't it? Possibly this is even more difficult for women than men because of how we were raised. Women were taught to be caregivers. We don't give up that role easily. For many of us, it was how we defined ourselves; it was where all of our good feelings came from.

Getting used to the idea that we don't need to do for others except by choice can be considered the next phase of our education. It may take concerted study, in fact. Many of us came by caretaking so naturally that stopping it feels disrespectful and irresponsible, but let's be willing to explore all the things we can do besides care for others. The process will allow us to see the real gift of freedom that now belongs to us. We have earned this.

I can spend today doing only what I choose to do.
I will appreciate this. I've earned it.

JANUARY 4

You know that if you live long enough
you will have to deal with these years of retirement.

Some people look forward to retirement. They put off many dreams until that long-awaited time. We all know some who died all too early after retirement and whose dreams went unrealized. We can't be certain the same won't happen to us, but we can control how we will spend the important days that do remain. Wasting even one is folly.

Many of us think of travel when retirement rolls around. Perhaps that's because vacations from our jobs always felt too short or even stressful because we knew what awaited us upon our return. Travel can begin to feel like work, too, if we have a steady diet of it.

There is no right way to handle retirement, but getting involved in some activity with others is a good beginning. Problems can easily result from being too narrowly focused, particularly on ourselves. Taking notice of others, especially considering ways we might ease their lives, quite mystically eases our own. How does this work? we wonder. Perhaps all that matters is that it does.

> My day will be as full and exciting as I make it.
> Connecting with others will bring me pleasure.
> I may brighten their day, too.

JANUARY 5

*It took me quite a while
to rethink my daily patterns in different terms.*

DON KENNETT

None of us knew what our lives would actually be like after retirement. We envisioned trips, long naps, time for hobbies, and freedom from stress. We knew we might get bored or feel lonely part of the time, but most of us pushed the fear away. Now that we've arrived, how is it? It's surprisingly different than most of us imagined.

Some who dreaded retirement have never been happier. Perhaps they have been more successful at turning over their direction, their plans for each day, to their inner voices. Others who couldn't wait for the freedom to play and travel may have hit unexpected snags. Health failed them or death claimed a loved one who they had planned to "play" with.

It goes without saying that no day will unfold just as we might have imagined. It is our good fortune, however, to have the wisdom to know that only those opportunities that we can handle will come to us. A lifetime of experiences have taught us this. We haven't always had an easy time, but we are here.

I may have a schedule for how I want today to unfold.
I will be at peace if some other plan emerges.

JANUARY 6

Retirement is a good time to explore
those things about yourself that you don't know yet.

LOUISE JEROME

This idea might seem foolish to some. Surely at our age there are no surprises. But on the contrary, many of us have been so busy with our occupations, families, and community activities that we have given little thought to our interior spaces. What a wonderful opportunity we now have to inventory who we really are, what we like about ourselves, what we'd like to change, what we'd like to accomplish in the next few years, what legacy we'd like to leave behind.

Perhaps not everyone is eager to pursue the introspection that is suggested here. Maybe we haven't commonly shared our inner fears or thoughts or feelings with others or even looked carefully at them ourselves. If that's the case, it's not unusual for this exercise to be unsettling. A slight change in perspective is all that's needed, however. We can gain this by a little willingness to seek the help of God.

The upside of this exploration is that we can more meaningfully and intentionally experience the remainder of our lives. That's an exciting opportunity. Who knows what we might discover about our real selves?

I am much more than I may appear to be.
I'll savor this idea today.

JANUARY 7

Age is opportunity no less
Than youth itself, though in another dress.

HENRY WADSWORTH LONGFELLOW

Our definition of opportunity reveals, quite subtly, our attitude about life. Thomas Edison, for example, saw every "failed" attempt to perfect the incandescent light as drawing him closer to the real thing. Every experiment was a profitable opportunity for more knowledge. We, no doubt, have friends who laugh off mistakes, no matter their gravity, sure that their achievements lie just around the corner. Every moment is viewed as an opportunity for learning and advancement. It's a mind-set. No more and no less.

Perhaps we haven't all *lived* our errors this easily. Our past behavior does not have to determine our present perceptions, however. Only we control how and what we think. Maybe in our youth we were easily led by our peers. Or domineering parents or bosses scared us into accepting ideas that didn't fit us. But it's never too late to formulate our own opinions or follow whichever opportunities appeal to us the most.

I have no better opportunity than now
for making a change in how I think and what I do.
The past is not the present.

JANUARY 8

When you take a walk, are your ears open?
Are your eyes open?

JANICE CLARK

One of the gifts of getting older is that we are not so busy any-more. We have the time to read that stack of books on the desk. We can organize the family album; the pictures have been accu-mulating for years. Perhaps we can offer to help a neighbor who is not as agile as we still are. And most important, we can finally take time to smell the flowers. For years we said we were going to slow down. Now we can.

In our youth, we probably didn't appreciate the beauty of nature. We were too busy running through it. We may even need a little practice to become adept at absorbing the smells and sounds and sights of nature. But what a pleasant undertaking.

The glory of the living world around us convinces us, per-haps like nothing else, that a Supreme Presence has had a hand in it. Noticing this work of art can make each of us feel special, too. As the saying goes, "God doesn't make junk." The treasures are everywhere.

Having the time to really notice
my world is a blessing of old age.
Today, I'll try to see something I've never seen before.

JANUARY 9

I'm too active to sit still.
Sometimes I wake up at five A.M.

HOPE SHOAF

One day a neighbor shared that the older he got, the earlier he got up. He didn't want to run out of time before doing all he still longed to do. Being excited to arise every morning is a blessing; however, it's also a feeling that can be cultivated if we don't naturally enjoy it. Appreciating the many good things in our lives is a beginning.

Perhaps we've had more than our share of hardships, or so it seems. That makes it hard to feel grateful. But we're surrounded by men and women who have suffered far more than we have. We sometimes need that reminder to improve our perspective.

No doubt we've all heard that we are never given more than we can handle. Additionally, our experiences are defined by the growth we deserve. In the midst of chaos, we're not always relieved even when we remember this, but it's true. Our opportunities for giving to others aren't over. We're still here, after all.

Waking up joyfully isn't so hard
once I put my mind to it.

JANUARY 10

Doing nothing, that hurts you.

JOHN ARNOLD

Doing nothing as a steady diet would wear thin after a while, but doing nothing once in a while is good therapy. We need to let our minds and bodies rest. Being always booked for an activity gives us too little time for reflection about our lives. We have come a long way. Taking the time to appreciate that during our quiet spaces will enhance our self-perception.

Not a one of us has had an unsuccessful life. We may not have accomplished every goal we've set for ourselves, but we can believe that we did what really needed to be done by us. There has been a divine plan at work even though we were unaware of it. The same continues to be true. We will be nudged to pursue hobbies or volunteer activities or even part-time jobs if that's the plan for us. This certainly takes the guesswork out of our lives. It makes us know we are pretty special, too.

I'll do whatever calls to me today.
As long as it's not something that will hurt
another person, it will be right.

JANUARY 11

We are so saturated with everything—money and luxuries—
that we have lost sight of the real essential things
that make for a full, happy life.

JEAN WILL

We have many friends who worked years of long hours to acquire things to make them happy. Quite likely we followed their lead. And to be sure, buying cars and clothes, houses and furniture, cameras, and tennis racquets did give us brief moments of happiness. But they failed to sustain us for long, so the next shopping spree periodically beckoned.

Are the passing decades changing us? It's certainly okay to enjoy the pleasure of nice clothes, a car that runs well, a cheery home, but we are learning that greater happiness comes from good health, the company of loving friends, and having meaningful activities in our lives. And we have the wisdom to pursue these, now. Some might say we always did; however, we were easily blinded by our material desires. They still may glimmer, but years of experience reveal their emptiness.

Simple pleasures sustain me now:
hearing the voice of a friend;
reading a quiet, loving passage in a book;
reaching out to someone who is in need.
Today is full of opportunity.

JANUARY 12

My philosophy is "simplicity in everything."

MARIA REGNIER KRIMMEL

The idea of simplicity is akin to a rainbow. Simplicity has many hues, and most people have a specific understanding of what it means to them. It's really not necessary to have a definition that satisfies everybody, but it's important to decide the value the idea has had in one's life. To Maria it meant living an "uncluttered" life; not collecting either friends or things that couldn't be attended to frequently.

To some, simplicity has meant voicing few viewpoints, collecting few possessions, and nurturing few dreams about the future. To others, simplicity was seeking the solution to any situation from one's inner messenger, not complicating potential outcomes by involving too many other voices. Probably everyone would agree that simplicity implied sticking with what was known when making a decision and waiting for the future to unfold in its own time.

As we age, we may value simplicity even more. We have tired of our many decisions; we have felt encumbered by our many possessions. Our too-busy social lives have left us drained. There's no shame in wanting to slow down. We've earned the right to step back, to simply say no, if that's our wish.

I'll take stock of how I really want to spend this day.
I can keep it as simple and quiet as fits my mood.

JANUARY 13

*Hugging and kissing and all that kind of stuff is just
not always true love. Actions speak louder than words.
You show love by everything that you do.*

VIOLET HENSLEY

Many believe there are only two emotions, love and fear, and
that any action one takes that is not loving is really a cry for love,
a cry that's born in fear. Looking at our experiences, particularly
our relationships, bears this out. How fortunate that we still
have the opportunity to act lovingly rather than fearfully every
minute of the day.

None of us appreciates a hug or kiss from a "well-wisher"
who we know is insincere. Therefore, let's be vigilant regarding
our own acts of kindness. Are we simply performing, hoping to
manipulate a situation? Or do we honestly feel the love and
kindness we have expressed? Many might say that "acting as if
we love" is the next best thing to really feeling it. However,
discovering and honoring our oneness with all others is a better
step to feeling sincere love, and that's our goal, after all.

**I have no better time than right now
to explore my willingness to love. If I'm not willing,
where is my fear coming from today?**

JANUARY 14

Example is the lesson that all men can read.

GILBERT WEST

Patterning our lives after others is familiar. Maybe as kids we emulated "toughies" or the teacher's pet. As we grew, the criteria changed, but we sought role models, nonetheless. The career we chose and the family relationships we developed may have been inspired by the example of another. Today may be no different. Seeing our friends and acquaintances pursue paths unlike our own gives us ideas to explore. How lucky we are that teaching is never done and learning is merely a decision.

The only thing that has actually changed is our age. The opportunities for growth continue to flow. Our purpose for being here remains the same. Our responsibility to ourselves never abates. It's comforting to count on these things. It makes our choices simpler.

There's always the right step to take, the right response to make, the right attitude to foster. But if ever we're in doubt, the impulse to forgive and to love will never be wrong.

**My action today may be an important example for a friend.
I pray to choose my steps and words wisely.**

JANUARY 15

A fine old age can never be taken for granted.
It represents perpetual victories
and perpetual recoveries from defeat.

ANDRE GIDE

Our lives are a series of failures and successes. We hope we have had more of the latter. However, our failures may have proven to be our best lessons in life, and isn't that, finally, success?

We really aren't the best at judging what's good or bad in our lives. Our vision is really short-sighted and definitely ego-centered. Perhaps someone else's success, in the moment, depends on our failures. Does that really mean we have failed? On the contrary. Hindsight is generally required before we can fairly assess any experience. It's human nature to want to make an immediate judgment, but those judgments are seldom accurate.

Our histories consist of innumerable experiences that were given to us by design. Some felt good and others caused us pain. Going on with our daily lives, in the face of all experiences, constitutes ultimate victory, and we have all managed that.

I am guaranteed a victory today.
My attitude is in charge.

JANUARY 16

*As you grow old, try to grow kinder
and more broad-minded and more generous.*

ALPHA ENGLISH

As we age, our athletic ability declines. Our memory fails us more often. We tire more quickly, too. And developing the enthusiasm to explore uncharted territories requires more effort than when we were young. However, in spite of these admitted shortcomings of old age, we are never too tired or too forgetful or too bored to be kind to our friends and fellow travelers. Indeed, this is one area that we can show marked improvement in as we advance in years.

Knowing that we can get better at some things is exciting. The good news is that we can practice these attributes as often as we want. Every encounter with another person gives us the chance we need to be kind. Being more open-minded to the opinions of others is also a decision. And maybe we can't be more generous financially, but we can always be more generous in spirit. That's of even greater value to the well-being of the human family. Growing old *is* growing better. We can see that now.

**I will have many opportunities to hone my skills today.
Each person I encounter will be the better for it.**

JANUARY 17

I just see a need, and I try to fill it.
I see a problem, and I try to solve it.

J. M. SPICER

Being alert to the world around us is a learned response. Fortunately, we are never too old or too young to acquire and then practice this art. But what's the point in being alert, some might wonder, particularly when we're on in years?

Assuredly, nothing says we have to contribute, to pay our dues, every day of our lives. However, the less involved we allow ourselves to be in the events surrounding us, the fewer reasons we'll have for getting up each morning. In the final analysis, being involved with others, regardless of our level of activity, keeps us thinking and that keeps us alive.

We've survived into "old age" not by accident. Good diets helped. So did healthy exercise. But even more important, perhaps, was our zest for living. And that we can still muster if we put our minds to it.

I will willingly help a friend today, if asked.
Giving loving attention to someone else is an easy way
to stay alert and alive.

JANUARY 18

The difficult task may take a while to accomplish;
the impossible one will take a little longer.

ANONYMOUS

Is nothing beyond our capabilities? Most of us would say, no. However, none of us knows that for certain. Just maybe we *can* do whatever is our heart's desire. Perhaps all we lack now or have ever lacked are the inclination, the perseverance, and the faith to proceed. It's a small enough challenge if we're willing to take a bit of a risk.

We have all met women and men who are pursuing activities we envy them for. We see them taking up bridge or volunteering at a nursery school, taping books for the blind or answering phones at a crisis center. Do they possess something we lack? Or are they simply more willing to explore the unknown?

Let's follow their example. We really have nothing to lose. In fact, hindsight may illustrate that they were in our very lives at this time intentionally, as our teachers. Tomorrow may offer us the chance to be teachers, too.

Commitment and perseverance
will lead me to new accomplishments.

JANUARY 19

Sometimes two minuses make a plus.

EDITH SHANNON

What appears to be a problem sometimes turns out to be a most beneficial circumstance. We live only in the present, and it generally takes the perspective of hindsight to get the full meaning of an event. Over the years, we have learned that some of our best lessons actually caused us pain while we were in their clutches. What a relief to be able to see, now, that they had their silver lining. This principle still holds true.

We have had a lot of years to learn to take our experiences in stride, giving them no more weight than they deserve. But it's easy to forget that it's the accumulation of them all that defines who we are. The lost jobs, the friends who left, the hurdles in a marriage all played their part in the people we've become today. We are who we need to be right now.

> I can't let a setback set me back today.
> Whether I'm sixty or seventy or eighty,
> I am evolving right on schedule.

JANUARY 20

I'm developing every day,
always working toward the next plane.

MONTY CRALLEY

Age is limiting only if we decide so. Monty Cralley, at eighty-eight and mostly blind from macular degeneration, still paints, still writes, still gardens, and best of all, still praises God for every day of life. Knowing that we grow and change and contribute to lives around us, regardless of our age, is a gift of insight. It's one that's available to all of us. However, not everyone claims it, thus we all get a bit cheated.

How many years of days have we awakened with fear rather than rejoicing that another day has beckoned. It's not unusual to feel fear. For many it's perhaps more familiar than peace or happiness. Understanding where fear comes from may help to dispel it. Some would say our sense of separateness from others is what creates fear. That's an acceptable explanation. And it's no more than a change in perception to begin seeing us as one, as united, rather than separate. Feeling our connection dispels our fear. The truth is so simple.

I am never too old to explore new ideas.
My associations with others will have new meaning today.
I am one with everyone.

JANUARY 21

*I think a person ought to live every day
as if it's going to be their last and plan as
if they were going to live forever.*

HELEN MORGAN

We really don't know how long we might live. The life span of our parents and grandparents might be an indicator, barring freak accidents of nature. But even that is no guarantee. Our best plan is to make every minute of every day count. How we do that varies, of course, but living in the moment is a good place to begin. Stopping to smell the flowers or listening to the chatter of squirrels takes on added meaning when considered in this context.

How can we claim the richness of only the present and still be prepared for the possibilities of the future? It seems contradictory. But thinking ahead in specific ways, like buying groceries for a special birthday dinner the day before, saves us from the anxiety of last-minute rushing. Making out a will to specify how our assets will be divided is being responsible. It doesn't mean we are missing out on what this day offers.

Common sense can be our best guide in how we travel through the hours of any day. This approach will give us gifts we hadn't planned on. That's the real fun of life.

I am only sure of right now. I will live wisely.

JANUARY 22

*I feel at this age I can go overboard
and be as ridiculous as I want.*

MIRIAM HOFMEIER

A real blessing of growing old is the freedom it gives us to be who we really are. Of course, we could have been our real selves our whole lives. No doubt some of us were. However, far too many of us struggled to impress others with the person we thought we ought to be, and in the process, we lost a lot of real living. Fortunately, it's never too late to project the real us.

Do we know for certain who we really are? Age is no guarantee that we do. Living through others is not so uncommon, unfortunately, and if that describes us, then we still have the task of discovering who we really are. But let's think of it as an adventure rather than a task. It's a journey, one that promises to be full of surprises.

We have earned the right to speak our minds. We have earned the right to whatever beliefs appeal to us. Most particularly, we have earned the right to spend our days fulfilling whatever dreams we want. We're lucky. Living this long has its rewards.

**Being as silly as I want to be today feels good.
I have it coming!**

JANUARY 23

I don't feel old. I have aches and pains,
but I still feel like I'm in high school.

JOANN REED

How old a person feels is a matter of attitude. Oftentimes, it's an attitude that was instilled by parents. If they grew old quite joyfully, they probably imparted a cheerful spirit to their children. If they hated the passage of time, they likely fostered resistance in their children. In any circle of acquaintances, a few will be far more enthusiastic and young at heart than others. Which ones do you gravitate toward? Do you impart an attitude that attracts others?

Feeling young can mean many things. Perhaps it means physical fitness to some. Maybe it means the cultivation of new ideas. Having no fear of new circumstances, being willing to take risks is more common among the young. Are we like that too? Staying young can mean nothing more than continuing to be involved in our communities. We don't have to do anything really but be present and alert.

There is another consideration, though. Must we continue feeling young although growing old? There isn't a right answer. What's best is that we feel however we want. Some days we may want to wallow in our oldness, claiming that we can't handle a certain task. And that's one of the blessings of old age, whether we feel young or not. We need to do only what appeals to us.

How I face today is up to me.
I can be excited and involved or reclusive.

JANUARY 24

*The thing that bothers me most about aging
is the lack of energy. I used to have so much.*

HELEN CASEY

No matter our age, none of us has as much energy as in our youth. It's the negative attention we give that fact that makes it an issue in our lives. We've earned the right to take frequent naps, to slow our pace, to say no when invited to join in an activity that doesn't appeal to us. Perhaps we haven't considered this a gift, but it is. Age has finally accorded us the freedom to do only what we really want to do. This means we can conserve our energy and use it to please ourselves.

Remaining active is important, however. Perhaps we can't move around as easily as before, but we can keep our minds stimulated, and we can define active however we want. While our bodies may grow old, our minds can keep working. Thinking new thoughts and sharing new ideas with others is life-enhancing. Exercising the mind, at this age, is at least as important as exercising the body was in our youth. We'll never be too old to flex this muscle.

I'll seek out a good conversation today.
If no one is handy, I'll read a book and look up
all the words I'm not familiar with.

JANUARY 25

All my yesterdays run together.

CLARA GLENN

Age doesn't demand that our memories become fuzzy, but they commonly are. We often fret over this. We could, instead, make light of it and simply appreciate that we worked our memories overtime for many years. There is no requirement that we have long memories anymore. Our age gives us this freedom.

There are some plusses to having the past run together in our minds. For one, it prevents past tragedies from gaining too much focus. Also, we are able to see how really insignificant many of our trials were. That's a good reminder that our current worries will barely be remembered, even a month from now.

Only today deserves our attention; this gives us an easier set of circumstances to handle. Being caught in the past can hinder our present decisions. The past may offer something to inform our present, but *this moment* is unique, not like the past at all.

> My past is over. My future is irrelevant.
> My present is all that matters.
> And it is designed especially for me.

JANUARY 26

You really need to take care of yourself because you won't be
good for anyone else unless you take care of yourself.

HARRY BARTHOLOMEW

Do we merely assume we are taking good care of ourselves? It's perhaps a good idea to list all the ways we think this is true. Do we get enough exercise? What is enough, anyway? Are we eating the right foods and enough of them? How about rest? Do we take naps when needed, as well as get a good night's sleep? What about laughter? Some would say there's no better elixir than a good laugh. Of course, we have to be willing to laugh at ourselves, on occasion, to make the most of it.

Taking good care of ourselves is much more in our control than we might have imagined. While it's true that some of us need a devoted caregiver because of our infirmities, we are able to laugh at will and to eat what's good for us. We are also very much in control of how we feel about the circumstances of our lives. Whether we think we have it good or bad has a great deal to do with the details of each day.

We're not much fun to be around if all we do is moan and whine. Neither response ever takes good care of us. And both of them hinder the day's experiences for our companions, too.

The best thing I can do for me today is smile at my life,
my friends, my remaining dreams.
I can show I care.

JANUARY 27

When they take your smile away
they might just as well shoot you.

VIOLET HENSLEY

Violet is one big smile. And it's not the result of having an easy life. On the contrary, she has worked doubly hard all her life to support her family. However, she has a joyful attitude, and it has made the difference in her life. Now in old age, she still works hard making fiddles for sale and performing music; but she loves every minute of life, and when you're with her, you love it too.

Why aren't we more like Violet? The answer always rests within us. We have decided how to respond to life's trials. We were never forced to dread, hate, or appreciate our experiences. We were, and still are, solely responsible for our interpretation. The Violets of the world opted to have more fun. Fortunately, it's never too late for us to make a different choice even though we may have to work hard to break an old habit.

How do we begin having more fun? The first step is deciding to leave the past behind. No matter what our experiences were last year or in our childhood or even this morning, they don't have to determine what our experiences will be in this next hour. Having more fun is clearly a decision that is coupled with action. Any one of us can do it as well as we want to.

Smiling at myself in the mirror is good practice.
Offering one to the first person I encounter strengthens
my desire to offer more.

Let every man be occupied
in the highest employment of which he is capable
and die conscious that he has done his best.

SIDNEY SMITH

Doing something that we feel good about never loses its importance to our lives. Whether we're fifty or eighty we like to matter. And it need not be a prestigious occupation for our work to be important. In fact, who are we to decide what kind of job is truly important? The most menial of tasks may have a profound impact on a particular man or woman today, and that's what really counts in God's grand scheme.

It is said by some that the highest order of employment is the offering of love and acceptance to the people on our paths today. For us to define employment solely in terms of career is shortsighted. Every minute we're awake we're busy with something, and that means we're employed.

A broader definition of employment gives every one of us a chance to put in a productive day. Knowing that our presence, our words, our willingness to listen to someone else has made life better for them makes it better for us, too.

I will go to bed fulfilled
if I have shown love and respect for others today.

JANUARY 29

I just pictured in my mind what I wanted to do.
You can use that same formula in
accomplishing anything in life.

IDA BELLEGARDE

The imagination is a powerful tool. With practice we can perfect our use of it and the results will astound us. Research has shown that athletes who visualize a practice session on the field or mountain or course hone their skills as effectively as those who practice "in the flesh." This may be hard to believe, but it's nonetheless true.

If this formula has worked for others, it can work for you too. But how do you begin? First, consider what you would like to do. The next step is to sit quietly, close your eyes and imagine, in detail, the activity you want to pursue. Stay quiet with this image until it feels natural. Take special note of the sensations you feel throughout your body, the colors you see around you, your inner voice's message. Absorb the experience fully before coming back to reality.

Repeated "journeys" with your mind will make any activity feel familiar, and enough familiarity makes success possible.

I am not prevented from doing anything I really want to do.
Using my imagination to experience it the
first time will get me started.

JANUARY 30

An artist is primarily one who has faith in himself.

HENRY MILLER

"I'm not an artist," you might be saying. But there is another perspective: some would say we are all artists. Our accomplishments attest to that; our medium has simply differed. Another way of interpreting this message is that when we have faith in ourselves, we can create rich lives. The key, of course, is nurturing faith in ourselves. What are the steps to take?

Not everybody grew up with encouragement. We may have reached adulthood by the skin of our teeth. Having confidence in ourselves took effort and we often failed. But life is made up of effort and failure and more effort again.

Artists are many things, but first and foremost, they are comfortable in their daily activities, which may be at an easel, or in the kitchen, or in a classroom. It may be with others or alone. They seldom doubt what they can offer today. We are all artists. Just as surely as we are alive, we have a gift to offer others.

> I will revel in my accomplishments today.
> My artistry has been revealed to others
> even though I may have failed to see it.

JANUARY 31

This continuing need to produce
is at the center of the creative spirit.

DANA STEWARD

What does it mean to have a creative spirit? Unless we paint or write or knit or carve, we assume we aren't creative, but that's defining the word too narrowly. People who walk a spiritual path generally believe that we are all gifted in some way. Perhaps that's a better understanding of creativity. No one else can do what we do in exactly the same way. That makes each of us creative.

Keeping busy, or at least having the drive to keep busy, is a good indicator that our inner creative spirit is calling. We've been told before that being alive implies we're *not done yet;* therefore, let's investigate the inner urge and get busy.

How we define *produce* can further complicate our understanding of creativity. To many, to produce means making something that is concrete, that can be held, perhaps. But can't we *produce* a serene environment by how we interact with people? Let's broaden our definitions and see our perspective change. We'll appreciate our contributions more.

I will have the desire to do something today.
My spirit is calling. I will listen and *do.*

FEBRUARY

FEBRUARY 1

There are many things people can do
if they're not afraid.

EDITH HUEY

Fear can be all-consuming. Some of us have been controlled by fear throughout much of our lives. It may still dog our steps. For that reason it's helpful to dwell on a few of our achievements, including the things that may not seem so important. In this way we can remember that even with fear hounding us, we accomplished great things.

Our family is raised and we provided the home. With no hesitation, we offered comfort to loved ones in need. We carried our load in the workplace. We planted gardens, built bookshelves, sewed curtains, made photograph albums. We planned reunions, organized vacations, kept the car in good running condition. The list of our accomplishments is long, very long, even though we may have been filled with fear. It didn't immobilize us. It doesn't have to now, either.

Let's begin a simple project today. Sorting through old clothes to donate to the thrift store is manageable. So is cleaning the cabinets in the basement or garage. Pulling weeds from around the bushes gives us a new focus, too. It's not what we do that counts as much as just doing something.

I refuse to let my fear be in charge today.
I can fulfill any wish I truly long for.

FEBRUARY 2

You can always solve a problem
if you just think about it so you can understand it.

CEDELL DAVIS

Few problems have really complicated solutions. But because we nervously dwell on a problem itself, we cloud the solution. It helps to remember that we have had years of practice at solving problems. There is no reason for them to overwhelm us now. The difference may be that today we have fewer people to talk over our problems with. But that can be good. Remember, "too many cooks can spoil the soup."

Having a problem can be a positive experience, particularly if we are intent on solving it. We exercise our minds when we have a problem. We reach out to others while seeking a solution. Both activities strengthen our connection to the human community.

We inspire others when we grapple with a problem successfully. We are models for each other. Just as we patterned our lives after people we admired in our youth, others look to us in old age. Every circumstance is an opportunity to set a good example.

I am in a unique position today.
Whatever comes to me allows me the chance to demonstrate
for others that solving problems is manageable.

FEBRUARY 3

Life is so much easier
if we don't feel sorry for ourselves.

HELEN CASEY

Our willingness to feel sorry for ourselves is related to our level of faith. When we cherish the knowledge that God has always been present, we can pull ourselves through any difficult experience. Some might say that our difficulties multiply as we age, and many situations are harder for us to handle. Perhaps we have less income and our bodies are less agile. But nothing has to get us down, and nothing will if we go to the ever-present Source for whatever we need.

When we decide to feel sorry for ourselves, we have effectively filled up our minds with thoughts that prevent us from hearing the inner voice of strength. If we listen to it instead, we'll not be overwhelmed by any situation that's happening. It might help to recall an earlier period in our lives when our faith walked us through a hard time. Perhaps we got fired or a marriage filled us with pain. When we sought comfort, it came to us. It still will. We need not feel abandoned, which is what we're feeling if trapped by self-pity. God didn't go anywhere. Only our minds left.

> I will recall the Power of the Presence
> anytime I am scared or frustrated today.
> Comfort will come to call.

FEBRUARY 4

People are as happy as they decide to be
before and after retirement.

FRAN COYNE

Happiness is a decision. It always was. Isn't it sad that so few people choose it daily? What we realize is that we love being around those individuals who always seem happy. The miracle, too, is that many of their circumstances have been difficult, yet they are happy anyway. What mystery did they know that we had failed to learn? Nothing more than the power of their minds. They knew, perhaps instinctively, that no external circumstance had absolute control over how they felt or acted.

It's important that each of us take an inventory of our responses to the many situations that have troubled us over the years. Can we see that we might have reacted differently? Perhaps that seems impossible in some cases. The unexpected death of a spouse or friend, lost jobs, problematical children certainly deserved our feelings of anger, sadness, or disappointment. Or did they? Letting any experience determine how we will feel takes away our freedom of choice. That doesn't mean we should feign happiness when we don't feel it, but it does mean that we can cultivate happiness as our overall perspective on life.

I can seek to feel happy today.
It's all in my mind.

FEBRUARY 5

*All that retirement means is that you stop
working a particular job; you don't retire from life.*

PAT AND LOUISE JEROME

Not everybody responds to retirement in the way the Jeromes
have. Some people do, in fact, appear to retire from life. We have
all known a relative or former friend who "sat down to die," no
longer interested in life, no longer challenged by the dream of
unrealized goals. They have the right to withdraw from the
world, certainly, but how unfortunate. There is so much living
and giving yet to be done by all of us, or we wouldn't still be here.

We still have contributions to make. That's a pleasant reality
as long as we don't try to do others' contributions, too. There's
something very important for each of us to do today. Quite
possibly, the most important thing of all will be to encourage
someone to join us in whatever we had planned, someone who
was going to hide out at home, unengaged by the world. It's not
our job, ever, to force someone else to do something against
their will, but many times people lose their confidence about
trying new activities. They may need our encouragement. Let's
give this idea careful consideration today if we know someone
who is unmotivated.

**I will consider sharing my plans with someone else today
and hope they join me.**

FEBRUARY 6

I guess all work is leisure time to me.

VIOLET HENSLEY

The attitude a person cultivates is solely an individual matter. Money doesn't determine it. We have all known wealthy, resentful people. Health doesn't determine it either. Nary a one of us hasn't met a disabled man or woman who still encounters the day wearing a smile. Deciding to feel blessed, thus content with life, comes from our interior spaces. We do reflect to others whatever we feel within.

What kind of people are we? The good news is that whoever we have been doesn't need to limit us anymore. We aren't committed to being depressed or fearful or angry unless we have given our power over to that emotion. And even if we have, we can take it back and be serene and hopeful instead.

I am in charge of my perspective today, like every day. Beginning with a prayer for peace will help me attain it.

FEBRUARY 7

I was fifty-six years old when I retired,
and I felt that I should still be working.
I felt I was doing something wrong.

SANDY WARMAN

Guilt ruins so many years of experiences. No doubt parents and other authority figures introduced us to guilt in our youth. But it's not likely they still hover over us. Yet, the guilt does. Did feeling guilty become a habit?

For many, that's exactly what happened. The good news is that habits can be broken, some more easily than others. The bad news is that guilt is one of the more difficult habits to break. It simply *seems* to come over us. Of course, that's not really how it happens. Our willingness to feel guilty comes first. Our acceptance of guilt and then nurturing it comes next. Whatever is left of an experience or the whole day is easily transformed when we've let guilt monopolize our minds.

There is a solution to guilt. It's realizing that we can replace any thought we harbor with one that benefits us more. Guilt is nothing more than an unpleasant thought that we manufactured. It has no life of its own. We can discard it. Now.

I am as free of guilt as I choose to be today.
Whatever I was taught in the past need not decide my present.

FEBRUARY 8

If a man can carve something out of wood,
he is just as much a creator as a man who works with words.

CLARA GLENN

It's really not *what* we do in life that matters, but *how* we do it. To more clearly understand this, let's take an example. We can all remember dreading a project that needed doing—maybe mending some pants or replacing a screen in the back door. First, we couldn't find our glasses to thread the needle, then we stuck ourselves with the needle, drawing blood that promptly got on the pants. Or we hit our index finger with the hammer as we attempted to install the new screen. Our recollections are endless. Interestingly enough, our personal attitudes always directly controlled the success we had with the project.

What does this mean to us now? It suggests that if we are fully attentive to whatever we pursue, our experience of it will be significantly different. We are competent to handle anything that needs our attention. In most cases, we'll be more than competent. And if we have a real desire to do the job, we'll excel at it, providing we give it our undivided attention.

> I am a creator of something today.
> Maybe it's a friendship or a poem.
> They are equal in the eyes of God.

FEBRUARY 9

What you desire with a burning desire,
a continuing burning desire, you will draw to you.

JEAN WILL

Our thoughts manifest themselves. That's both a powerful realization and a haunting one. Does it mean that we are to blame
for the bad as well as the good experiences in our lives? Some
wiser than ourselves would say yes. However, if our lives have
been fraught with pain, that response doesn't comfort us. Let's
settle, instead, for coming to believe that we have gotten what we
needed for our growth, and it has taken many forms. We will
continue to get whatever we need to make us whole.

Our journey has been full of surprises, right? Probably few of
us imagined the turns our careers took. Nor did we anticipate
the travels, the friends, the struggles in the midst of joys that our
families experienced. And yet, all that we have come to know has
benefited us. All that we have lived through enriched our contributions to others.

We may not be conscious of our souls' supreme desires. We
must trust, however, that they have come to us in the right way
at the right time. They will continue to do so.

My experiences have always been right for me.
Even when I didn't like them, they were right.
The same will be true today.

FEBRUARY 10

I play while I work and I work while I sleep. I depend on the functioning of my subconscious imagination to do my work.

EDITH SHANNON

Our minds are never at rest. It's rather nice to know that someplace within we remember everything that caught our attention, even when we weren't conscious of it. Learning to tap into this well of information comes with lots of practice and the willingness to get quiet, really quiet.

It's our attitudes that make play of work. Keeping our thoughts and composure joyful prevents even the dullest task from boring us. Being open to the possibility that fun is an outlook we can foster changes us quite profoundly. It also keeps the channel to our interior imagination uncluttered with the negative. We will always know how to proceed in every instance if we let our inner knowing guide us. The subconscious imagination is never asleep.

My inner self stands at attention always.
I will let it answer my questions, make my decisions.

FEBRUARY 11

*You start preparing when you're thirty
for the person you'll be at eighty.*

JANICE CLARK

We can't get away from ourselves, at least not entirely. Who we were at ten and twenty and forty and fifty remains as threads in our tapestries. Many of us shudder because some details of our personal panorama weren't so very pretty. But that's the way life is. We are what we are. And yet, we have examples of favorable changes, too. How we were never kept us from becoming who we wanted to be. This truth continues to reign in our lives.

We all know women and men who continue to be enthused about even the tiny happenings in the passing of a day. A bird's flight from the porch to a nearby tree to feed its young, the laughter of children passing the house on their way home from school, the family reunions, large or small, bring smiles and memories that comfort. Probably we envy those folks, unless we happen to be *them* already. In either case, imitating others or serving as their role models helps to strengthen our positive responses to life's details. No matter how old we are, there is still joy to be felt. And there is still time to change and grow.

> There is no rule that says I have to be
> and think and act the same way my whole life.
> Today is a clean slate. I can be who I want to be.

FEBRUARY 12

The most important thing to me now is my health.
I hope it holds out.

RUTH CASEY

Our priorities change as we age, don't they? It's not that health wasn't important when we were younger, but we probably took it for granted. Serious health challenges didn't hinder most of us. Even at this age, we may have been spared many of the conditions that have plagued friends or other members of our families. If that's the case, let's not only count our blessings but be particularly mindful of how we treat our bodies. Nutrition and exercise have a lot to do with how they perform.

Our health becomes the bottom line as we grow old. Nothing stays the same; that we can accept. We have less energy. Our hair thins. Spicy foods upset our stomachs. The list is endless. However, if we lose our health, every aspect of our lives has to change. We can survive the changes, certainly, but they aren't always easy to handle.

How can we prepare for the inevitable health changes? For one, we can nurture our relationship with God as we *know* God. Having faith in a Source outside of ourselves assures us that we'll not be alone regardless of what the future holds. The comfort that offers is immeasurable. Let's make this a top priority.

I can affect my health today by what I eat, how I think,
how I move. I will be very thoughtful regarding my input.

FEBRUARY 13

Inspiration starts in the home.

ALPHA ENGLISH

What does being inspired really mean? Alpha would say it means having the faith to tackle difficult tasks. She surely had it. In a time when few women went to college, she did and with honors. Then after a lifetime of teaching in a small Arkansas town, she began writing plays and a history of African Americans for the benefit of young and old alike. She was inspired. Her example inspired others, too.

But what if we didn't grow up in a home where inspiration was nurtured? Did that mean we couldn't develop it? Taking notice of how we have solved problems and approached the unknown in our lives indicates the level of inspiration we acquired from somewhere. What's obvious is that we did create it somehow. Any accomplishment we can point to is evidence. Nobody tackles anything without some inner drive that says they can. That's inspiration.

Some of us did have more than others. Some of us still do. The good news is that we can "trade" inspiration with each other. We can give it away when a friend is in need, and we can borrow it back when we're feeling uncertain about a direction or a task. It matters not where we get it. It never did. It was simply easier for us if it was one of the gifts passed on in our homes.

My inspiration can come from anywhere today.
Those who are closest are the obvious "carriers."

FEBRUARY 14

*I think having to come up the hard way
really inspires you to keep going.*

IDA BELLEGARDE

Many people would agree with Ida. However, there may be some who grow old with resentment for how hard their lives were. Those men and women aren't inspired at all. It is also true that many who grew up with a silver spoon are nonetheless inspired to contribute their fair share, or more, every day.

Attitude is no doubt the one most significant thing that inspires a person to keep going. We all know someone who has had more than his or her share of tough luck, maybe even life-threatening health problems or family traumas. And where are they on a regular basis? Still busily involved with the welfare of others. Nothing keeps some people down.

We must not feel like we don't measure up if some situations get us down, however. It's okay to sit back some days. No doubt we have done enough, and doing what fulfills us daily is what really keeps us going. All of us can handle that.

I will get back at least equal to what I put in today.

FEBRUARY 15

I thought my life was completely filled
and that I didn't ever need anybody else in it,
except an occasional friend, until I met Harry.

EDITH HUEY BARTHOLOMEW

Isolation can become seductive in old age. Perhaps our occasionally ailing bodies initiate it. Or maybe depression. Finances can sometimes keep us from activities that would be good for us. The willingness to manufacture motivation may even be a necessity, but once we get involved with others, the desire to stay involved will simply happen. Having others in our lives lets us focus on ideas and people outside of ourselves. That's a good remedy for the blues.

Needing others isn't a failing. Unfortunately, we may have been told otherwise years ago. Perhaps that message has ruled our perception ever since; in which case, seeking out others and determining how we can offer something of value in exchange for companionship may have to be a learned behavior. Thank goodness old dogs can learn new tricks. Whether it's a newfound friend, a live-in companion, or the addition of a pet to our household, having something to focus on outside of ourselves will reward us many times over.

Whoever I meet today has something to offer me.
I'm not alone.

FEBRUARY 16

My husband and I have grown closer in retirement.
We want to end up friends when we get finished.

MARIE BURNS

The adjustment to retirement strains the relationships of some couples and even some good friends. Being together for extended periods on a too-frequent basis may be trying on the nerves. After all, we all have our foibles, thus we all need a little separateness. We had plenty of it earlier in life, and that offered a good balance to our relationships.

The assurance of ending up friends, as voiced by Marie, happens because we nurture and appreciate the differences between us. It happens because we are willing to let one another pursue interests that may be solitary. It happens because we are willing to listen to and respect the opinions and perspective cherished by those in our company.

Friendship is an art. It takes patience and honesty. It takes willingness and silence. It can happen between any two individuals. It's a gift we all deserve many times over before "we are finished." Having a spouse who is a ready partner for friendship indeed makes us lucky. Let's not squander the opportunity.

Being a friend to someone today
is my opportunity for real contentment.

FEBRUARY 17

Being prepared for retirement is an important step.
I think it has helped us enjoy it.

JIM BURNS

Many retired people share a common complaint: lack of purpose. The good news is, it can be easily addressed. Purpose can be as simple as showing concern for another human being. This gives us the freedom to do anything with our time and feel that we are bettering the world. It's how we respond to the other people that counts, that guarantees purpose.

Certainly we can plan ahead by putting aside money, by designating certain activities for our less active years, by discussing with our spouses or other loved ones what their picture of our retirement is. And yet, what we do and how we do it moment by moment is the key to a happy retirement, regardless of the plans or lack thereof.

I can prepare for this day and give it purpose.
That's enough to focus on, perhaps.

FEBRUARY 18

I used to think that what you did for a living determined how people evaluated you, whether they liked you or not.

JOE CASEY

Unfortunately, Joe's assessment may still be true for some people. In earlier days, we probably all asked most new acquaintances what they did for a living before seeking any additional information. We may have moved on when we weren't impressed with their credentials. Now we look back on that response with regret. Wisdom comes with maturity, it seems, and finally we have learned that a person's worth isn't measured by the work they pursued. No doubt we missed getting to know some really interesting people.

We're no longer closing the door on potential friendships, are we? This doesn't mean we have to like everyone equally, nor does it mean that an acquaintance with very different values has to become an intimate friend. But we can make thoughtful choices regarding the friendships we want to cultivate. Watching how potential friends treat others as well as themselves, listening for their opinions, taking notice of how willingly they allow others to be different from themselves, taking a special interest in how they perceive the world around them are good indicators of whether to pursue a friendship. Let's not bypass someone who reveals a loving heart. Their former profession surely counts no more.

> People I may want to know will be present today.
> I will listen to them with a loving heart.

FEBRUARY 19

My entire life used to be based on what people thought of me.
That's not so true anymore.

SANDY WARMAN

Most of us focused too much on what others thought of us, didn't we? Sandy's experience is all too familiar, but it's best if we don't criticize ourselves for that at this stage. Rather, let's acknowledge that our concerns about others' opinions might have even prompted us to make more sensible choices on occasion. Whatever contributed to our evolution played its part. If we're not satisfied with the outcome, we can make changes that will affect our future now.

It was pretty difficult to be insulated from the opinions and criticisms of others when we were attempting to make our marks in the world of work. Not uncommonly, we all wanted friends and respect from our peers. This wish hasn't entirely changed for most of us; however, we are less concerned than we used to be. One of the benefits of growing older is that we can "grow into ourselves" more. We can claim all of our parts more easily, thus we can let the opinions that others have of us roll off.

This freedom may not be second nature to us yet. We have to get accustomed to the idea that we're fine just as we are. Having a spiritual program can help. Having friends we can trust to share our concerns with helps, too.

I do care what others think. That's okay.
However, I need not be controlled by them today.

As you get older, you should get wiser,
but I don't know that you do.

LOUIS FREUND

Getting old doesn't mean always making the right decisions. On the contrary, we may make any number of wrong decisions simply because we think we *should know everything at our age.* Asking for advice from others, whether children, counselors, or other professionals, sometimes gets harder as we get older. Perhaps we got too used to others looking to us for advice, and we think asking for help now negates all the ways we were able to help others in years past. Of course that's not true, but we may believe it.

Doubtless, there are many things we are wiser about now than when we were young. We know that who we are *inside* is far more important than how we look *outside.* We know that listening to the hearts of others always provides messages from God. We know that *this too will pass* whenever the hurdles seem too high. And we know that we are never given more than we can handle, providing we look to others for support or suggestions. We are wiser now. We will get wiser still.

My wisdom is guaranteed if I am open to it.
The people in my life today are conduits for it.

*I don't want to get too relaxed. When you get too relaxed
you're not interesting, you don't want to face a challenge.*

ALPHA ENGLISH

Some days we don't want to face any challenge. And that's okay.
We've earned the right to sit it out occasionally. On those days,
perhaps we can curl up with a book or write a letter to a friend
or just sit at the kitchen table and enjoy the sights and sounds of
nature. Nobody can make us conquer the world if we'd rather
rest. Getting old gives us real freedom.

We soon discover, however, that the more we retreat from the
life that beckons, the more difficult it becomes to get involved at
any level. We need to remember that we are here for a purpose,
and it's doubtful that we're fulfilling that purpose if we are
always in repose.

Finally, we can conclude that a balanced response to the call
of life is the healthiest. Let's take time to be quiet and attend to
the soul. What we give when we are nourished will be more
nourishing to others as well.

**I will thoughtfully choose my level of involvement today.
Caring for myself will help me give more to others
when the need is there.**

FEBRUARY 22

When I decide I like something,
I give everything I can, everything I have to it.

TOM HARDING

Eagerly arising every morning is a wonderful blessing. How many of us are so gifted? If you aren't one of them, perhaps attitude is the culprit. We really are as happy as we make up our minds to be. Being reminded that it's never too late to get happy through delving into something new is helpful.

Having a passion for something, such as history, gardening, photography, or woodworking is a sure reason for awaking with enthusiasm every day. Just because some of us haven't developed hobbies during our more productive years is no reason to avoid them now. On the contrary, there may be no better reason to find a hobby than the fact that we've failed to nurture our creative spirits up to now. For some of us, the fun is just beginning.

Not knowing how to begin a hobby need not stop us. Let's quiet the mind and seek guidance and direction. It will come. Absolutely, it will come.

Liking whatever we are doing today is a decision.
Any activity can become our passion if we so desire.

FEBRUARY 23

We're not going to live forever,
but I think we should have the attitude of "Why not?"

HARRY BARTHOLOMEW

Taking our focus off of the future and placing it instead on whatever presents itself today adds a richness to each moment that can't be measured or duplicated. Dwelling on our deaths or the ill health that might befall us leaves us no free time to laugh and learn from all the experiences that are presenting themselves. The end will come. Of that we can be sure, but why let thinking about it *discolor* every minute that remains between now and then?

Most of us have no idea what our real purpose has been in this life, in these bodies. It's quite freeing to give up the need to know why we're here. It's far more fascinating to simply acknowledge that we are here, and the friends and strangers who walk with us are all that matter minute by minute. Figuring out nothing more than this lets us give our total being over to whatever experience has called to us, as though it's all there ever was or ever will be. Nothing appears the same, from the past or the present, when we see it this way.

I have all the time I need to do whatever comes to me today.

FEBRUARY 24

Longevity comes from working at something you like,
such as service, creativity, and a good marriage.

MONTY CRALLEY

A long life isn't absolutely guaranteed from doing all these things that Monty suggests; however, the degree of joy we have experienced in life is very likely in proportion to our commitment to some of these things.

There has never been much we had absolute control over. How we longed to control our spouse, children, friends, and co-workers. But, alas, they resisted. The quicker we gave up our attempts, the more joy we began to realize, and the more time we had to focus on rewarding work, a fun hobby, or a fulfilling marriage.

It really isn't the number of years we live that counts, but the quality of our days. Some of us have lived many decades in misery, and we hated our work, lacked friendships, and resented our spouses. If it sounds all too familiar, make an immediate decision to be kind to someone today. It might be the beginning of a new life.

> I am so lucky that each day is an opportunity
> for a new beginning, a new outlook.
> Today can be whatever I want it to be.

*I know that death is as much a part of who I am
as my birth, my job, and my retirement.
It's just the beginning of a whole other experience.*

FRAN COYNE

Not all of us look to the final stage of our lives with acceptance. Fear about dying is common. Possibly, the older we get, the greater the fear. There are innumerable reasons for this. If we grew up in shaming environments, we may expect death to punish us. If we grew up in agnostic or atheistic homes, we may fear the nothingness that we've been taught to expect. Or maybe we simply fear the uncertainty of what it will be like. No one has come back after death to give us the specifics, although people who have had near-death experiences have interesting tales to tell.

If we have fear about death, it might help to ask our friends how they feel about it. Those who are like Fran might have some good suggestions or some stories of their own to relate. Perhaps we can seek the counsel of a minister, even if we don't attend church. Few ministers would deny us the opportunity for solace, regardless of our beliefs. Seeking books on death or near-death experiences might be a good first step. Prayer, even when we may not believe in it, will offer some comfort, too.

Today I will examine my feelings about death.
I will share these feelings with someone close to me.

FEBRUARY 26

*I have the innate feeling that this is not all there is—
that there is a better life.*

RUTH CASEY

Not everybody shares Ruth's belief. Nor does that matter. However, each of us must decide what we do believe, because it flavors how we interpret this life. If we think this life is all there is, we may be extremely anxious about our missed opportunities or our failures. Actually, we may want to reconsider what our belief systems are doing for us, or to us. Might we find ways to feel greater peace here, now? Particularly if this ends up being all there is, wouldn't it be nice to enjoy it more?

To many, it's a moot question whether or not there is a hereafter. We still have to interact with other people, resolving conflicts and agreeing to solutions for the many problems that impact all of us now. If there is more than this life, some of us merely hope it's less fraught with struggle. Those who agree with Ruth quite possibly perceive this life as merely the training ground for our much deserved serenity.

Believing that a better life awaits us perhaps lessens the sting of the present turmoil. It doesn't really change it, however. Finally, we have to seek peace in our own way, but we may have something to learn from another person's perspective on life. Perhaps we should ask.

**What do I believe about a hereafter?
Today is a good day to contemplate this.**

FEBRUARY 27

*I am a relatively simple person who believes what he sees
and that things are purposeful and beautiful
just the way they are.*

DON KENNETT

If we all shared Don Kennett's view about life, it would take the sting and the anxiety out of the many experiences we hadn't counted on. The simple belief that all is well, all is as it should be, profoundly comforts us. Why do we resist believing it?

The kind of spiritual upbringing we had provides part of the answer. How comfortable our parents were with their lives also contributes to our visions. A household that looks upon all experiences as opportunities for growth and contribution is far different from one that sees only disaster and foreboding. The surprising thing is that two families may see the same experience in such different ways. This is not unlike the wisdom that beauty is in the eye of the beholder.

How I see today is up to me.
My power, in this respect, is awesome.

*I've found that you can't draw road maps for the Lord.
I've tried that.*

JANICE CLARK

The attempt to control is such a predictable human response to every situation, regardless of age. Fortunately, the serenity that develops when we give up our control makes letting God be in charge rather appealing, but most of us have spent decades learning and then relearning this. Have we, even yet, mastered this idea?

Let's review our most recent behavior; it will indicate our willingness to let God take charge of the events and people in our lives. Were we in even a tiny conflict with anyone in the last twenty-four hours? If someone's opinion differed from ours, did we walk away, allowing him or her to feel okay about the choice he or she had made? How about being put on hold when trying to make a phone call or getting stuck in the slowest lane of traffic? Did we use that time to think prayerful thoughts about people we love or to ask God to help us be more accepting of those who trouble us? If we can't answer yes to these questions, perhaps it's time to reflect on our distance from God's loving will. When we are in partnership with it, our lives will look and feel far different. Shall we try to seek more peace today?

**I can be as peaceful as I make the choice to be today.
Letting God handle all my affairs is the way.**

FEBRUARY 29

Don't take life too seriously.
We were put here to laugh.

HELEN CASEY

Not everything that has happened in our lives is laughable. And we shouldn't pretend otherwise. However, it's pretty common to take most experiences far too seriously. Every event in our lives was a small blip of time, nothing more. How we responded to it is what gave it its meaning. Even a tiny shift in attitude or perspective makes all the difference in how we interpret and incorporate the blips, even now.

None of us has been spared the friend who whines and moans over everything. Nor did we escape the acquaintance who was sure she had all the answers. The perpetual critic often hounded our steps, too. But none of these folks had the power to steal our laughter or ruin our perspectives of a situation without our willingness.

Nothing has changed. We are still in the seat of power when it comes to how we see our lives, how we feel about the blips, what we decide to do. Making light of most circumstances will give us better payoffs than exaggerating them. Hindsight taught us that.

I can look for the light side today.
When in doubt, I can recall a funny story from my youth.

MARCH

MARCH 1

You can finish a painting,
but how do you finish a career?

LOUIS FREUND

Adjusting to this stage of life comes easier some days than others. For decades we defined ourselves according to where we worked rather than how we felt or what we fantasized or thought about the daily trials of living. Perhaps that was appropriate then, but now we have the opportunity to explore new dimensions of ourselves. Who are we, really? What do we honestly believe about the universe? About God? About death? About the younger generation?

Our careers, whether as homemakers or assemblymen, absorbed our visions of life. At last we are free to dream, to pursue a hobby, to try new philosophies of living. We can even try one path for a while, feel finished with it and travel a new road, all with no explanation necessary. We never imagined the joy we can now expect daily. Doing whatever we want, on our timetable, finishing whatever we choose to, or stopping in the middle of a task is all up to us now.

Finishing a career is really a treat when I realize it means
I can do whatever I want for a change. Today beckons.

MARCH 2

*I got myself into such a tight knot about finding a business
that I thought I was having a heart attack.*

SANDY WARMAN

When we don't seek spiritual solutions to our problems, we magnify them, and ill health commonly results. If that occurs, we have forgotten that we are never without spiritual guidance. Fortunately, it is never too late to relearn that whatever we need will come to us when the time is right. This was true in our youth, and honest hindsight reveals it. A principle such as this always remains true.

None of us have been spared anxious moments in our lives. Perhaps we've had more than our fair share. Was that simply due to bad luck? Some would say yes. Others have come to realize that one's level of anxiety is directly proportional to our willingness or *unwillingness* to seek spiritual guidance. Maybe we've enjoyed extended periods of anxious-free living—and its opposite. How pleasant or fearful the hours pass today is proportionate to our willingness to rely on spiritual solutions.

**I will move serenely through today
if I remember that spiritual guidance is ever-present.**

MARCH 3

Something needs to be done in the course of a day.

EDITH SHANNON

Where did we learn to be productive? Perhaps from parents who expected chores to be done. Or maybe from the popular refrain heard in every classroom by every child: "Get busy!" The stories we read as children usually lauded the fruits of being industrious. The message was everywhere. And nothing has changed.

Being productive isn't a failing. In fact, without committing to productivity we'd never have attained any goal we set for ourselves. Our past accomplishments wouldn't have materialized. But a lesson we deserve to learn—and it's never too late—is that we can define "getting something done" as loosely and as imaginatively as we wish. This is surely one of the rewards of old age.

Feeling as though we have made a difference is what we really yearn for. How we make that difference is as varied and optional as our minds can fathom.

**Something as simple as smiling at a stranger
is getting something done. I can brighten
someone's world so easily today.**

MARCH 4

*My philosophy on exercise is that whenever
I feel the need to do it, I lie down until the feeling passes.*

TOM HARDING

We can all chuckle over Tom's statement and perhaps share his opinion, but we also know that we're paying the price in old age if we never got much exercise when we were younger. Weak bones plague many of us, and falls can incapacitate us for many months. How fortunate that we can work our bodies a little, and it will help. We don't have to walk three miles daily or run up and down stairs, but we can stretch and take short walks or at least lift very light weights with either our arms or legs. We can't undo years of neglect, but we can limit the continuing damage of no exercise.

There's another payoff from exercise, and it's an unexpected one for many: one's mental and emotional mood gets better when exercise is part of one's routine. There's a biological reason for that. Exercise releases endorphins in our brains and we feel energized. Feeling better for whatever reason is not something any of us want to scoff at.

If committing to an exercise program is uncomfortable, just make the decision to do something each day, one day at a time. Remember, it doesn't have to be much; even a few minutes is a beginning. That's all we need to do to get started.

> Today, I'll get my exercise in, no matter what.
> If nothing else goes right all day long, at least
> I'll feel good about that accomplishment.

People do need to have a purpose,
some direction in life, both before and after retirement.

LOUISE JEROME

Getting up every morning is far more exciting when we can anticipate being engaged with people or activities that interest us. Mattering to the world around us is important. Even when we aren't consciously aware of it, we matter to everyone we come into contact with. This has always been true and nothing has changed.

While still occupied in a profession or as a homemaker we didn't often doubt that we had a purpose. We had a place to be every day and tasks to be completed. We might not have considered that what we did made much of a contribution to the greater world, but we knew it counted, nonetheless. It's not as easy to believe this now. Maybe that's because we aren't currently involved in any specific activities that touch other people. But few days pass that we don't have contact with at least one other person. Quite possibly, that's the only purpose we have right now: being present to that one individual, whoever he or she might be.

Our purpose need not be *grand* to be important. God has need of each one of us. We are still needed, absolutely. All we have to do is "report for duty." We do that by awaking each morning.

I look to today with anticipation.
God has a job for me and I'm ready.

MARCH 6

Most of the real artists I know
do not sit around waiting for inspiration.

JANICE CLARK

It's been said that "inspiration comes from perspiration." In other words, creativity is an acquired trait that we hone with effort. The good news is that all of us can "perspire." Each of us is as artistic, as creative, as we put our minds to being, and the richness and variety in our lives has been the result of our personal sweat equity. This remains true even today.

Knowing that we can pursue old or new hobbies is exciting. Nothing stands in our way but our willingness to proceed. But if we haven't painted or written poetry or worked jigsaw puzzles for a long time, we may fear we can't do it any longer. Even worse, if we've never done hobbies before, we can be intimidated by the mere idea of them.

Getting started on a project, any project, for fun will influence how we perceive the myriad possibilities for fruitful aging in our changing lives. We'll come to appreciate this as the best of times, if we're so inclined.

My interests might not be clear to me yet,
but some quiet reflection will give me direction.

MARCH 7

*There's a relationship between creativity
and longevity, you know.*

MONTY CRALLEY

Monty's statement may not be an absolute. We may have known creative individuals, some very successful in fact, who died an untimely death. And we all know old codgers who don't do anything creative, who moan and complain incessantly about life, politics, the neighbors, and they are still very much alive and healthy at eighty-five or ninety. However, Monty is an excellent example of this principle. He's still going strong, writing and painting and enjoying opera almost every day, and he's nearly ninety and legally blind. Best of all, he loves life.

The attitudes we have spent years cultivating are finally what really counts, regardless of how long we live. The medical profession is quick to give credit to one's outlook when a health challenge occurs and is averted. Certainly, that may not always be the case, but how willing we are to seek the silver lining in every situation does leave its mark on our condition. In a very important way, our willingness to have a better outlook on any circumstance might be considered the most creative effort we can make.

Being open to new ideas and new pursuits will give my life
added meaning. Today's experiences just may offer me
an opportunity I shouldn't pass up.

Art is not a thing; it's a way.

ELBERT HUBBARD

We have all known people who lived with the flow of life. They didn't try to control every outcome of their circumstances. They refrained from making decisions for others. They took each experience as an opportunity to collect new information and adjust their perspective on the possibilities for change and growth. They were good role models even though we didn't imitate them.

We can see now that they lived "artfully." They didn't fight every decision; they didn't resist every change; they didn't seek people to join their side against the opposition. They saw no opposition, in fact. They simply were. They simply lived.

Now we can simply *be,* too. Joining the flow is akin to appreciating the balance in a wonderful painting. Our eyes move from one side to another, taking in the shadows along with the highlights. And we are satisfied. Moving through the day can be just as satisfying.

**Every day creates its own rhythm,
and I can join the dance.**

MARCH 9

*My hobby provided some income and a focus for my life
while my husband was sick and after he died.*

ALICE MERRYMAN

Regardless of the role hobbies played in one's past, perhaps it's time to consider developing an interest in something new. Crafts of all kinds appeal to some. The choices are endless. Working with organizations that need volunteers may be more to your liking. It matters little what someone chooses, but getting the focus off ourselves, being engaged by others or in an activity that lets us forget ourselves for a time, is where the real value lies.

That Alice got busy with her crafts ultimately expanded her reach far beyond her small farm in Arkansas. Life took on new purpose, which was important at the time her role as wife was changing so dramatically. As our lives change, due to retirement or the death of loved ones, we need to seek new challenges to feel present in the world around us. Are we prepared for the changes that are bound to come?

> Today will offer me some time to assess
> if I'm doing what really matters to me.

*I am not a worrier, although I do have concerns
about some of the people in my life.*

RUTH CASEY

Some might say there's little difference between having concerns and being worried. Perhaps the difference is in intensity. People who worry a lot allow their minds little time to have any other thoughts. They are always focused on the minutiae of a particular situation or person. Being concerned, on the other hand, generally means feeling compassion.

Is there anything wrong with worry? We can all think of friends who wear the badge of worry proudly. Maybe they think this makes them more caring people than we are. Do we think that, too? If the answer is yes, it might be well for us to remember that worry is the opposite of faith. Our worries can't change a situation, but our faith can change us and, thus, how we perceive the situation.

Worrying doesn't change anything for anybody, except the worrier. Worriers have more stress in their lives because of it, and stress can hinder their health. They have fewer hours to feel joy each day because they crowd the pleasant thoughts out of their minds. There's really nothing to be gained by worrying, ever. God has offered to handle our lives for us. Why not give God a try?

**If I begin to worry today, I'll try to remember
that God will take care of the situation.**

MARCH 11

To enjoy retirement you need inner peace.

JIM BURNS

To many of us, inner peace sounds elusive, mystical perhaps. We often associate peace with prayer and a connection to God. For many it is gained that way, but peace can be our gift through other avenues, too.

How we treat other people contributes to how peaceful we feel. Giving time lovingly to another, listening to someone's need for understanding or acceptance, and sharing a personal experience that might offer a new solution to someone who's in trouble are all ways to claim some peace for ourselves. There isn't any mystery to it. Perhaps it seems that way, because we feel it so seldom.

If the enjoyment of any time in our lives rests on peace, can we ever really be certain of it? Most would say no, but that's not giving ourselves enough credit. The attitude we cultivate, in turn, cultivates our inner peace. It always comes back to how we look at the world around us. We're always in charge of that, which means we'll always have as much peace as we desire.

Do I really want peace today?
Only I have the answer.

MARCH 12

You need few basic things for a vital age:
purposes and projects, and bonds of intimacy.

BETTY FRIEDAN

Feeling needed is what it all adds up to. We didn't doubt our value when we were raising our families and bringing home a paycheck. We knew we were needed when a child or parent or spouse came to us for advice. Friends sharing their innermost secrets with us made us feel special, too. But now, none of these things may be prevalent in our lives. It's not unusual for people our age to feel worthless. The responsibility for changing that feeling rests with us.

If being involved, whether on the job or with friends, gave our lives meaning when we were young, we at least have an understanding of how to regain that sense of well-being now. We certainly don't need a job to do it, but we do need to make an offering of some kind to the world at large. And we must have a friend, a confidant, we share ourselves with fully. Knowing that we make a difference in someone's life, anyone's life, gets us out of bed and on the bus every morning.

It's not all that hard to find a project or a friend. We simply have to want to.

I will enrich my life by sharing it with someone else today.
I don't even have to know who this person will be
until I "get there."

MARCH 13

There's one thing you can't give away.
You can't give away a smile. It always comes back to you.

VIOLET HENSLEY

We have had years of experience with the results of smiling. How many times have we felt better simply because we smiled, even at a stranger? Smiling is somewhat like yawning. When we see someone do it, it initiates one in us, too. But how often are we the initiators of a smile when we catch the attention of someone? Seldom. And what a shame.

As kids we probably heard that it took more muscles to frown than to smile. We usually were told that in the midst of pouting and the message agitated us. Whether or not it's a truth based on research doesn't really matter. Smiling simply feels good. It inspires the same good feelings in others, too.

Life could be simpler than we choose to make it. We really don't have to assess every situation before determining what expression we'll wear. We need not search for a hidden meaning in every action or expression of the others we're with. We can awake each day, decide that we'll respond to our experiences and the people in them with respect and friendliness, and put on a smile, just like we put on lipstick or a cap when it's chilly out. Some of life's decisions are simple. Let's relish them.

My first smile will be at me, in the mirror today.
If I savor it, it will set a good tone for the rest of the day.

MARCH 14

We need to laugh at ourselves,
to not take ourselves too seriously.

HARRY BARTHOLOMEW

The older we get, the easier this seems to be, doesn't it? What have we finally learned? For one thing, we can see now that most of our earlier worries never came to pass. Unfortunately, the hours wasted can't be regained, but we can fill our time more productively now. Let's not be confused by "productivity" though. It's not necessarily synonymous with "serious." It simply means making the minutes of our lives count for something. And making someone else laugh may be the most significant contribution we can make on any one day.

Everytime we take ourselves too seriously, we influence how everyone else experiences us as well. Certainly there are serious situations that need our attention. Sick friends, late unpaid bills, appointments with the doctor need our more serious side. However, most of what happens in a day is of little lasting consequence. There's no need to make a federal case out of a forgotten name, a misplaced billfold, an overcooked hamburger. Laughing at our mistakes, our poor memories, even our missed opportunities does more for our current state of being than if we'd been perfect every instance.

Laughter will shake me free
from whatever might ail me today.

MARCH 15

I admire humor and wit.
I think we develop those qualities we admire.

JOANN REED

Having a well-developed sense of humor can make it possible for us to survive the most difficult of times. If we shift our perception a bit, choosing to see the lighter side of a situation, or if we are willing to laugh at our own foibles, "disasters" affect us far differently. This doesn't mean we shouldn't take life seriously, nor does it mean there aren't real tragedies. But most tough experiences are exaggerated in our minds. We have the capacity to perceive them differently. Let's consider our willingness.

Medical research has recently established that laughter is a healthy exercise, that it can actually change the outcome of an illness. Watching funny movies, as therapy, was tried successfully by one well-known journalist who then wrote about his experiences. He cured his disease and lived many more years. It's not known exactly how this works or why, but the proof is in the evidence. If laughter can completely alleviate, or at least reduce serious conditions, surely it can change the many tiny troubles that hinder us. It's worth a try. Right?

As JoAnn suggests, admiring someone else's sense of humor is the first step to improving our own. Might this be a worthy pursuit today?

Having a good laugh at myself or with someone else
will change how I see everything today.

MARCH 16

*My parents believed in honesty and hard work,
and they passed that on to me.*

MONTY CRALLEY

Most of us can think of a number of things we can credit our parents with. For some of us there may not be as many good legacies as bad, however. But time has marched on and we can't redo a bad past. Nor does it help to continue rehashing it in our minds. Our parents simply passed on to us what they had learned. If it wasn't all good, let's hope we learned enough from it to break the pattern before we passed it on to our children.

Let's focus on the blessings and the positive experiences in our lives. While it's true that we learned something from every experience, even the ones that seemed vile at the time, the more pleasant ones helped us interact in a more hopeful manner with others. The more hope we had, the more hope we inspired in our friends, too. There was no better quality to pass on to others.

We are still passing on ideas and impressions to others. Every opinion we share, every favor we perform, every moment we intently listen to someone talk about themselves is our opportunity to pass along something positive to a person who needs us. Our work isn't done.

I will pass on something I can feel proud of today.

MARCH 17

We didn't have any money growing up,
but that isn't the essential. We had happiness.

HELEN CASEY

One of the most important lessons in life is how "valueless" money really is. While it's true, we need enough to take care of our physical needs; more than that brings little additional benefit. There are literally millions of wealthy, unhappy people in this world. It's trite and profoundly true that money doesn't buy happiness.

Where does happiness come from? Let's take a brief inventory of the times we have laughed in the past week. Were we opening envelopes containing money? That, of itself, is laughable. But the point is that happiness resides in our minds, not in other people, in possessions, or in wishes. We make it ourselves. We know this, certainly. But we forget it just as certainly.

The benefit of remembering this is that each day can be as much fun as we decide to make it. Being old or infirm or poor doesn't demand that we be unhappy too. What a powerful idea this is. And it's available to us every minute.

I am in charge of the kind of day I'll have today.
This has always been true, but I'll respect that thought today!

MARCH 18

Children need parents or other adults
to stand behind them.

ALPHA ENGLISH

The majority of us probably had either parents or teachers who offered suggestions about how to live more successfully. We may not have followed their example all that well, but the guidance was there. And we have survived many decades, so we haven't done all that badly even if we weren't good listeners. Our need for guidance, on occasion, is still a reality. Depending on the severity of our situation, it will behoove us to choose our confidants carefully.

Having others we can turn to brings us such comfort. No matter how old we are or how successful we were in our prime, we don't know all the answers. We never did. Two heads are generally better than one, and if we add a third, the wisdom of our inner voices, we'll likely make better decisions. Every day we'll be asked to make choices, decisions, changes in our lives. We'll do it more confidently if we have developed patterns of seeking help and comfort from those who are close and who care.

In a sense, we are always children. Our need for support and help is the hallmark of being human.

I am in need of a "parent" no matter how old I am.
What a blessing that I always have God to turn to.

MARCH 19

When you're younger, you are so vulnerable. There is a certain strength that comes from having dealt with life.

VIRGINIA ERICSON

Other than our own deaths, there is little we haven't experienced by now. We've known the turmoil of adolescence. We've felt the pride that accompanies career advancement and the disappointment over a missed promotion. Worry over the safety of our children and our parents is familiar. We've missed opportunities that would have changed our destiny and reaped rewards that we hadn't expected. Life has been full; our gift has been to grow confident and wise.

Having lived through so many ordeals prepares us for even the most uncertain of times. In this way we fare better than the really young. Their growing pains lie before them still. Knowing that no experience will get the best of us, or least not for long, offers us a peace that can only be felt, not explained. This is the gift of age.

Occasionally a challenge may seem too daunting. Let's remember that the decades have shown us that we are never given more than we can handle.

I'll not be given a bigger task than I can handle today. Recalling my past will give me the preparation I need.

MARCH 20

I am perfectly happy living,
but I look forward to dying.

TOM HARDING

What we believe about death defines how we approach it. Being afraid is all too common. But trusting that there is a loving Supreme Being can alleviate fear. We all know men and women who fit comfortably into either group. The choice for one or the other is ours to make. As a matter of fact, we have the freedom to make the choice daily if that's necessary. But by looking at our past, noting in particular the many times we were plucked from harm's way, we find pretty good evidence for believing that there is an all-powerful Presence who cares about us.

Life is an education. We've honed skills, mastered ideas, developed new theories, offered guidance to others who knew less than us. Surely our busyness has not been all for naught. We have had reason to live. In the same regard, it is just as possible to begin earnestly looking at our attitudes and beliefs toward death. We have worked too hard as life students for anything less.

Believing in God gives me peace.
Living and dying are the whole of life. I will not be afraid.
I will be protected. My friends will greet me.

MARCH 21

I think there is fate in how our lives work out.
I feel we have very little control.

MARIA REGNIER KRIMMEL

Few of us would wholly disagree with Maria. We might not label our lives as *fateful,* but we recognize there is something apparently going on besides just our personal dreams and expectations. Many of us find comfort in calling fate the hand of God. That gives us a sense of security when we don't know what lies ahead.

What is true for all of us, regardless of our beliefs, is that we have been fulfilling a purpose here. There is great comfort in that realization. It assures us that we can expect the future to be equally satisfying.

Need we do nothing in regard to where we are going? Some would say yes. But most of us prefer to believe that we have some responsibility for facilitating our movements. Doing nothing, being passive in every way, is deadening. Surely we weren't born to live this way.

> I may not know just where this day will lead me,
> but I can be willing to trust my fate.

*Due to my health problems,
I went from being completely active to zero activity.*

JAMES CASEY

While young, we neglected to value our physical well-being, our agility, our levels of energy. It gradually or, in some cases, instantly disappears. It forces us to take stock of who we are now and what we can still do with our lives. To go on in a meaningful way, we have to give careful thought to this. We may live in denial for a while; that's generally part of our process. We may be stuck in anger, too. But getting to acceptance and even gratitude for what our lives now mean is the eventual outcome we seek.

If physical activity is no longer possible, if we are rooted to a wheelchair or dependent on an oxygen tank, we can at least still communicate with others, by phone or letters or audiotapes. Being in "relationship" with other people can take many forms, and each of them is valuable and quite unique to each person and each circumstance. Giving good counsel, being an intent listener offers another person greater value and comfort than perhaps any other service we might have performed in our younger, healthier years. That's good to remember. Being limited by our physical conditions doesn't limit our value to the human race, ever.

I am here by design.
Whatever my condition is today,
I still have something of value to offer others.
I'll not forget this.

If I could do my life over,
I wouldn't have sold my business so soon.

SANDY WARMAN

We probably all have regrets of some kind. Being alive means having made mistakes; however, we usually made the best decisions we were capable of throughout our lives. We never intentionally screwed up. What many of us need help with now is accepting that the past was perfect as it was. No matter what we did or failed to do, it's okay. If we are caught in the trap of lamenting the past now, we'll fail to appreciate the present; and in the future we'll probably feel regrets about it, too. Let's stop going over the past in our minds. What's done is done, and we learned lessons we needed to learn.

It's so much more sensible to take this approach to life, isn't it? Why is it so hard to do, though? Perhaps because it became a habit to second-guess ourselves. Few of us were ever as confident as we longed to be. We took the critics in our lives too seriously. We always had available the comfort of a Higher Power, but too often we sought our answers from the intellect only or from other fallible human beings. Let's let the past go. It's done. It controls us no longer except in our minds, and we can change them instantly. What's standing in our way?

I can let go of regrets and bring a fresh perspective
to all my activities today.

When I knew I was going to retire,
I made a long list of all the things I wanted to do before I died.

FRAN COYNE

Having a plan for our lives makes sense regardless of our age. We did lots of planning, no doubt, when we were younger. Deciding which occupation to pursue, whom to marry, whether or not to have children, and where to live were all considerations that we made plans for. Some situations occurred that were unexpected, but generally we gave some thought to our direction in life.

Retirement works best when we approach it in the same way. We've been tightly scheduled for most of our lives. Thus one of the joys of retirement is that we can be more selective about what we do and when. But there is a downside to all of this freedom; we may begin to question our usefulness. Our busyness with work and family activities gave us little time to consider this before.

Appreciating the opportunity to pursue new avenues now that we have the time changes how we perceive our lives. We begin to see that we're a long way from "being done." And that's exciting. At least a half a dozen ideas of what we'd like to do come easily to mind, and that's a beginning. Just keep adding to the list and then take one at a time. The joy comes in living out the dream. If some pursuit isn't as fun or as challenging as we'd hoped, we can quit, immediately. We're the boss!

Today is a new opportunity.
I can do whatever appeals to me for as long as I choose.

MARCH 25

Once the garden was laid out,
I knew I should find something else to do.

MARIA REGNIER KRIMMEL

Must we do something all the time? We probably know some who think so. And maybe for them that's right. We must not compare ourselves to others, however. We did enough of that throughout our lives. In those comparisons we seldom measured up, right? Now we have the freedom to do only what we want to. If that means being busy fourteen hours a day, that's fine. The days we want to lie around and read a book, nothing more, are fine, too.

The best thing about being busy is discovering we still have a lot to give the world. It's not uncommon to retire and feel like we're useless. Depression dogs a lot of people initially. Discovering the right rhythm for this phase of our lives takes time. But exploring our imagination about all those activities that sound fun and then choosing one to pursue is a good beginning. Nothing says we have to do it forever. The really good part of this phase of our lives is that we can quit whatever we're doing whenever we want to.

What I do today is my choice.
Perhaps I made a plan yesterday that no longer appeals to me.
I can change my mind.

MARCH 26

*After my husband died and I was searching for things
to fill the empty spaces, I got the piano.*

ALICE MERRYMAN

In our youth, we had few empty spaces to fill. Most of us ran
from pillar to post just trying to keep up with our lives. Jobs,
families, children, friends crammed the hours in a day. We
longed for the time when life moved slower. And now it's here.
Funny, we're not quite as excited about the slowdown as we'd expected to be.

Why is that? Was being busy all the time our way of avoiding
what we might learn in the quiet spaces? We can't avoid them
now, can we? But we can assume there is only good in them. We
know this is true because with age has come wisdom, and we
have come to believe that our attitudes are everything. With
good attitudes, all experiences, the noisy ones along with the
quiet ones, inform us of information we need.

Any change in our circumstances can be an opportunity for
opening a new door. As we grow old, many circumstances in our
lives will change. But let's rejoice for the freedom it gives us.

**I can begin a new activity today. What I did or didn't do
when I was younger need not control me now.**

> *Since my husband got sick,*
> *my main objective has been to make more friends.*

RUTH CASEY

Recognizing our need for the support and companionship of friends is important at any age. It's doubly important when we get older and feel less courageous about handling all the new and unexpected circumstances that visit us. The feedback we get from others can make the difference between making a decision in a state of fear or a state of peace.

There are other reasons for making new friends, too. One of the most important ones is that no friend lives forever. If we have limited our list to just a few, the death of any one of them leaves a big void. Certainly, we can't protect ourselves from the grief of loss, nor should we. Grief is a natural emotion that we need to acknowledge, but we can move through it more comfortably if we have the support of others who understand the sadness of loss.

Having women and men to laugh with and make plans with grows in importance, too, as we age. Our interaction with others staves off boredom and dull-mindedness. We don't lose intelligence as we age. Nor do we lose our sense of humor. However, both need to be exercised. Friends help us do that.

> I will make plans with a friend today.
> We need each other's companionship.

MARCH 28

Another advantage of being older . . . you can get a parcel
of time that's big enough to do something.

LEE ERICSON

Our lives resembled the compartments in a desk before we retired. We had specific responsibilities and certain times to do them. An occasional hour was all we could steal for a leisure activity. Often then we were too tired for much. Hobbies? Sure we thought about them. We probably even knew a few men or women who found time for them. Now, our time has come.

But how do you develop a hobby if you've never had one? We may feel intimidated initially. Have you ever even asked yourself the question, "What would I most like to do for fun?" Start making a list. We all have dreams. All we need to do is choose one and begin. It's probably best to keep our first choice simple. We want to experience success, not frustration.

The daily gift of our present situation is that we don't have to rush. No boss is hounding us. No paycheck hangs over us. We have the time we need to do what we want. Let's rejoice.

I will not run out of time today.
Tomorrow is only a sleep away.

MARCH 29

*I plant a seed about what I want to do
and then watch it take different directions.*

FRAN COYNE

Fran's openness to accepting God's involvement in his hopes and dreams makes his life far more peaceful than many of our lives may be. Trusting in a spiritual solution, the *right* turn of events for a particular situation, means having the willingness to lay our own willfulness aside. God will always have a better plan for us than we can imagine. This has always been the case, throughout our lives. It's likely that on many occasions we thwarted God's plan and caused ourselves undue pain. Have we decided to listen and to trust God's involvement now? It's never too late to try this approach.

Ruminating about the many years that have passed gives us the opportunity to see our struggles and our successes in the workplace and in the home in a new light. Those times and circumstances that caused great pain for us and others need not have been so devastating. Our resistance to the change that beckoned gave rise to our troubled state of mind. Many of us simply couldn't let go of trying to control every detail of our lives and others. God is the best manager. Do we finally understand this?

**My job today is the same as every day that I have lived.
I consider what I'd like to do, and then let God
decide how and if it needs to be done.**

I think women have come a long way.
We have come into it by just stepping in
and doing something that we were forbidden to do.

CLARA GLENN

There are few things we are forbidden to do. That's one of the blessings of old age, regardless of gender. Family and friends aren't as intent on trying to control us as they might have been in the past. We have also *earned the right*, so to speak, to tackle whatever activities appeal to us now. We're not so afraid of failure as we might have been in our youth or when pursuing a career. And we don't care as much what others think about our choices or pursuits. There are myriad payoffs to getting old.

Having the freedom to decide exactly what we want to do with the day or hour or summer is a real treat. We have earned this reward because of our willingness to do whatever needed to be done when we were younger. Most of us did far more than was expected of us on many occasions. Fear may have motivated us. It seldom hinders us now.

Excitement generally accompanies the anticipation of forbidden activities. Fortunately we don't have to relinquish excitement just because so little is forbidden anymore. Excitement is a matter of attitude. We can have as much of it as we want. Whatever we set out to do today will benefit from our willingness to get excited.

I can be as fulfilled as I choose today —
whether my projects are big or small.

MARCH 31

Retirement has been too busy at times.
I've had to check with nine organizations when I wanted
to travel rather than just my secretary.

PAT JEROME

Most of us looked forward to lots of free time when we retired. Whether we had been employed out of the home or as home-makers, our time was seldom unstructured. The notion of hav-ing to answer to no one appealed to all of us, no doubt. And then we added the role of volunteer. We often found ourselves over-committed, busier perhaps than when we were still employed. How did that happen?

Many people fear having too much time on their hands, so they get involved with organizations that need extra, unpaid help. Most of us have reaped meaningful rewards from just such involvements. But we have to take frequent stock of how we want to spend our time. We can get so busy that we fail to allow any time for the flexibility we'd looked forward to in retirement.

Learning to say no when we're called on to "do just one more thing" for even the worthiest of organizations may become nec-essary, and it may not be easy. When we were still "gainfully em-ployed," we knew we could only handle so much with grace and devoted attention. The same is still true. Let's take stock now.

Am I busier than I want to be today?
Only I can change that.

APRIL

APRIL 1

*Since we've retired, for the first time in our lives
we do exactly as we please.*

ANN CRALLEY

Not everybody considers the freedom referred to above as a blessing. Some need more structure to keep from being bored or depressed. That's not bad; however, it limits our creativity. Having nothing on the agenda can push us to explore new activities, perhaps even engage strangers in conversation. We can never be certain just what might be in store for us unless we are willing to take risks, to be available for unplanned journeys.

Never before in our lives were we as free as we are now. Our careers have ended. The kids are grown. We have worked hard and we deserve the freedom that's ours now. What we do with it day by day will be as enriching as our minds can imagine.

Let's take just this day, one day at a time. If we could do anything, what would it be? Perhaps our first idea can't be realized, but that's not reason enough to quit dreaming. Let's be daring, just this once.

**Taking a risk to do something new today just might be fun.
What have I got to lose?**

APRIL 2

Everybody has what it takes to express himself.

JANICE CLARK

Talent has been bestowed on all of us. We doubt this only because, regardless of age, we compare ourselves with others too often. We fail to see that our callings are unique, not quite like anyone else's, and that we aren't really comparable to them. We've been told this for years. Why do we disbelieve it anyway?

There is no time like the present for changing our philosophy about life. But how do we begin? Let's start by accepting the fact that we are blessed with gifts that are unique to us. Next, let's assume that the people who come into our lives—who have been coming into our lives for decades—are in need of what we, and only we, can give. Additionally, let's continually extend compliments to others for their achievements, quietly being thankful for our own as well.

We can learn to believe in our strengths, seeing them as our special talents, by earnestly deciding that they are so. It's a simple, but profound, change in attitude. We can do it.

My talent can be expressed in many ways today.
The easiest is to lovingly acknowledge the presence of others.
The rest will follow.

Coming back to writing after all these years was difficult.
In a way, it was like catching up
and dreaming old dreams in a fresh way.

DON KENNETT

Putting aside an activity, even one we love, is sometimes necessary. It never means we can't pick it up again. We aren't always able to control what we'll do with our lives. Unexpected opportunities beckon that can't be ignored. What we can be certain of is that we'll be drawn to what we need to do day by day.

"Picking up where we left off" is an expression common to us all. However, because we have seen and thought and felt many things since we were last involved in the current pursuit, we will see it in a new way today. Coming fresh to the table promises us the growth and understanding we're actually ready for now.

We sometimes fear we will have lost our touch if we have put an activity aside for some time. We may have to redevelop our skill, whether at writing or tennis or gardening, but that's not bad. What we bring to the experience now is wisdom that we didn't have earlier. Who knows what that may mean to our ability level?

How I see anything today is, at the very least,
slightly different from yesterday.
That's good for me and my experiences.

*Painting requires letting your unconscious go to work.
My wife taught me that.*

MONTY CRALLEY

Monty is a painter who approaches his work so gently, so intuitively. He allows his inner spirit to guide the brush. The end product pleases his heart.

When it comes to putting a brush to canvas ourselves, or a pencil to paper, or flowers in a vase, or any creative pursuit, we must learn to let our hearts influence the outcome. We can approach projects however we want. We don't have to get bogged down in technical concerns or how others will judge our work. All that's important is that we enjoy it. Finding something we enjoy, something about which we can feel passionate, is the real pursuit anyway.

**Do I feel passionate about anything right now?
Let me give this careful consideration today.**

APRIL 5

What we've sown, we will reap.
These are the harvest years.

JEAN WILL

We can't undo the seeds of fear or doubt or rage we may have planted in our children or other family members in years past. Our consequences may rear their heads with regularity. And when they do, we have to seek forgiveness.

Likewise, our good deeds toward family and friends reap benefits too. It's particularly helpful in these, our golden years, when "this harvest" is bountiful.

It's good to remember that as long as we're alive, we're still sowing and reaping. We are never done and each day presents us with additional opportunities to ensure better harvests for our future. Celebrating this empowers us to remember it before we take any action. In this way, we can ensure a future that we'll want.

The good deeds of our youth are not forgotten.
Today's good deeds will bless us in our tomorrows as well.

APRIL 6

Life is getting to be different, but I still have goals set and projects. I've got a closet full of them.

ALICE MERRYMAN

Laziness is the prize some claim when they get old. That's okay if it really pleases them. However, most people feel better when they are involved in something beyond themselves. One of the most treasured gifts of older age is that we have the freedom to pursue whatever draws our interest. While working long hours and raising a family, we had to shelve some dreams for a better time. The better time has arrived.

Not everyone has a closet full of projects, but we all have one or two ideas we've thought about pursuing. Maybe we've considered taking a drawing class or chronicling the history of our family. Gardening is rewarding for those who do it. Agencies of all kinds need our help as volunteers. We still have our wisdom to contribute. What's most often needed is mere common sense. We don't lack for that, certainly, or we'd not have arrived at this rich old age.

I'll talk with a friend about my life today.
New ideas will come to me.
New ideas mean new directions, too.

APRIL 7

*I know I'm not going to just sit down and fold my hands.
These are good years now, but I've never seen the time
when I didn't think that the next year would be better.*

J. M. SPICER

Attitude is everything. But we are sometimes lazy about taking control of how we think and act. It's okay to take the day off occasionally; however, letting a poor-me attitude become habitual is far too easy. We have all observed others who have mastered this, and they are not much fun to be with.

It's not really all that difficult to set a positive tone for the day that's unfolding. Smiling at ourselves in the mirror is a first step. So is making a phone call to a friend. Listening to music we love or reading an inspirational passage in a favorite book chases away the dread we might be feeling.

But if it lingers and none of our attempts lift our spirits, talking over our worries with a friend or counselor might be necessary. Pursuing such a solution is a practical step.

Abraham Lincoln said,
"We're just as happy as we make up our minds to be."
This gives me hope today. I'll share mine with a friend, too.

APRIL 8

My husband, my children, and my faith
have provided my best memories.

HELEN CASEY

Spouses and children understandably make up many of our "good" memories. Most of our adult years have been devoted, quite specifically, to them. Pointing to one's faith as a "best" memory is perhaps less common, but how fortunate that it's been true for some, like Helen Casey. That her faith is a good memory implies that it has served her well, of course. If we haven't all shared that experience with our faith, let's consider why we haven't and then decide if we'd like to change that part of our lives now. It's not too late.

What can having faith do for us? The kind of worry that destroys our appetite and disrupts our sleep loses its hold on us if we have faith. Wearing ourselves out trying to plan outcomes for all our activities can be a thing of the past, with faith. Giving up the awesome burden of trying to control the other people in our lives gives us a new perspective and so much freedom. Faith means having trust that we, and everyone else, are always in good hands. Recalling the past, knowing that God was in charge, uplifts us even if we didn't acknowledge it then.

How lucky I am that I can develop more faith, even at this age.
Faith can free me from my burdens.

APRIL 9

My spiritual life has changed in the last few years.

JAMES CASEY

Most of us have expanded our understanding of "the spiritual life." We may have grown up in religious homes. At our age, that wouldn't be unusual. But now we realize that didn't necessarily mean we were encouraged to be spiritual. The idea of "spirituality" might have been suspect, even. To our parents it may have sounded like the occult rather than a church affiliation.

What spirituality meant to Jim, and perhaps means to many of us, is having a relationship we nurture with the Creator, however we define that. It means believing we have an inner voice that is eager to offer us guidance whenever we are at a loss about what to do. Practicing a spiritual life also relieves us of the burden of worry about the future. We know it will take care of itself, in the same way as we'll be taken care of.

As we move through life, we continue to be confronted by conflict and problems over which we have no control. That's the learning curve, nothing more. We'll always be on this path. The good news is that our response to the struggle will change in proportion to our willingness to seek God's help.

How I see God and my life should keep changing.
Will I do my part to open my eyes wider today?

I think my peace comes from my good fortune.

JIM BURNS

How we define "good fortune" is a significant indicator of one's attitude. While winning the lottery might be judged as good fortune by all of us, virtually every other occurrence will be evaluated in a very individualistic way. What seems like a wonderful situation or opportunity to one might greatly frighten his or her neighbor.

Peacefulness is a feeling everyone deserves. Thank goodness it's attainable. Perhaps we're beginning to realize that it always was available even though it didn't seem within our grasp. The fault was never the result of external circumstances, even though that was where we laid the blame. Finally, we're becoming willing to see that we will have all the peace and good fortune we want by simply taking charge of how we interpret the experiences that trouble us.

We're never too old to develop a positive outlook on life. Some say, "I'm too old to change." But that's not true. Let's offer a good example to a friend who is still stuck in the chaos of a defeated perspective. Our demonstration of the attainment of peace may be all this person needs.

Peace can be enjoyed by me today, regardless of circumstances, if I shift my perception ever so slightly.

APRIL 11

It seems that everything that has happened to me
has been accidental.

MARIA REGNIER KRIMMEL

No one would argue that we aren't allowed to think of life as simply accidental. That perspective is shared by some of us, in fact. However, it can result in unnecessary worry because its very nature doesn't foster the idea that we're protected from life's dangers. Isn't it preferable to think that we have a willing guardian?

Perhaps it's too big of a shift in perception to move from a viewpoint that's similar to Maria's to one that says all aspects of one's life have been planned in every detail. But maybe we can adopt a view that rests somewhere between these extremes. We obviously still have some life yet to live, so why not live it with less worry and consternation? By believing that we have been watched over, at least in some respects, we can cultivate a level of acceptance that whatever is happening on any one day will ultimately be good for us.

Hindsight assures us that this has been true. On many earlier occasions, particularly in our youth, we were certain our lives were over. When a relationship ended or a job was lost, we were devastated. But something better always came along, didn't it?

There is purpose to what happens today.
I may not immediately like a circumstance,
but it will grow on me.

APRIL 12

Many of us resist the changes that happen around us. We get comfortable with how things are, thus fearful about how they might become. Commonly, we don't think we have changed much over the years, except perhaps in appearance. Yet one of the most obvious ways we have changed is our reaction to the way the world and people around us are changing. It didn't bother us so much before, did it? Why does it now?

The reasons are varied and many. Confidence often wanes in proportion to the aging process. We lose strength, perhaps. Our memory is not as sharp. Our energy dissipates far more quickly than when we were in our prime. Thus we feel more vulnerable. With vulnerability comes uncertainty, the nesting ground for fear of change. It would help us to inventory all of the changes we've "survived" in our lives. The acknowledgment, alone, will give us strength and hope about living through whatever changes are in store for us now. They will come. And we can handle them.

Change is the necessary order of this world.
I have been doing it all along.
I can do it quite successfully now, too.

APRIL 13

I have thought on many things
And after thinking find
One's world is not a stable thing
But a product of the mind.

IDA BELLEGARDE

Understanding and accepting Ida's philosophy simplifies our lives. It guarantees that what we dwell on, we'll experience. Another way of saying it is, "As we think, so we are." This puts us in the driver's seat, so to speak, but not all of us want the responsibility for how our lives are unfolding. We have had and we will have whatever experiences we desire in this life. That's a thrilling, awesome, sometimes fearful thought.

Often we have marveled at how easily some others go through life. They seem to avoid the calamities that befall us. Considering Ida's simple poem for a moment gives us another perspective. Those who sail through life have quite probably *pictured* a different set of experiences for themselves. They are not favored by the gods; they simply use their minds to a sweeter advantage. Rest assured, we can do the same.

Today is mine to picture and enjoy.
A moment's contemplation will give me what I long for.

APRIL 14

The only time you have is what you take.

HARRY BARTHOLOMEW

We all know folks who never have time to join us for dinner or movies or socializing. Probably we can't imagine what keeps them so busy. Are we envious? Perhaps we're not busy enough. It's not always easy to take up the challenge of a new activity alone, but sometimes it's necessary. We can't wait for others to free us from our own boredom. It's nice to have companionship, but ultimately, we need to find satisfaction with our own company. When we've mastered that, we'll more fully enjoy every minute we get to spend with a favored companion.

The opportunities we missed in the past won't come again. But that's okay. We'll have additional ones beckon as we're ready for them. Just because we're in the "sunset" of our lives doesn't mean the fun and adventure has ended. It's quite possible that the best experiences haven't even called to us yet. Take time to listen to the requests for our involvement. Seek out activities you always dreamed of doing. You'll discover that your time will be well spent. We never know how many more days we'll have. We only know we can live this day to its fullest.

I'll have no time for boredom today if I follow my whims.

APRIL 15

Nothing gets old but your clothes.
Only giving up and giving in makes you old.

EVA WINES

Attitude is what makes us feel old. The number of years we've lived or the infirmity we suffer isn't nearly as important to our perception of age as is our attitude.

No doubt we know someone who has given up. We may have had bouts of depression and immobility too. We will experience whatever we choose daily. In the midst of a bout, it's not always easy to remember that we and only we have the power to discard it.

When we feel like giving up because we are tired and lonely, what might we do instead? Writing a note to someone we miss, calling a friend who seldom gets out or picking up a book we always meant to read takes us outside of ourselves. We'll find treasures there that we hadn't counted on. Our lives are only as gloomy as we make them.

I have control of my thinking today. I do every day, in fact.
I'll adopt a positive attitude today.

APRIL 16

*We've lived long enough to see the things we have been
interested in come full circle, and it's very gratifying.*

LOUIS FREUND

Louis Freund's experience may not match our own. We haven't
all had lives that flowed smoothly from one experience to the
next, from one era to the next. But we are coming to understand
the part many seemingly unfortunate occurrences played in our
development. That may not seem gratifying, but at least we
don't live in total darkness about the meaning of our lives.

Very few of us have done everything we set out to do in our
youth. Some of us fear we have missed key opportunities, but it's
really never too late to open a new door. The experiences that are
right for us will still be available to us if we have the right frame
of mind and the willingness to pursue them. We aren't too old to
try something new. That's merely a lame excuse many use when
they don't really want to travel a new path.

How do we get inspired to try something new? Try dreaming
a bit about the past. What comes to mind? No doubt it will be
something that brought you joy. Why not explore a related activity today? After all, as we've all heard, this is the first day of the
rest of your life.

**I have twenty-four hours to fill however I want today.
That's an exciting thought.**

APRIL 17

I have no fear of death. I'm prepared to go.
As Father Adrian said, it isn't death we fear, it's fear we fear.

HELEN CASEY

Reading the obituary column before anything else in the morning paper has become standard practice for many of us. Years of friends and acquaintances will be found there eventually. We wonder if they were ready to die. Some bearers of wisdom claim that no one dies without his or her own consent. Some go so far as to say we are in on the planning of our deaths throughout our lives, but we simply haven't lived consciously in those spaces of our minds.

It's going to happen. But how we prepare for it or even think about it defines the rest of our lives. That's an awesome reality. It frightens some; however, it can free us up too. It's all in how we interpret it.

Regardless of our age, we have done a lot of living to get to this point. We have met with success and failure. We have lived with dread and joyful enthusiasm. We have had periods of peace and times of turmoil. Death may have seemed appealing on occasion. It may even now. Accepting it as another stage of our lives diminishes our fear.

I am ready to follow God's call today.
Whatever it is will fit my divine assignment.

APRIL 18

*My retirement hasn't been easy
because it came earlier than I'd counted on.*

BUD SHERMAN

Bud's story is not unusual. Many of us reading these pages were forced out of our jobs, and that situation can leave a lingering sense of self-doubt in our minds. But we can get beyond the pain of the experience with some willingness. Having a good support system around us will help. So will having a belief in spiritual "salvation."

We won't ever have all the answers we deserve regarding the circumstances in our lives. Over the years, many things happened that felt unfair or that we didn't understand. Depending on their nature, or how they affected us, we easily assimilated them or perhaps denied them. We generally got beyond them, at least. Some of our friends perhaps handled the mysteries in their lives more easily than ourselves. Might they have relied on a spiritual answer to those situations they didn't understand?

The point here is that some believe a spiritual perspective can always be adopted if confronted by an uncomfortable or frightening experience. Relying on a spiritual explanation might not change the experience, but it will change how we see it. And isn't that all that really matters?

**I have experienced much that I hadn't counted on.
Today may offer the same. I'll seek spiritual solace if necessary.**

APRIL 19

One of the reasons I want to give up some of my volunteer activities is so I can take advantage of other opportunities that might come my way. Right now I'm too busy to do that.

PAT JEROME

Opportunities seem to come to busy people. Why is that? We have all heard the adage, "If you want something done, give it to a busy person." Generally speaking, busy people tend to be organized and efficient. Busy people, even though retired, still tend to get the most done.

Let's remember that if we fall into this category, we're not required to maintain a certain pace. When we go too fast, when we take on too many activities, we might miss unexpected opportunities. Those opportunities are not simply happenstance; they come to certain people quite intentionally. That doesn't mean, of course, that they have to be taken advantage of, but there is something special in them for us or we'd not have attracted them. *Opportunities are invitations to dance with God.*

Am I eager to pursue a unique opportunity today?

APRIL 20

*I squandered a lot of time over my life
and now I'm trying to make up for it.*

TOM HARDING

This is a feeling common to many of us. Perhaps we did waste lots of time and effort when we were younger, but so what? We did only what we knew to do at the time, and it seemed to be right then. To lament endlessly over past failings prevents us from making the most of the present. And how lucky we are to have a *present* to be a part of!

Trying to make up for our lazy past just doesn't work, no matter how reasonable it may seem at the moment. That might be our natural inclination, particularly if we're really excited about a hobby or some class that we're taking, but pushing ourselves beyond our energy level or our ability to sustain concentration will only overwhelm us in time. When that feeling sets in, we feel defeated rather than exhilarated. We don't need that, and we can avoid it quite easily.

Pacing ourselves in whatever pursuit we choose will ensure our success. That doesn't mean we're going to write the great novel or be another Grandma Moses. But we will find joy in our lives. No matter how much or how little we think we had in the past, we can chart a new course for ourselves now. Let's get busy!

I can use today as I choose.

APRIL 21

I felt I was doing something wrong when I retired at fifty-six, but I didn't know how to ask for help.

SANDY WARMAN

No doubt we'd all change some aspects of our lives if we had the chance. But giving too much of the present over to lamenting the past negatively influences today's experiences. The past cannot be redone. Of course we know that. So why is it that we harbor such disappointment in ourselves?

Some think it's simply the human condition to heap judgment on ourselves. It probably has seemed that way because so many do it. It's not a given, however. It's a decision, one that we can refrain from making. Regardless of which decade we're living now, it's never too late to form a new habit of thought. Any moment is the right moment to begin forming a new habit.

Let's consider, for instance, the accomplishments we've had in our lives. We all have examples to point to, and each of them related, in some way, to a previous failure or success. There has been a thread running through our lives that has tied our experiences together. And we've needed every one of them. Let's not lament the past. It served us well. It brought us here.

Today I will appreciate the journey that brought me here.

I believe in doing the things you want to do before it's too late.

FRAN COYNE

One of the realities of life is potential infirmity as we age. Some of us will remain physically fit and agile throughout our lives, but many of us will begin to experience the health problems associated with aging. That certainly doesn't mean we become housebound and unable to pursue hobbies or volunteer work, but we will have some limitations. We need to be realistic about the inevitable future and pursue activities that are more demanding now while we still have our strength and health.

What are those activities? No one can answer that question for us, but we know what our dreams and our current capabilities are. Being honest with ourselves is a necessity. Retirement is a benefit most of our ancestors didn't get to enjoy. They often worked until death. Having the time and the health to explore new interests is a wonderful opportunity. We all know men and women who are sitting idly, depressed because their lives seem empty. Perhaps one of the things we can put on our list today is to try to interest someone else in joining us in an activity.

Today I am called to get involved.

One of the best parts of retirement is
that you can do things when you want to do them.

THELMA ELLIOTT

Retirement is full of many small pleasures, along with the bigger ones. The freedom to do what we want, when we want, is one of these. What makes this so special? No doubt it's because we were constrained by time and responsibilities for so many years. Simply not having to live according to someone else's timetable is such a treat.

There is a downside to all this freedom for some, however. Having too much time on our hands breeds boredom, or worse, a sense of worthlessness. Many of us avoided wondering about our worth when we were still actively involved in our profession or in raising the family. Our busyness meant we never had time for personal contemplation. Now, maybe it seems that's all we have to do.

If we're fortunate, we have made friends with men and women who can assure us we are worthy human beings with a job still to do. And if we don't have those kinds of friends around us, it's our job to find them! Richard Bach, the writer, said that if we're still alive, our work isn't done. That's a comforting thought. The good news is that we can do our work whenever we feel like it.

I can plan for today however it suits me.
I'm the boss at last.

APRIL 24

For me it was a miracle when I turned my letters to the kids
into newsletters that I sent to dozens of friends every month.

JAMES CASEY

Some people can always turn a negative into a positive. That's just their nature. Jim was one of these. He lost his voice box to cancer, so he began writing letters by the dozens. The letters evolved into a monthly newsletter that many looked forward to. He wasn't destroyed by his condition; he turned it into something that benefited others as well as himself. Do you share Jim's outlook on your current condition?

What some of us may need is a shift in perception. It sounds easy enough, doesn't it? But it takes willingness, a lot of it, to seek to see the good in a circumstance that has negatively impacted us. It helps if we can believe that every situation is the right one for us to experience. It doesn't matter if we really understand this or not. We simply must make the decision to see each experience as an opportunity that will change everything about the rest of our journeys.

We do get what is right for us. This has always been true. Let's make sure we honor this principle today.

How I see my life today will determine my level of contentment.
If I need a shift in perception, I need only seek it.

APRIL 25

Now I can let my imagination take flight as I sit and do some thinking, pondering. After a while, ideas begin to come to me ... and I have this tremendous energy.

MONTY CRALLEY

Asking the inner voice for direction each day guarantees it, as long as we are quiet and patient. And the ideas that flood our quiet minds perfectly match the talents we have been given. What we have done with our lives and what we are still destined to do reveals our purpose. It's easy to discern it when we are quiet and hopeful.

Having the energy to pursue our passions will always come if that's our wish. Most of who we are, what we do, and where we are going relates to our attitude. Being tired, bored, scared, or unhappy are decisions, nothing more. Coming to grips with this reality has the potential for changing every aspect of what remains of our lives.

Those among us who are having fun are our guides. We can follow their examples. They haven't been *given* better lives; they simply are better at using their minds. We can copy them and laugh more too.

My mind bestows energy on my body.
I'll do as much or as little as I please today.

APRIL 26

I'm old now. I've had my turn to run things. It's time
for others to take over, but I'll always be available to help.

ALPHA ENGLISH

Having the wisdom and the grace to know when it's time to step
down isn't experienced by everyone. We seldom fail to recognize
when someone else has missed his or her cue. But do we "stay
too long at the party" ourselves? It's not easy to see our own
shortcomings. A good rule of thumb is that when we see something we don't like in others, regardless of what it is, we can be
pretty sure we share the trait.

Perhaps it's helpful to recall how we felt when we were first
trying to assume responsibility for an activity or event and an
"old-timer" had all the answers, even when we hadn't asked the
questions. It's our human tendency to repeat their mistakes. We
need not feel ashamed of this trait but simply recognize it. We
learned many valuable things in this lifetime. It's not unusual to
think we should share them all with the next generation, no
matter their age or level of experience.

Our job is never done. That's the good news. It simply
changes. Some even believe that with age comes the most important of all jobs: being examples of the attainment of peace.
This is a lesson everyone needs to learn. Let's show someone
how it's done today.

My greatest achievement is knowing peace.
I'll reflect this willingly many times today.

APRIL 27

*My philosophy is to do a little shifting
and give somebody else some encouragement
to do something besides sit down in an easy chair.*

VIOLET HENSLEY

Is there something wrong with sitting down in an easy chair? If that's where you are right now, don't get up, not yet at least. Resting, meditating, contemplating our lives and the future all happen best in easy chairs, so we're not admonished to stay out of them altogether. Let's not languish in them, however. We still have lots of living to do or we'd have passed on like many of our friends.

Knowing that we're "not done" is our first certainty today. And we know that's also true for those we're traveling among. But just because we're surrounded by people doesn't mean they are all eager to be involved with life today. Here's where we can help.

Offering words of encouragement to a friend who wants to learn a new skill or take an exotic trip is worth our effort. It may well be that that's our foremost "assignment" today. It's assuredly not an accident that we have the friends and acquaintances we have. They are part of our divine unfolding. That means we're part of theirs as well. Let's help each other.

**I have been here a long time. I am still called to fulfill my part.
Even though I may not fully understand it, I am needed today.**

APRIL 28

If you argue with a person who is unbalanced, after a few minutes it's hard to tell which one of you is unbalanced.

JIM BURNS

Differing opinions and perspectives add a richness to life. There would be no incentive to broaden our understanding of anything, to change how we perceive people or circumstances, if we found ourselves in agreement with everyone every moment. So being in absolute agreement isn't the goal; however, being willing to accept others' opinions freely, without the need to change them, is. The curious thing, of course, is that when others don't try to change us or our opinions, but honor whatever view we have, we feel more willing to open our minds to something new. And vice versa.

The lucky among us learned long ago that it was no reflection on us when others didn't agree with our opinions. Some of us are still struggling to believe that. A good way to check out this idea, though, is to take note of how certain admired friends respond to adversity or a very opinionated person. We always marvel at how they can smile and walk away from a conflict. They have no special talent. They have merely learned, earlier than ourselves, the more important quality of respect and acceptance. "Being right" is always a matter of degree and perspective. Being at peace is always a matter of choice.

I can choose peace rather than trying to "sell" an opinion today.

APRIL 29

*I'm glad I worked hard all my life.
I passed that on to my children. I wanted them to have
to work. It builds character.*

ALICE MERRYMAN

Hard work may not be considered a blessing by all of us, particularly when our work has been unappreciated, but it always helps to develop one's character. Even if we hated our job or our boss, we managed to figure out how to tolerate unpleasant situations, and that's character-building. We can see this better now than when we were younger, no doubt. Pointing this truth out to our children might not have been particularly appreciated either. Fortunately, hindsight is a wonderful teacher for all of us.

One of the good things about years of hard work is the contrast we are now privy to. Having more time to do nothing, if we're so inclined, or to pursue a wholly new line of work or play, is generally recognized as a blessing. Those among us who still dwell on problems of the past or complain about the present maybe don't want to experience the joy that's available to us.

Being glad for whatever kind of life we had might be considered wisdom. What our work was, who our families were, the achievements we aspired to, all made their mark on our lives. This will hold true for our futures, too.

**Today is an open book. What I decide to do today
influences tomorrow, too. I will make a good choice.**

APRIL 30

I am living out my life in accordance with my faith.

RUTH CASEY

Does faith in God guide your actions as it does Ruth's? It's certain our actions are guided by some set of beliefs. If our memories of past situations are troublesome, maybe it's because we allowed our behavior to be controlled by certain beliefs that did us harm. How might we define our beliefs for a friend today? Are we at peace with them?

Belief systems don't simply occur in our lives mysteriously. We consciously choose that which we adhere to, whether we realize this or not. Sometimes our families foisted their beliefs on us, even when they weren't comfortable to us. Until we were old enough to decide what fit us better, we may have had little recourse. Later, we may have adopted beliefs that matched those of our peers—even though these beliefs contradicted our personal ethics.

Acknowledging the existence of an underlying set of values gives us both security and relief. It means we don't have to spend many valuable hours worrying about the right thing to do in every situation. The actions that fit our belief systems will be obvious. Let's be willing to monitor how our beliefs impact the lives of those around us. It's never too late to consider changing them.

Today's experiences will reflect what I choose to believe.
Does that promise me peace?

MAY

MAY 1

I try to plan my life one day ahead.

TOM HARDING

Living such a focused life isn't all that easy, is it? Depending on the kind of occupation we were in, we may have been responsible for creating budgets and strategic plans that projected us well into the future. Limiting our attention to this day may leave us feeling unprepared for the future. And yet, aren't we lucky that we don't have to plan for others anymore?

It makes sense to give some thought to the next day if we are expecting to share it with a friend. Otherwise, simply savoring each moment as it comes can be quite rewarding. If we're too intent on what we think we should be doing, we miss the spontaneous opportunities that are bound to arise. It's not wrong to think ahead about the afternoon or evening. It's not wrong to think about next week or next year. But we don't need the aggravation of worrying about the future. We did enough of that when we were younger, trying to succeed in careers, trying to raise a family.

Now that we're free of the daunting responsibilities of stressful work, let's not complicate our lives by getting ahead of ourselves. Who knows what tomorrow may feel like? Let's wait until it's here to make our plans.

**Today is all I really need to consider. In fact,
I don't even have to think of the whole day. What a treat!**

MAY 2

*I don't think you're suddenly going to begin to look at
the world with new eyes when you're eighty if you haven't
been doing it when you're thirty.*

JANICE CLARK

We are creatures of habit as evidenced by our getting stuck in
old viewpoints long after they have quit serving us. However,
that fact doesn't restrict us for all time. Anytime we want to
cultivate a new idea, an alternative approach to a situation, we
are free to do so. Janice may be right regarding some people she
has known, but we are capable of freshening our perspective at
any age.

We have all known some elderly men and women who have
the spirit and enthusiasm of the very young. Unfortunately, we
have also known the reverse. How sad to observe the forty- or
fifty-year-old person who has quit living. Their whining belies
their age. Who will we be? The choice is always available to us.
And we can remake it as often as we wish.

What a relief to know that if we're old and resentful today, we
still have the opportunity to be young and full of laughter
tomorrow. We maybe can't do everything we used to do, but this
decision is still in our power.

**I will open my eyes to whatever I choose to see today.
Yesterday's experiences have only the power I give them.**

MAY 3

Even though I'm nearly ninety,
every day I have something to do.

MONTY CRALLEY

Every person reading this book realizes the importance of having something to do upon arising each morning. Many of us have been out of the work force for decades, but we have still needed to be busy. Having something to do keeps us engaged in life. Having too little to do, too little to think about but ourselves, leaves us bored.

There are so many untried activities that we've considered doing at some point in our lives. Maybe we didn't have the time or the money. Family obligations or our need to advance on the job left us too few hours for play. For most, that's no longer the case. We've been given a reprieve from many obligations. And regardless of our financial standing or the state of our health, there's at least one activity we always said we wished we could do. Let's seek to remember it.

If nothing comes immediately to mind, perhaps sorting through old photos will trigger a memory. Talking with a friend might help, too. In fact, something that currently interests him or her might be the reminder.

I'll not tarry long in bed today.
There's much to do and I want to get started.

MAY 4

Many people think they can't paint,
but I think everyone has artistic ability of some kind.

EVA WINES

Many of us probably don't agree with Eva, particularly if we haven't tried to paint or weave or write or throw pots. We mistakenly think that others have talent, never ourselves, but that's because we misunderstand what talent means. Talent is really just an inclination; it develops from a desire to pursue some activity that we then proceed to cultivate with a passion. It's not mysterious. It doesn't just happen. We persevere because we feel good when involved in the activity. When we define talent this way, we realize how right Eva is. It's just that many of us haven't followed our passion yet.

One thing we all have plenty of in this later stage of life is time. While raising children or working, we seldom allowed ourselves much time off to explore the more playful side of our nature. But time is what we have most of now, and we are free to use it as wisely or as frivolously as we choose. Coming to understand that we do, indeed, have talent, that it has simply lain dormant until now, is perhaps one of the most exciting aspects of our lives presently. If we haven't yet realized this, dare to believe it now. It will change every minute of the rest of your life.

Today is a good day to pursue one of my dreams.

MAY 5

*The creative spirit creates with
whatever materials are present.*

M. C. RICHARDS

Perhaps we commonly associate creativity with artists and gauge ourselves as deficient. Not many of us gained great acclaim as painters, writers, photographers, or sculptors. But every one of us is creative. That's an absolute. We can be certain of this because no two humans ever approach a problem or an ordinary experience in exactly the same way. Each of us creates our own perspective, our own response, one that fits our individual histories.

Coming to understand this broader definition of creativity allows us to appreciate what we have been bringing to the table all along. This, in turn, eases our concern about how appropriate or creative our responses to any experience today might be.

Because we respond to the details of our lives quite methodically, we fail to notice our creativity. It's time to trust that creativity has always been there. It always will be there, too.

I will discover a creative solution for every problem today.
My artistry is my birthright.

MAY 6

Every artist dips his brush in his own soul,
and paints his own nature into his pictures.

HENRY WARD BEECHER

Our perception of any experience, even the smallest detail of an ordinary event, is quite exceptional. No other person will share our particular vision. Frequently that results in arguments. The need to be right is a common affliction. If only we could appreciate the richness of sharing and combining our views.

Because of our age, we may assume we have more wisdom than others. On occasion, we will. However, we have something to learn from all souls who cross our path, or they wouldn't be there. Understanding this is real wisdom.

What a dull world this would be if we all shared the same perception of every event. There would be nothing to discuss, no opportunity to expand our minds, no reason to interact at all. Instead we are blessed with opportunities for conflict and growth, the deepening of relationships and character development, choices, and decisions. All because we each see what we see.

How I see an experience today is unique
but neither right nor wrong. I will remember
the same holds true for all my friends, too.

MAY 7

I'm a little leery when people try to tell me
what I should believe about God.

HARRY BARTHOLOMEW

Each of us has to decide for ourselves what God means. The kind of religious education we had in our homes no doubt influenced us in our youth. Depending on how strict it was, we may still carry that influence. But over the years, we have met many people from differing religions, and we have been introduced to many ideas that run counter to our own. Are we able to see the value in that or are we still bothered by foreign ideas?

Being exposed to ideas that differ from what we were exposed to in our youth is natural to the maturation process. In that regard, we could say we are still maturing. The new ideas are ever-present, aren't they? How do we respond? Are we threatened by them or do we embrace them? Being willing to trust that listening can never hurt us may prove to be enlightening. Just because we have passed our prime, maybe decades ago, doesn't mean that we can't experience a significant change in opinion or even character.

We simply can't be sure that whatever we believe currently is the absolute truth. We don't have to adopt any idea about God or anything else that bothers us, but choosing to not even listen closes the door to an opportunity. Let's not make this decision lightly.

Am I leery of others' opinions?
Perhaps I can be more trusting today.

MAY 8

*I've lost so many people in my life: my only brother,
my husband, one child, a sister, her husband, and their son.
Being spiritual has helped me handle all that.*

ALICE MERRYMAN

Anything we have to handle, whether a monumental tragedy or
a simple loss, is made easier if we believe that a Power greater
than ourselves is watching over us. Some among our group of
seniors have always known this. A few of us have not accepted
this idea yet, perhaps. Our families of origin, along with teachers
and peer groups, influenced our belief systems, and changing it
doesn't come so easy the older we get.

If we aren't feeling peaceful on a daily basis, if we are fearful
or full of dread about what the future holds, we might find relief
in a change in perspective. That's all a belief system is, in fact. It's
a perspective that explains how we see the world. If we struggle
to handle the uncertainties of this changing world, or if we feel
overwhelmed by what's expected of us, deciding to look at our
experiences in a new way makes sense.

Maybe you think you can't change your mind at this late
date. But that's not true. The one thing we can always change, regardless of how old we are, is what we hold in our minds. No one
has the power to put an idea there but ourselves. Is it time to
make a change?

Do I feel peaceful and unafraid today?
I can with a change of mind.

MAY 9

*I think if you accept what comes in your life as the way
God wants it for you, then it's much easier to carry on.*

HELEN CASEY

When tragedy occurs, it's pretty hard to accept that God wills it for us. That might not be the most appropriate interpretation, in fact. We have free will, which means we have to take responsibility for the events in our lives. Tragedy may have resulted from any one of our actions. However, if we look to *a Power greater than ourselves* for the strength to survive it, we will come to understand that God has been with us always, in tragedy as well as triumph. That's the lesson.

We don't have to be happy about all that befalls us. That is an attitude we can cultivate, however. Deciding to "wear a happy face," just might take the sting out of the circumstances that trouble us. Just imagine shrugging your shoulders instead of stomping in rage when an expected check doesn't arrive or when rain ruins your plans for a trip. We're not too old to learn something new. It may seem that way, and we may be resisting this very idea, but giving it half a chance is worth the effort.

**I may not like the idea that God wills everything that
happens today, but if I trust I'll survive it,
with God's help, I'll be at peace.**

MAY 10

I believe that things just came to me.
I did make use of them; however, I didn't go looking for them.

MARIA REGNIER KRIMMEL

Most of us can look back on our lives and concur that we took advantage of opportunities that came our way. Certain opportunities may have slipped by us, for a time, but it's likely they returned, too, perhaps in a somewhat different form. It is believed by many that whatever we did with our lives was quite necessary, unique, and part of a much wider plan that involved the lives of everybody in our circle. We can find comfort in that idea.

If our past was purposeful, then our present must also be intentional. Just knowing that we haven't outlived our worth gives us pause to rejoice. But many of us struggle in this stage of our lives to figure out what we should be doing next. We struggle simply because we haven't yet mastered how to listen to our inner guide. Much of our lives we "accidentally" followed our calling. There is no shame in that; however, we can more confidently move into the future if we practice listening for guidance *in the present*. Making an adjustment such as this in our daily lives can offer us real excitement, too. It isn't the same humdrum process that we'd grown accustomed to, or maybe even become bored with. Let's practice.

I have always had a guide.
I'll be more conscious of it today.

MAY 11

*You can't go to church on Sunday
and be a devil on Monday.*

VIOLET HENSLEY

Actually, you can do just that. We all know folks who seem to, anyway. Just because we act as if we are loving doesn't mean our actions are coming from our hearts. For some, that has been an effective way to manipulate. But occasionally, "the act" will become real and the love will too. What good fortune for our companions.

It's no fun to be nice one day and mean the next. Not really. We don't escape the pain we inflict on others. We may not feel it in exactly the same way as they do, but we feel it nonetheless. The reverse is also quite true. Being genuinely nice to others warms our hearts as well.

Life can be understood on very simple terms. What we give out comes back to us. What we think manifests in form. What we fear has power over us. When we love, we'll discover love all around us. Our purpose in this life will become clear when we nurture the love in our hearts.

Today will reflect my mind and my actions.

MAY 12

I plan for each day ahead of time,
but I'm willing to give up my plan and do something quite
spontaneous if the opportunity arises.

TOM HARDING

Most of us had far too few opportunities to be truly spontaneous when we were in our prime. Our responsibilities generally kept us on a demanding schedule. That was appropriate then. Being freed from a rigid schedule fits us now. However, most of us need to find a balance between too much and too little to do. We want to have plans but we don't want to pass up "God's unexpected dancing lessons" because we're too busy. We can choose to look at this stage of life as particularly rich because of our many opportunities coupled with few responsibilities.

Tom hasn't been given any window on the world that's not available to the rest of us. We need to ask ourselves whether we are taking advantage of our days in a way that really gives us pleasure. Or are we merely checking off the hours of each day as they pass? Let's be honest about this. If we are content with how our days are spent, we may not need to make a change. If, however, we feel time as a burden, let's seek the "dancing lessons." They are always just around the corner. We merely need to change our perception.

Opportunity knocks every day.
Am I a willing receiver today?

MAY 13

I didn't really have a plan for a career, but I learned how to run our business quite successfully one day at a time.

JOANN REED

Whether we had a specific plan for how we anticipated our lives unfolding or reacted to our opportunities spontaneously, we finally had to take whatever came in small increments anyway. Life only happens a day at a time, regardless of who we are. Being "leveled" in this way is good for one's humility. It's also a relief to many of us. Living way into the future prevents us from appreciating whatever is happening at this moment.

So much of our lives is in the past now. Even though we may be blessed with a number of good years ahead, we can't take them for granted. There can be joyful excitement in that realization if we decide to squeeze the thrill out of every minute that comes to us. If we are practiced in living just one day at a time, we'll not find this difficult. But many of us got caught in the struggle to control outcomes, circumstances, and people far into the future throughout much of our lives. Living a day at a time now feels like taking a giant step backward.

With practice, we'll realize that living more slowly actually extends whatever life we have left, because we'll be able to truly experience each of the moments. Learning this, at any age, is a gift. Let's rejoice in it.

Today offers me twenty-four hours of moments to be appreciated. I will do my best to love them.

MAY 14

*I visualize the things I'd like to do
and they fall into place.*

FRAN COYNE

The power of visualization is a bit mysterious, isn't it? How it works, perhaps, isn't so important. That it does work is attested to by many. Athletes often credit their superior performance to the power of visualization. Golfers commonly talk about imagining their ball's trajectory before every shot. Therapists tell clients to "see" themselves calmly handling situations prior to the actual circumstance.

Today may be a good time to experiment with this tool. Consider something you'd like to do. Perhaps take a trip, plant a garden, paint a picture, or organize the hundreds of photographs that have accumulated over the years. Take a few quiet moments to "observe" yourself getting organized and a few more moments "watching" yourself follow through with the activity. The meditative process acts as a motivator, pushing us forward into the activity. It also seems to help ready us for the arising opportunities that will enhance the actual pursuit.

We can't rationally explain how this process works. But do we need to? Books are filled with examples of success. Rather than doubt the possibility of our success with any activity that appeals to us, let's try visualization first. It's probable that we can add our stories of success to all the others.

**I'll close my eyes and imagine what I want to do next.
That's the first step to success.**

MAY 15

*I believe if old people sit down,
they've just had it.*

ALICE MERRYMAN

Alice was a good example of one who never sat down. At eighty-seven, after recuperating from surgery and a stroke, she built a picket fence around her house. The next year she tore down a garage, single-handedly. Some people believe you don't ever have to quit. What an enlightened attitude. Generally the people who live this way not only continue finding their own lives exciting, but they help to inspire others around them, too. One truly inspired person fortunately has an impact on four or five others every day. Communities as well as families can change when this is the situation.

The reverse is just as true. The interminably negative individuals we encounter on our path, if mimicked, will change our perspective on how life can be. A situation that might have been hopeful can feel quite hopeless if we fail to appreciate its value to us. Alice knew that everything had its purpose and its silver lining. Consequently, she looked forward to every day with anticipation and willingness to "get her work done." And this outlook allowed her to grow very old and remain very happy. It can do the same for us.

How do I see my life, moment by moment?
Today is a good day to begin monitoring my perspective.

MAY 16

*My philosophy is, don't go to the doctor too often
because they just find things wrong with you.*

RUTH CASEY

We have all needed medical services, probably hundreds of times over the decades. However, some people think we "create" unneeded illnesses by our constant focus on "imagined" health problems. Seeking validation for them comes next, and a physician will generally strengthen our belief in their existence. Does this mean we can actually make ourselves sick?

The mind is powerful. It's far more powerful than any of us imagine, and it's all too true that what we focus on long enough can come to fruition. Hindsight will support this principle. The positive aspect of this truism is that we have always been the creators of our thoughts. Whatever we carry in our minds has been our choice. Happy, healthy images have manifested when we exercised them. The reverse has been just as true.

What does this mean for us now, today? Simply, it means that our thoughts contribute to our well-being or our discontent every moment. Perhaps we have health challenges, but we can take control over the emphasis we give them in our lives. This determines, finally, how we'll feel all day long.

**I may not feel wonderful today,
but I don't have to let that be my focus.
There are many more pleasant things to contemplate.**

MAY 17

If I don't have something to look forward to,
it's bad news.

CATHERINE PAUL

Do you have something to look forward to? Part-time jobs, volunteer activities, visits with children and grandchildren, travel plans, hobbies, daily prayer and meditation, chatting with friends—the list of what might occupy our attention is vast, indeed. However, it's not the quantity of things on our list, but the quality of the experience that matters. If we find ourselves doing something that we don't really enjoy just to stay busy, we should reconsider our commitment to it. Life is too short to spend precious hours in ways that don't give us joy.

If we're not having lots of fun now that we have more time for it, what should we do? The best solution is to query our friends about their lives. What inspires them to get out of bed each day? Maybe we can ask to join them in whatever they're doing, at least for a while, to see if we'd enjoy it too.

There's no shame in seeking the help of others. Some of us recoil at the idea, perhaps, but it's good to be reminded that we're gathered into families and communities for a reason. We learn from one another. We are both teachers and students, being one or the other at every moment. Let's not shy away from letting someone teach us today.

Did I get up with a willingness to teach or learn
something new today?

MAY 18

If I can't walk someday, I'll just have to do the next best thing, whatever it is — get me a buggy perhaps.

ALPHA ENGLISH

Trusting that we are being taken care of every moment of our lives is a decision. Not everybody makes that decision as easily as Alpha did. But simply knowing one person who has enjoyed a worry-free life because of it gives us the courage to consider making the decision, too.

The impetus for deciding to trust may best come from reflection on our past. How many instances can we recall nearly suffering grave injury but we were spared? Or the myriad times we were desperate because of a personal situation, only to have it seemingly resolve itself after we prayed a bit? Trusting that we are being watched over guarantees that we'll figure out how to move forward regardless of the circumstances that befall us. Our lives are a testament to this. This is true of our past. It will be true of our future, too.

Wearing life like a loose garment eases our journey. Alpha's perspective is easy to adopt. It's all in how we look at life.

**I will find what I seek today.
I can only see what I am willing to see.**

MAY 19

The most important thing I've learned in life is to love others and accept their love in return.

JIM BURNS

After decades of living and learning, is love really our most important lesson? Perhaps we doubt this. Whatever trade or profession we mastered provided well for us and our families. Surely education counted. And what of the thousands of simple tasks like driving a car, riding a bike, cooking a meal, balancing the checkbook? The list can go on endlessly. Let's not discard anything that we have learned as without value. In fact, every example we can think of has played its part. The point here is that *how* we did our tasks, regardless of their significance, is what really matters. Doing anything, whether great or small, with a mean heart leaves its mark. The converse is likewise true.

How does love really enter into the ordinary activities that engage us? Easy. When someone pulls in front of us in traffic, we can bless them. The snotty clerk at the grocery needs a smile. The friend who whines about her misfortunes deserves a hug, perhaps. We can refuse to offer anything but love in every circumstance. It may seem impossible; after all, there are so many situations and people who irritate us. But giving only love changes each person and every situation. And the one who is changed most of all is ourselves.

Knowing that I can change any situation by what I bring to it thrills me. Today will be a test of my skill.

MAY 20

*I'm never so happy as when
I make someone else happy.*

MONTY CRALLEY

Why does making others happy bring us happiness? Or does it? Not everybody gets good feelings out of caring for others, perhaps, but when we think about friends who are truly happy, we realize that they are usually thoughtful and pleasant people. We all learned the Golden Rule when we were youngsters. Is it so surprising to discover how true it remains?

Another rule we learned as kids was that it took more muscles to frown than to smile. Whether that's really true or not isn't important. What really matters is that bringing a smile to someone else nearly always results when we offer one first. Spreading a little joy is an easy task, and there may be fewer tasks that we can accomplish with each passing year. How nice to know we'll always be good at that one.

Wise souls dictate that there is no greater work to be accomplished than bringing happiness into the lives of others. Let's be assured that whatever we have done in the past really isn't grander than what we are able to do right now.

**Doing a good deed for a friend or a stranger today
does me a good turn too.**

MAY 21

I always felt that if just one person got something good out of my newsletter, it was worth all my effort.

JAMES CASEY

We never really know what we may do or say that will help another person. When we reflect on our own lives, we realize that many times we received help or guidance quite inadvertently from someone. Perhaps they weren't even aware of their roles in our transformation. Obviously, we have helped others in exactly the same fashion. We can feel confident that if we are attuned to our hearts, if we have quieted our minds, we'll be shown how to respond to every person or circumstance that comes our way.

It's probably best that we aren't aware of all the specific "good" we might have done already. It might make us arrogant or powerful rather than humble, and God makes better use of us when we are quiet and unassuming. We can trust that God will not quit using our services as long as we are willing channels. There are many things we can't do quite as well in these latter years of our lives. We don't have the stamina, perhaps, or the eyesight, strength, or disposable income. The list of our limitations may be very long. But we'll always have just what is needed by the other people on our paths if we listen for God's direction.

Growing old is as exciting as I make it.
I have more time to listen to God and other people.
What will I hear today?

MAY 22

I know this: It's not just experience in age;
whatever you can do best will bring itself to light.

EVA WINES

Perhaps you don't feel that you do anything well. Oftentimes, we make only half-hearted attempts at whatever we do. Then, we have ample evidence that we're not doing so well. We can change that experience, though. A bit of effort and a measure of patience will nurture noticeable improvement. But what does it mean that whatever we can do best will come "to light"?

We get urges to try our hands at something every now and then. Mostly we ignore them. If we're attentive, we're aware that the urges repeat themselves. They are coming "to light." We then must make the choice to follow them or not. What's in store for us, if we actively acknowledge them, is fulfillment like we'd never known before. It's not accidental that we are called to do certain things. No one else has exactly the gifts we've been blessed with. We must offer ours to the world for its realization, and ours, too.

I can point to many accomplishments in my lifetime.
What brings me the most pleasure is undoubtedly God's
special assignment for me.

Aging is not easy, but what's our alternative?

HELEN CASEY

The kind of attitude we developed over our lives determined how we saw every detail of each experience. Even now our attitude holds us hostage. The misunderstanding that many of us have is that we think we can't really change how we see our world. Nothing is further from the truth. We can make a large or small shift in our perceptions instantly. The outcome is that everything about our lives changes from that moment forward. Thus, how we perceive the aging process is controlled by our willingness to look at it again.

Helen has aged gracefully. At eighty-six, she still finds time for making new friends, three bridge clubs a week, daily mass, and frequent communication with her children and relatives. She carries a positive, hopeful attitude with her wherever she goes, which inspires others, young and old.

It wouldn't appear that aging has been hard on Helen. But the truth of the matter is that she has suffered many losses. What she has managed to hold onto though is her faith in God and her willingness to see every "glass as half full."

How lucky we are that we can "tinker" with our attitude for as long as we're alive, and if we aren't completely happy, we have work to do. As Helen says, there is no alternative to aging, except death. What happens now is up to us.

I am only as old as I decide to feel today.

MAY 24

Some things we think are bad may be good.

HARRY BARTHOLOMEW

Making hasty judgments about people can be detrimental. We quickly decide if an invitation to dinner is worth our time, or maybe we pass up an opportunity to engage in a book club or get acquainted with a prospective friend simply because we are a bit fearful. Does it really make sense to so quickly dispense with the people or the possibilities that beckon when we have so much time to spare?

While it is true that some opportunities may not be good, we can't make educated judgments about anything without at least a modicum of exposure. It's *by design* that we are still here, in this life, in these bodies. Perhaps we should be more open and trust the Grand Designer. Quietly seeking our inner voice will tell us what to do.

No doubt we have all regretted passing up opportunities after hearing of another's experiences with them. That doesn't have to be the standard for our lives, though. Careful contemplation coupled with some quiet meditation will always guide us appropriately. Taking the time to fully consider an option allows us to cull the good from the bad.

I don't have to accept every invitation that comes my way, but I can be open to new options.

MAY 25

My humble beginnings
have made me very grateful today.

JIM BURNS

Gratitude doesn't depend only on humble beginnings, even though that's the case for Jim. Rather, it's a mind-set. It may not be automatic to many of us; however, it can be cultivated. For starters, we can take a moment to remember all the friends and family members who are still present in our lives. Calling them to express our love, dropping them a note of appreciation, or walking into the next room to give them a hug will trigger it. Gratitude always takes willingness on our part and a little effort.

Those of us who have had seemingly horrendous experiences may find it hard to be grateful. And there are lots of us in this category, but we must be seeking another perspective or we wouldn't be holding this book right now. That, in fact, is the miracle of gratitude. It happens with just a tiny bit of effort, just like the effort we're making right now. Perhaps we can acknowledge that we're grateful that we still have sight or the strength to hold this book. That's a beginning, and that's all that's necessary.

I have many things to be grateful for today,
even if they don't come immediately to mind.
Just looking around this room will offer some examples.

MAY 26

*I didn't have much self-esteem before I entered
the work world, but I have it now.
I don't think retirement will change that.*

JOANN REED

Self-esteem isn't natural to all of us. That's often an unfortunate circumstance of how we grew up. Some families were better at helping their children realize their self-worth than others were. The more confident the parents were, the more easily they could help their children develop confidence. Fearful people seem always to breed fear in others too.

However we feel now is very much related to how we have spent our lives. If we got good feelings from our work, we may feel content now, knowing we were successful. Or perhaps the reverse is true. Maybe we long for the days when we were more in the thick of things.

Taking an inventory of how we feel now is important. We can only change those elements of our lives that we understand. Until we look carefully at them, we'll not know what to do differently. One good aspect of growing old is the familiarity with change that we have all experienced. Making some additional ones now is really no big deal.

**If I'm not really at peace with who I am now,
I need to look at how I spend my time and with whom.
I can make whatever change will help.**

*Getting used as a sounding board for problems
has been all too common to us in our retirement.
It can become overwhelming.*

LOUISE JEROME

Being sought as a problem solver makes us feel valued, doesn't it? We never outgrow the need for knowing we count in the lives of others. But we can get too involved in others' concerns too. It's not unusual for us to become too available; it's habitual, both for us and for those who grow to depend on us.

The less busy we are, the more we may seek the dependence of others on us. It may be the main way we feel engaged in life. It's not wrong to be of service to others. The best we have to offer anyone may be a willing ear, but some may seek more from us.

We need to set some boundaries, perhaps. We may need to be clear with others and ourselves about our proper involvement in their problems. Listening, simply that, can never be wrong. Oftentimes, anything more will be. Let's be careful about our entanglements today.

**Today I will be aware of the difference between being a good
listener and getting overly involved in others' problems.**

MAY 28

*I wasn't prepared for retirement
so I floundered a long time.*

BUD SHERMAN

Not everybody is faced with a sudden, unplanned-for retirement like Bud was, but floundering, at first anyway, isn't unusual. Even men and women who think they know what they want to do after retirement struggle to find meaning in their activities. Having a particular job, with a familiar set of expectations and a timeline for doing the work, gave our lives a definite structure. That was comfortable for most of us. We simply don't have that anymore regardless of how we fill up our hours.

In time, we'll come to appreciate the freedom we have now. For some, the change has already occurred. Maybe an additional activity for our retired years is to help those in our circle of acquaintances who haven't found their way yet. Floundering is so debilitating. If we can help even one person feel more hopeful and find greater peace with the life he or she has now, we'll have performed a service every bit as important as any work we did in our past.

We deserve to feel content with our lives, with our accomplishments, with whatever the future holds. There is something special that still needs to be done by each of us, even now. If we haven't figured it out, perhaps we should pray for guidance. It will come.

**I won't flounder for long today.
If I'm uncertain of what to do,
I'll seek spiritual guidance.**

MAY 29

I'm disappointed that my husband and I can't work together in retirement. It's just too much togetherness.

BEVERLY SHERMAN

Many of us anticipated the ideal partnership when we retired. Buying a small business or perhaps running a resort was a dream that appealed to us as a couple. Accepting that it isn't all that ideal to be thrown together every waking minute is difficult now. At first, some may wonder if it means we don't really love each other. But let's not complicate our lives with doubt. When we look honestly at the past, we realize that for most of it, we had many separate activities. That was good. It allowed us to come together with fresh ideas all the time.

Too much togetherness can be stifling. Talking openly about it with our significant other is not always easy, however. Hurt feelings are common. Seeking the counsel of a professional to help us walk through changes can diminish the defensiveness we might feel. We do need to make this stage of our lives more satisfying for both of us. It's not a mark of failure to seek help to see our possibilities in a different light. Let's be willing to get help if we are struggling. Our future deserves it.

Does today excite me?
I'll seek the counsel of someone if my answer isn't yes.

MAY 30

Every day is a different day.
You never know what it will bring.
That's the exciting thing about getting up every morning.

ALPHA ENGLISH

No doubt we have all hit spells when we didn't feel the urge to get the day going. Pulling the covers up around us seemed far more inviting. There's nothing wrong with occasionally resisting the next twenty-four hours. We do need variety in our lives. Even a healthy, fun routine is still a routine. Shaking it up is good for us. But if we make a habit of avoiding whatever plans we've made, we need to take an inventory of our feelings. Depression isn't foreign to most of us. Chronic depression needs to be addressed, however.

If we begin to feel blue about our lives, let's make sure we are expressing our feelings to a friend. Generally, there is a simple solution. Maybe we have forgotten to pray and meditate regularly. Perhaps we have become self-absorbed. Being appreciative of others generally changes how we see every aspect of our lives. Recounting with a confidant or in a journal all the blessings and achievements we've accumulated over these many decades often pushes us out of the doldrums. Let's remember that most days surprised us with their outcomes. We never got exactly what we expected. This is one certainty about life that we can always count on.

Today is bound to surprise me in how it unfolds.
I'll appreciate what comes my way.

MAY 31

Creativity can be anything: painting or writing or
visiting people in hospitals. We can all do something.

MONTY CRALLEY

Getting outside of ourselves is our assignment. Being constantly
self-absorbed stunts our imagination, which in turn, extin-
guishes the flame of creativity. It makes us boring people. It isn't
that difficult to get intrigued by new activities. We succeeded
well enough when we were employed. We'd never have been able
to do our work had we always been focused on ourselves. What's
holding us back now?

Lots of folks think they don't have the artistic ability to pursue an activity such as painting or writing. If only they dared to
try, they'd find there's really nothing needed but a little willingness and the humility to practice something new. Humility requires that we let a source outside of us show us the way. If we
have always felt we had to be right, that we had to know all the
answers, it won't be easy to be guided in this way.

Fortunately, we have other creative options to consider besides artistic ones. Reading to a blind acquaintance, playing
cards with a group at a nursing home, writing letters for an un-
well friend are all avenues open to us. The point is for us to think
of someone besides ourselves. Our opportunities are limited
only by our unwillingness.

I can be inspired today by doing something different.

JUNE

JUNE 1

I often think I'm not doing enough with my life.
I paint, I golf, I dabble, but is that enough?

ABBY WARMAN

Nobody can answer the question posed by Abby but ourselves. The point is, are we content? If we hesitate even a moment before replying, perhaps we need to reconsider how we're spending our time. There are few if any specific assignments at this juncture of our lives. However, we aren't through interacting with others; we still have a key part to play in this life. It's that part that most of us want to feel good about.

The solution to fulfillment is simple: Express only love to the others in our lives. It's not *what* we do, ever, but *how* we do it. Some very wise voices would say this has always been true. Many of us matured with a far different set of values, though. Let's consider letting this philosophy guide us for a while, as a test, perhaps. What we're striving for is to be content with how we're spending our lives. If focusing on giving only love and acceptance to others gives us pleasure, could we want for anything more?

There is nothing anyone can do that's more important than helping another person feel loved or forgiven, if that's called for. Whether we are working part-time or merely at play, our opportunities are unending. We'll know we have done enough if we have welcomed them.

Today I can offer love to someone quite easily.
Both of us will be rewarded.

JUNE 2

I'm afraid I'm not going to find something to do,
and that feels terrible.

BUD SHERMAN

Must we always be busy? Fear is not an uncommon response to the early stage of retirement. We are so used to being on the go with our jobs, our families, our social lives, and other commitments that not having the overbooked feeling is sometimes frightening. We generally defined ourselves by our many activities. Who are we now that we have little we have to do?

It might be the best medicine in the world for our fearful psyche to have no direction for a time. Too many of us seldom took the time to question what we really wanted to do with our lives. We got on a track and stayed there. Now we have this wonderful opportunity to step back and ask, "What do I really want now?" Some among us seek the counsel of a professional, even. There's certainly no shame in that. Retirement is an adjustment.

There are healthy ways to handle retirement and some not so healthy. We have probably all met a few who turned to alcohol to fill the hours. We have also heard of those who withdrew from all activities. And then there are retirees who volunteer for everything, fearing having even a moment of unscheduled time. Where do we stand today? If we're not all that content, let's talk to a friend.

Am I too busy or not busy enough today?
Let's think about that.

JUNE 3

When you retire you've got to try and do something or you will be miserable.

TOM HARDING

Many men and women long to retire so they won't have to do anything anymore. Is it true that we're miserable if we don't have something to do? There's no single, right answer to the question. It's an individual matter, but boredom will eventually set in if there are no distractions. Perhaps boredom isn't so bad! Those of us who have been on the proverbial treadmill for much of our lives want the sanity of no responsibilities for a time. That's okay. When we begin to get antsy, we know it's time to find an outlet for our energy. And that time will come.

How do we select an activity to pursue if we haven't come upon a hobby naturally? Talking to friends is an obvious first step. We may be able to join them in an activity, thus get involved quickly. Getting involved with others always gives us new ideas for how to spend our time. It matters not whether we have ever pursued any activity outside of work or the home before. We will get used to embarking on new territory, and we'll wonder why we stayed away so long.

Not everybody wants to pursue a hobby. Doing volunteer work fits the desires of some better. That we are seeking a way to fit into our world now that it has changed is what all of these endeavors are about. We'll find it.

I am open to new ideas today.

JUNE 4

Making a contribution to others, now that I'm retired,
is important to me.

JOE CASEY

Most people probably feel this way if they give the idea some consideration. Taking that next step to get involved is more difficult. Time is one thing that we have more of now. Maybe we aren't as secure financially or possibly not as agile and healthy as we'd hoped for. But we do have additional hours available to us because jobs and families demand far less. This freedom offers us many opportunities for pursuing other activities.

Why is helping someone else important? Many of us were raised to value self-reliance. Isn't helping others depriving them of necessary work? We may need a considerable shift in perception in order to see the importance of "doing for others." Just consider, for a moment, how much better off some of us are than others. Most of us still have decent health. We continue to be interested in new ideas. Obviously, our minds still function fairly well, and if we're really fortunate, we are able to laugh at a good joke and ourselves, too. For all of these reasons, we have something to give to others. Many aren't as lucky as ourselves, but we can help them by being available.

I don't have to give much to someone else today
to make a difference in his or her life.
I benefit also from helping others.

JUNE 5

You have to feel that you make a difference.

MONTY CRALLEY

Most of us made our marks in careers or as homemakers. We probably had daily evidence from our bosses, customers, spouses, or children that what we did mattered. Now the feedback is less frequent. There may even be days when we have no contact with others. The phone doesn't ring. The mail contains only circulars deserving of the trash can. Even television may not engage our thoughts. On those days we have to work a little harder to believe that we still matter.

Richard Bach, the author of *Illusions,* says that if we are still alive, we haven't yet fulfilled our mission. We still matter. Seems funny that an idea so simple can be so meaningful, but it is if we believe it.

We can decide to believe whatever makes us happiest. It will certainly be true for most of us that believing we count will give us greater comfort than thinking we don't. Why would we want to make our lives any harder? Don't we deserve to feel good? Of course we do. Let's go for it.

> I do make a difference. With every breath I take
> I add something to the universe.
> This is God's promise to me.

JUNE 6

Some older people seem to have nailed it all down.
Well, then they're not trying to advance any.
I'm still trying to advance.

EVA WINES

"Nailing it all down" might be interpreted many ways. Having resolved all the major conflicts in our lives may be one way. Being settled in our circumstances, whatever they are, can be another. Eva's words reveal how eager she is for new experiences. Unlike many octogenarians, she still seeks growth. She doesn't want to nail it all down. She sets a good example for others. Life doesn't happen to us. We co-create it.

Some days we are tired and feel we have done enough. Let someone else worry over the sick and dispossessed. The neighbors can greet the newcomers. The volunteer board doesn't need us all, after all. But when we retreat from everything, we shortchange ourselves, as well as others. Our involvement, our advancement, so to speak, is necessary to the evolution of society, of the planet, and most important, of our souls.

It's not happenstance that an opportunity to expand our lives has beckoned. Let's be daring.

I still have things to learn or I'd not be here.
I am ready.

JUNE 7

When I sold my business, it was a snap decision.
I would do it differently now.

SANDY WARMAN

We made many decisions throughout our lives that could have been handled differently. Hindsight is so enlightening. It can also be our nemesis. It's helpful to acknowledge that we each did the best we could with the information available to us at the time. This is true for our roles as parents as well as in our careers. The tendency to decide anything too quickly is human, but we are trainable, even at this age.

Sometimes we think that we should have all the answers, that we should never need consultation with others. This is not uncommon, particularly the older we get. But age doesn't guarantee absolute wisdom. Getting the input of others doesn't guarantee freedom from mistakes, either. However, two or ten heads are generally better than one. And we always have a Higher Power for help with the final decision.

It's helpful to remember that most decisions can be changed when additional information has become available. And even where that isn't the case, we know most things do work out for the best.

Regardless of the mistakes I might have
made in the past, I survived the outcomes.
It's important that I honor this truth today.

JUNE 8

No matter what's going on,
what we've sent out comes back to us enlarged.

JEAN WILL

Are we content? Do we have the people and the activities in our lives that we really want here? Hopefully we can answer yes to these questions. But if we can't, it's not too late to change our possibilities. What comes to us is a reflection of ourselves. When our experiences don't please us, let's ponder our role in them because we are reaping what we have sown.

We can cultivate better experiences. We have it in our power to change what we send out. That means that what we get back will be different, too. This isn't new information; we have known this our whole lives. It's called the Golden Rule. It's possible we never realized how much influence our behavior had on that of others, but we can get a good example of it instantly. Just offer genuine love and friendship to someone you have ignored lately and see what happens.

I will have as good a day as my attitude allows.
That's a powerful realization.

JUNE 9

You make your own life.
You learn by your mistakes.

HELEN CASEY

Accepting responsibility for all our actions is not so easy sometimes. Even after years of experience with this principle, we dig
in our heels occasionally. It's so human of us to want to blame
others, particularly for our mistakes. Let's not be ashamed of
that; let's admit it and move on. Time doesn't stand still and
we're not getting any younger.

Believing that we have made our own lives can exhilarate us.
Why? Because it also means we make what is left of them, too. It
is never too late to begin a new course of action, a new pattern of
thinking. Yesterday is gone. How we felt about whatever happened in a multitude of yesterdays doesn't have to consume our
attention today. That's a profound awareness, particularly if it
underscores every moment.

We all have acquaintances who wear their troubles on their
sleeves, and we seldom look forward to our time with them.
Those who seek the silver lining cheer us. Who shall we adopt as
our teacher this day?

I am in charge of the *important stuff* today.
How I think, how I act, what I dream,
and what I dwell on are in my power.

JUNE 10

*You'd be surprised what people can do
if they are encouraged.*

ALPHA ENGLISH

None of us have forgotten how good it felt to be praised for our report cards when we were kids. Nor have we lost the memory of promotions at our jobs. We no doubt remember the specific teachers, bosses, and other mentors who took particular notice of us. They comprise a significant percentage of why we succeeded in the first place.

Our need for recognition and encouragement has not diminished just because our youth has. Since we know that's true for us, we can safely assume it's true for our companions, too, those we know now and those we haven't met yet. We won't be motivated every day to complete a task started yesterday. But we always have the energy to praise others for their attempts at something.

It's a good feeling to know that we always have a purpose to fulfill. As long as we are living, there will be companions around us who need our recognition and encouragement. That may well be the most important contribution of our entire lives.

**I have a job to do today. All I have to do is open my eyes,
my heart, and my mouth in praise of another.**

Friendship means more to me than money.
Pass on friendship. I'd rather be on my death bed with
a friend than with a million dollars.

VIOLET HENSLEY

How good a friend have we been over the years? It took effort, patience, and willingness. It required that we put another's needs before our own, sometimes. It meant saying we were sorry and taking responsibility for all of our actions, even those we'd rather have forgotten. It meant being honest.

Violet's words speak volumes. We all have come to know loneliness in our advancing years. Losing spouses and any number of acquaintances has become common to us. And with each passing friend, we find ourselves closer to our own end. Having a friend to share the hours with, to share our memories and remaining dreams with, to share both laughter and tears with, makes every moment that remains of our lives more poignant, more purposeful.

If our friends are few, there is action we can take. Organizations of all kinds need us. So do schools and churches. People just like ourselves live behind thousands of closed doors. Let's seek someone out if we're alone today.

I am only as lonely as I want to be today.
I can make the first move toward someone else.

JUNE 12

I've got all my marbles,
but my body is gone.

THERESA MCCARTHY

Theresa is ninety and still actively painting. She paints when she can't sleep; she paints the whimsical images that dance around in her head. Because her paintings have been sold on behalf of a charity, and thus are in the homes of families who will never personally know her, Theresa will live on in the hearts and minds of hundreds of people for many years to come. She has left a legacy that won't be forgotten. We all hope to leave a legacy, don't we?

Deciding what kind of legacy we want to leave is worthy of careful consideration. For some, our talents or hobbies or professions have determined the legacy we'll leave. Others among us have nothing material to point to, perhaps. No books were written; no houses were designed; no children were parented. The "arts" didn't claim an investment of time. Nor did community organizations. But we all have a personal philosophy, and the manner in which we lived our lives is not soon forgotten. The examples we set, the examples we continue to set, in fact, are possibly the most important legacies anyone can leave behind. Are you at peace with how others will speak of you when you are gone?

Perhaps I can spruce up my legacy today.
How I interact with others will make a contribution.

JUNE 13

*Honesty and contractual obligations are two of the things
I value the highest and wanted to pass on to our kids.*

JAMES CASEY

Living consistently with a set of values has been important to most of us. It hasn't always been easy, either. Many times over the years we had peers or maybe co-workers who tried to pull us off track. We may even have a few memories of when we did follow another's path for a while. But we always knew by our discomfort when we weren't being true to ourselves.

Having a set of cherished values to pass on to our children meant a great deal to most of us. Our own experiences had impressed upon us the importance of knowing who we were. We felt our children needed to have the same awareness. But, alas, we often failed in our attempt to pass our values on to them. If we still suffer disappointment over this; we should remember how we developed our own values. Our parents probably instilled some of them in us, but each of us finally had to determine for ourselves what fit. We were able to be an example to our children, nothing more. And that was quite enough.

Feeling at peace in our old age with how we conducted ourselves throughout our lives suggests lives well-lived. Passing that example on to children and grandchildren is the best of all values.

How I live my life today is as important as how I lived it
every day up to now. My example isn't done yet.

JUNE 14

The most important thing that was passed on to me by my parents was love. I tried to pass that on to my children, too.

BEVERLY SHERMAN

Offering love to those who share our paths is the most important contribution any of us can make today. It was always our most important contribution, even though we generally thought our careers or homemaking roles were more important. Isn't it interesting that so few of us ever really understood what our *real purpose* was?

Some of us might wonder even now what's so important about passing on love. It's not that hard, is it? But honest reflection reveals how difficult loving others can actually be. To love unconditionally means we don't leave some people out and love only those who are easy to love. Passing on love means feeling compassion and offering undivided attention to all the people accompanying us on our journey today. It means giving everybody the benefit of the doubt if we aren't in agreement with them. It means being willing to let others have their own opinions without trying to change them or judge them.

Loving others is more complex than many of us imagined. The good aspect of this is that we can stay busy learning to love for the rest of our lives. We'll never be done making this contribution to society. That's pretty exciting.

Am I ready to love everyone I meet today?
I can become willing to embrace this purpose.

JUNE 15

*I've always been a people-oriented person
rather than a hobby person.*

LOUISE JEROME

Part of the unexpected joy of these later years in our lives is the freedom to explore activities that heretofore hadn't appealed to us. If hobbies hadn't appealed to you, perhaps the time is right to see if that's still the case. Most of us have far more free time than we'd counted on. The problem won't necessarily be in filling it up, but in selecting organizations or activities that truly spark our interests.

Are hobbies and being involved with other people mutually exclusive? Not really. In fact, most hobbies aren't solitary activities at all. Perhaps woodworking or knitting or bird-watching or photography start out that way. But sustaining our interest in them is usually enhanced by sharing our "findings" or showing our completed projects to others who can appreciate them.

But clearly, there is no wrong way to spend retirement. We don't have to get a hobby. We don't have to volunteer for organizations that we don't really care about. We don't even have to spend much time with other people. In fact, we don't have to enjoy ourselves at all. But what a shame when we don't. There's so much to be learned from others. There's so much we can give to others. Time is what we have a lot of now. Let's use it wisely.

**How I spend today is simply up to me.
What do I really want to do?**

JUNE 16

Being able to do what you want to do
when you want to do it is marvelous.

FRAN COYNE

Any of us who are already retired have this luxury that Fran speaks of, whether or not we take advantage of it. It may have become habitual to overwhelm ourselves with chores. Demanding jobs in our past may have contributed to that mind-set. Making a "to-do" list isn't bad, but it can make us feel burdened. On the other hand, choosing to do only what one wants to do may feel far too irresponsible for most of us.

We may have to practice taking it easier. Most of us didn't have the opportunity to be totally selective about what we did when we were raising our families or fulfilling the boss's expectations at work. It may seem impossible to believe we can do something or nothing on any one day, but trying to live this way deserves some effort from us. We have worked hard for years. Even if we loved what we were doing, we still deserve a different outlook now.

For many of us, it's hard to get used to the idea that no one is looking over our shoulders. In fact, for some of us there may be a spouse who is a bit demanding. But we have the right to negotiate what we'll do when we feel like doing it. We've earned this opportunity. Let's not squander it.

Asking myself what I truly long to do today is my first priority.
Setting about making the plan comes next.

JUNE 17

Everything changes—
but some things change more slowly.

JANICE CLARK

Experience has taught us that change is inevitable. But getting used to this has seldom been easy, particularly if we liked how the circumstances of our lives were going. And then, of course, there were less comfortable situations that we prayed would change. Sometimes they did. Often they didn't, at least not on our timetable. That change is simply a fact of life is never more obvious than when we look at old photographs or sort through the memorabilia that children have left behind.

The physical changes that have occurred in most of us are often distressing. Did we honestly think we'd be agile and full of energy forever? The death of a loved one is one change that we all must confront, more frequently as the years slip by. No matter how many friends we have lost already, the next one is still difficult. Saying good-bye is letting go, and it means we have to acknowledge that we all are changing and moving on. Nothing lasts forever.

In our youth, perhaps we celebrated that nothing lasts forever. Commonly, as we grow old, we long for sameness. Let's help each other remember the comfort of change. Our journey is about change. That's why we're here.

I will watch my life closely today.
It will not be the same tomorrow.
This journey moves me along moment by moment.

JUNE 18

*Growing up, I was very afraid of making
new acquaintances. I was shy.*

MARIA REGNIER KRIMMEL

It might have become a habit to fear the unfamiliar, whether a person or a situation. What we tell ourselves repeatedly is what becomes our truth. Are we satisfied with who we are now, with how we relate to the world around us? If not, we must determine to change the messages we keep playing in our minds.

It may seem impossible to change our personalities. Shyness is generally considered a trait that we simply have. But we adopted it, we nurtured it, and we can relinquish it. What's the point, some might say, if we have been shy our whole lives? For some, maybe there is none, but if you aren't content with the level of activity in your life, or if you aren't engaged enough with other people, perhaps you should consider the inner dialogue that has kept you occupied for these many years.

There is great relief in believing that nothing about our personalities is cast in stone. Being one way for decades, whether shy or overbearing, isn't the only way we can be. Trying on a new characteristic is as possible as our imagination allows. It may not be comfortable at first. In fact, it will probably feel awful, but we can be daring anyway. Why not?

I can use a new approach in how I treat people today.

JUNE 19

*My relationship with nature and plants
is almost like religion with me.*

MONTY CRALLEY

Feeling connected to something outside of ourselves is important to our perception of life. And being alive assures us of many new situations. Maybe it's a move to a smaller residence or our recovery from the death of a dear friend. Having to give up cherished possessions is a decision we all have to make at some point, too. But handling any of these circumstances is easier when we have a connection to the world around us; nature, for example, can always provide us with a sense of solace and familiarity.

The natural world comforts many of us. Just noting the cycle of life in the trees and plants helps us to remember that everything changes. Everything is transformed, but life and beauty are still present if we look for it. When we're feeling lonely, it helps to remember that God is still present and evident in the miracle of the natural world.

It doesn't matter how we define God or if we do at all. God may speak to us through the swaying tree branches or through people. Or we may get a glimmer of God in a passage in a book. That we do sense something larger and external to ourselves is what matters at the end of the day.

**I will continue nurturing my spiritual side today.
This will comfort me.**

JUNE 20

Even though we were poor growing up,
we weren't poor in spirit.

JIM BURNS

To Jim, spirit means being truly alive and eager to experience whatever the day brings. Perhaps we think it's not possible for us to be rich in that kind of spirit, but it is. There's a way that beckons to each of us. It's called prayer.

Prayer has no doubt been a part of our lives already. And we found many expressions of it. Some of us believed in its power more than others, but whether we wanted better jobs, more money, happier relationships, or more skill in particular activities, we quite likely beseeched the God of our understanding to help us. And providing we were able to trust God's guidance, we did get help.

Feeling a spiritual connection need not elude us. It's as close and accessible as a mere thought. How truly fortunate we are that no amount of money or good health determines our ability to be filled with the spirit of peace and happiness. We've heard it before, but it bears repeating: Attitude is everything.

I can cultivate a joyful spirit as often as possible today.

JUNE 21

Physically, I'm in tough shape, but I try to roll with the punches and do as well as I can with what I've got.

JAMES CASEY

If only we all had the outlook expressed by Jim. Does he have some special gift? Not at all. He has simply taken charge of his interpretation of life's unexpected detours. We can always assume control of how we see our lives. That's the miracle that awaits us all.

Aging means having problems, though some dilemmas are more serious than others. We all have friends who still laugh a lot, in spite of the gravity of their situations. Often we think, I wouldn't be able to do that. How is it that they can? Perhaps we should ask them. We'd likely hear them say that they decided to cultivate positive attitudes long ago, because negative attitudes only made situations worse.

There isn't any mystery to how some people get happy and others stay miserable. We recognize in an instant which category each person is in. Do we realize others label us just as quickly? Let's make sure that we're in the positive group.

**People will recognize me by my attitude today.
Who will I be?**

JUNE 22

Everything has changed: families, children,
even senior citizens. What they used to like doing at our
center doesn't interest them anymore.

ALPHA ENGLISH

Nothing is changeless, formless, and eternal in this material world. Serenely adjusting to the ever-changing environment and host of experiences that are common to us daily is how we might define wisdom or maturity. It's often quite difficult to accept the changing of others. Perhaps it feels threatening to us. Our companionship had probably grown out of a shared undertaking of some kind. When someone "moves on," it changes our lives forever. It often doesn't seem possible that we can be comfortable with all these changes.

If we take the long view for a moment, we'll be able to see that actually *nothing has changed,* that everything is and always was in a state of constant flux. That's life. Because many of the changes are tiny and because we have been the initiator of them, we don't even take great notice of them. Those people who have been affected by them certainly noticed, however. Perhaps we need to shift our perception about change, recognizing instead that it means people are dynamically involved in our lives. Were we entirely alone, there would still be changes: the weather, our moods, the condition of our health. But we'd not be particularly charged up about the changes because no one else "caused" them. Change is no big deal! Really!

I am ready for today and all its possibilities.

JUNE 23

I believe that a lot of things we think are bad may not be,
and if we live long enough we'll see that.

HARRY BARTHOLOMEW

We have all lived long enough to realize we misunderstood many of the circumstances we encountered over our lifetimes. Lost relationships that devastated us perhaps weren't right for us to begin with, but we hadn't realized it. The job opportunities we missed out on and felt saddened by made it possible for us to find a better career. The friendships that went sour no longer had something to teach us. But seldom, in the midst of the loss, did we realize the necessity for it. More often, we fought against it, certain that we'd been unfairly treated.

We are blessed with having to live only one day at a time. Additionally, we are blessed with "being told" only what we need to know, when we need to know it. We have lamented, our whole lives perhaps, the fact that the future is so uncertain. But it isn't, really. What's supposed to happen will; we'll find it out when its time has arrived. The changes that occur, the situations that seem tumultuous, are exactly as they need to be. Our perception, our willingness to trust that we're in good hands always will continue to see us through every day of our lives. This is how our lives have unfolded all along. Why would it change now?

Today holds my next lesson.
I'm ready for it even if I'm doubtful.

JUNE 24

*People who don't want to try anything new are a sorry lot.
I've known a few.*

TOM HARDING

Are you looking forward to trying something new today? Have you tried anything new in the last month? A new casserole perhaps, or a new card game? A new category of books, if reading is an interest? If walking is your pastime, how recently have you trod a new path? Making a new friend is such a wonderful adventure. Can you claim a new acquaintance or two over the past few months? There's so much to be learned, so much to be exposed to by just including a new personality, a new voice in one's circle of friends.

It makes little difference what new experience we may have. Simply making the decision to broaden our scope on life is the point of it all. We seldom ever realize how narrow our viewpoint, how limited our awareness of the world, until we include new activities and ideas into our everyday living. The easiest way to usher in the new is through an introduction to a person we'd not known before.

How can we tell when we need some new experiences, some new thoughts to consider? If we dread getting up in the mornings, if we find that we're mindlessly watching television or taking too many naps, it's time to seek the new. All we have to do is make our need known to someone and the unfamiliar will appear.

**Am I eager to greet today?
Or do I need a new idea to consider?**

JUNE 25

Being interested in something means I stay young
even though I have grown old.

ALICE MERRYMAN

A curious, interested mind never gets bored. It's constantly working on solutions to various situations; some mundane and some quite complex. Curiosity undeniably affects the outcome of any condition in our lives. First of all, we are willing to explore various ramifications of a particular direction if we are curious. We are also open to trying alternatives if we are faced with a problem. Additionally, we aren't filled with fear about taking a risk because we have dared to think of our lives evolving in unexpected ways. All of these descriptions of how one might function can explain why some among us seem to stay so young.

We have heard many times that growing old is nothing more than a state of mind. Who among us hasn't met at least one really old forty-year-old man or woman? We kid that they seem to have been born that way, and there's possibly some truth to that. For whatever reason, they failed to get the idea that one's perspective is "individually grown." They became, instead, who they mimicked. That could have happened to any of us. The bad news is that it still can. Staying young is a decision, but one that has to be fortified daily.

My interests are my lifeline to a fulfilled life.
Should I develop a new one?

I know I need something to do everyday.
It probably doesn't even matter what it is.

THELMA ELLIOTT

Being busy is what Thelma desires. That may not be true for everyone. However, it's important that each of us recognizes what we do need. Taking an inventory of how we're feeling and noting what we're doing will offer some clues regarding our contentment or lack of it. If we aren't fully satisfied, we need to make some changes.

But how do we know what to change if we're not as happy as we'd hoped to be? Talking about our dreams and disappointments with a friend will be enlightening and a good first step. Deciding to change only one detail of our lives at a time is a good decision, too. Seeking to understand the way others have made their choices about what to do makes sense also. It's not coincidental that we're in communication with a particular group of people. They are here as teachers. Assuredly, we are instructing them as well.

Making our lives matter, keeping them rich and interesting, appeals to us all. How we go about doing this varies according to one's personality. What we can all be certain of, however, is that it matters not what we do but how we feel doing it. We can gauge this easily.

Am I content with my life today?
If something is amiss, I'll talk with a friend.

JUNE 27

I need to leave society a little better off before I die.

MONTY CRALLEY

Do you share Monty's philosophy? Our past experiences may have left us bitter and unwilling to think of others. If that's the case, how sad for us. How sad for all the people we have contact with, too. But that's not the end of the story unless we decide as much. We can determine to change the attitude we have perfected over the years. In fact, that might be an exciting undertaking for us now. We certainly have the time to devote to a pursuit of this nature.

Some may ask, what's the point of leaving society a better place? What can one person really do? The fact is, one person's actions are noticeable when they inspire others to follow suit. That's where the real impact will eventually be felt.

Just imagine the breadth of the changes in society that might result if everyone of us did just one nice and unexpected thing for someone else every single day. It's such a simple decision and it would take so little effort. Let's not contribute to worsening the lives of others in spite of the experiences we might have had. Quite miraculously, our lives will not seem to have been so bad once we begin bettering the life of someone else.

**My age won't keep me from thinking
of someone else first today.**

JUNE 28

Each day is a surprise—
a surprise we eagerly anticipate.

ALPHA ENGLISH

Attitude is everything! Regardless of what we are told about any situation facing us, we will experience whatever we have made up our minds to experience. Reviewing the past reminds us of this. Fortunately, we have only the future ahead of us, which means we can change whatever our most common experience was, particularly if much of our lives didn't give us the pleasure that others seemed to get. One thing never changes. That's the level of personal power we each have over how we feel about any circumstance that catches our attention. When you stop to think about it, we couldn't possibly need anymore power than that, ever.

Likely, we all have recollections that trouble us still, in most cases because we felt attacked, discounted, abused in some way. What we didn't practice in those encounters was taking charge of how we perceived whatever was happening. Even when other people were treating us badly, it was always possible to see their actions as evidence of their pain, which was not our responsibility. At least we know this now. Isn't it wonderful that it's never too late to change how we see life?

Today is an exciting prospect.
I'll share my enthusiasm with a friend.

JUNE 29

I would make some changes in
how and when to retire if I were doing it over.

SANDY WARMAN

Many people sharing this book had a similar response to their retirement. Some were forced out of their jobs due to mergers or new management. Others took advantage of an opportunity for early retirement only to discover they weren't really ready for it. Health concerns may have prompted some to leave their occupations before the mandatory retirement age. Whatever the reason for the current set of circumstances, an adjustment must still be made, and it's difficult for many to make it. Has this been true for you?

There are many avenues one can travel in pursuit of the adjustment. Some may choose to seek professional counseling. Others may discover a support group that can help them explore the new possibilities that now exist. Having a companion in the home or close by eases whatever we're feeling, too. The main point is that we can ask others to help us shoulder our sadness or anger. We can always seek spiritual solace. We have never had to handle any of our struggles alone. Even though we may have forgotten to seek help, or thought we had to be strong and handle everything ourselves, that was never the case. Let's look to others now if the need is there.

My age today is not relevant to my happiness.
The decisions I make are all that count.

JUNE 30

The beauty of retirement for me
is that I don't need a goal.

JOE CASEY

Living without goals is hard, at least in the early stage of retirement. We may prefer a goal; it may be what gets us out of bed in the morning. Not having to have one to feel good about one's self is what Joe is referring to. That's what we're all shooting for, isn't it? But in the interim, having too little to do and minimal contact with others can be troubling. Not uncommonly, we begin to doubt our worth.

The absence of feedback from others is generally the way it is now. We may not have appreciated all the feedback before, particularly when it was critical of our work or the goal at hand, but now we long for some sign that others have noticed our presence or our attempt to succeed. Can we adjust to this change?

The answer, of course, is yes, but it takes time. Since we have a lot of that, we're on our way. There are other things we can do, too. We can set small goals, ones that relate to our personal well-being. Maybe we have always wanted to explore our family history or take a Spanish class. Volunteering at the neighborhood school or working part-time in a store might interest us. Doing something is what matters. It's okay to have goals. They're a must for most of us; however, not needing them is what the journey is now about.

Am I feeling lost today?
Do I have a plan for who I want to be now?

JULY

JULY 1

I think I've made a reasonable contribution in my eighty-one years. At least I did what I thought was best.

JAMES CASEY

We all hope to feel as Jim feels, and the truth of the matter is, we can. No matter how many times we failed or regardless of the many regrets we have, we usually did the best we were capable of as each experience unfolded. Let's put aside our doubt about this. We were never expected to be perfect. We may have had demanding parents and teachers and bosses, but as long as we put forth honest effort, we usually did our part. We deserve to celebrate this fact.

None of us is necessarily through making contributions. We may have figured we'd outlived our usefulness, but such is not the case. There may not be any grand schemes that need our attention or any major family concerns that await our input, but we aren't through yet or we'd not still be here. What might our part be at this stage of our lives?

If we aren't sure what our next assignment is, let's simply be quiet for a while and wait for the inner urging to guide us. Maybe all we're needed for right now is to befriend a lonely neighbor. Or maybe a great-grandchild is walking too close to the edge of safety, and we need to take his or her hand. We can be sure there is something important to do. Let's be ready.

I am ready to do my part today and contribute what I can.

JULY 2

Some of my grandchildren say they want to be like me.
That's a wonderful compliment.

ALICE MERRYMAN

It's likely we have all been role models for someone. Certainly we can look back on our own lives and recall those individuals we hoped to imitate. We probably made a few wrong choices along the way, too. That's not uncommon, nor irreparable. Those who have looked up to us might have taken with them some of our less attractive traits as well. We aren't responsible for what others have noticed and copied, but we are responsible for what we copied in others.

Are we still "forming" ourselves, or have we "arrived"? There's no simple answer. By this age, we hope to have settled on certain traits we'd rather not lose, but the more thoughtful among us realize that making select changes in our behaviors and attitudes can go on endlessly. *We're not done until we are done.* There's real excitement in that idea. It means ongoing growth and new experiences. Every time we change something, it impacts many other areas of our lives as well as others. Change engages us, and that's what life is about.

Watching others watch us will keep us on our toes. Let's not send someone away with one of the traits that we're ashamed of. Let's put our best self forward.

Do my friends and offspring think well of me?
Yesterday's impressions aren't necessarily today's.

JULY 3

My retirement years have been my golden years.
I'm developing every day.

MONTY CRALLEY

Monty is an amazing man. He earned high acclaim in his profession, a worldwide reputation, in fact. But his retirement has brought him his greatest joy: He has taken up painting and it has changed his life. These can be golden years for all of us. It's a matter of decision, first, then willingness to become a student once again.

We have all heard a friend say, "I can't do that. I'm too old." Generally, we have either offered a rebuttal or agreed with them. Often we weren't really convinced they *could* do that, even when we said otherwise. And that reveals a great deal about our own enthusiasm for trying something new.

The men and women who are still having fun living are likely pushing the envelope of new experiences. There is no time like now for taking a risk. Really, what have we got to lose? Are we going to get fired?

I have the freedom to try anything I want today.
I am my own boss. I don't want this day to end
wishing I'd taken a chance.

JULY 4

Life is such a mystery. It's a miracle, but it's also a mystery. How quickly it can go.

HELEN CASEY

None of us have been spared the death of a friend who was "terminal." The truth is that we are all terminal; from our birth on we are terminal. We simply don't dwell on it and it loses its reality. Remembering it on occasion is good for us, however. It prompts us to squeeze the pleasure out of every moment.

Learning to appreciate one day, one moment at a time is not so hard. Even though we may have spent years living in the past or the future, we can form a habit of bringing our minds back to *now*. Vigilance is all that's required and it's an excellent tool to master.

Aging sometimes means giving up favored activities. Singles tennis may be too much. Walking replaces jogging. Listening to books on tape is more restful than reading. Necessary naps replace unnecessary running around. We seldom joyfully give up who we were. But focusing instead on our current capabilities reminds us that life is not over yet. *Our time will come* when the time is right. Let's accept the mystery and love this moment.

I am here, now, by design.
Those who have gone before fulfilled their
plans just as I am fulfilling mine.

JULY 5

*The most important thing we are doing right now
is thinking nice thoughts.*

JIM AND MARIE BURNS

Just thinking nice thoughts sounds so simplistic, doesn't it? Surely there is more in life to contemplate than that. But the power of nice thoughts, the impact just such a simple decision can have on our lives and the lives of everyone in our company, is awesome. Having nice thoughts and only nice thoughts is a significant departure for most of us. Far more commonly we quietly or vocally judged every man, woman, and child in our presence. Stopping ourselves from judging, in fact, stopping a judgment in its tracks, will reveal how swamped our thinking has been by the critical, mean-spirited side of us.

Seldom do we cultivate a quiet, peaceful mind. Seemingly out of control, our minds race from one idea, one judgment, one negative opinion to another one of equal harm to ourselves and the entire human community. Perhaps we didn't realize that every thought we harbor has an impact, whether it's voiced aloud or not. We can't lay the blame for this violent, mean world solely on others. We've had a part in it, too. Every time we favor a nasty thought rather than a nice thought, we add to the turmoil around us. The good news is that we can choose between the two at will.

**I will add to the tenor of the world today by my thoughts.
I pray that I may choose them carefully.**

JULY 6

*Caring—you know that is a great thing. I don't like
to be around phony people. I like people who are genuine.*

ALPHA ENGLISH

How genuine are we? And how caring? We can usually recognize others' failed attempts at sincerity. But do we acknowledge our own failed attempts? Our inner voice informs us, but how well do we listen to it? How much do we honor its plea for loving others?

Caring about others isn't really very difficult and doesn't take any extra time. It's little more than a decision. Being willing to do it is the only hurdle. Do we gain from not doing it? Actually, we lose a great deal. When we withhold love from others, we actually are devoting some of our precious time to harboring negative thoughts. And they multiply. The time for living that we lose in the process multiplies, too.

There are men and women we all long to be around. What draws us to them? Even a brief inventory of their qualities reveals that they have a zest for living. They offer us genuine attention. We know they care. Do they have some special talent that we lack? On the contrary, their decisions have been different, that's all.

> It's wonderful knowing that I make the
> decision to give or withhold love today.
> I will emulate those I admire.

JULY 7

My whole life was based on what other people thought.
Now I don't concern myself so much with that,
and it's a great new freedom.

SANDY WARMAN

If we hadn't judged others, would we have been so concerned with others' judgment of us? Probably not. We may have been obsessed with our comparisons to others when we were younger. No doubt it was because that was how parents and teachers attempted to mold our behavior. There were always good examples of behavior around, and they were pointed out to us. The authority figures in our lives meant well. It's simply been difficult to break the habit of always looking at others and evaluating how they are doing, thus how we are doing, too.

Why is it that we care less about this as we age? Probably it's because we have experienced so much. We have known many personal successes and failures. The wisdom of aging has taught us that we are so much more than the momentary achievements. Fortunately, the times we didn't measure up are indelible on our minds only. It's a joy knowing that others don't really care about who we were, or what we did. How we respond to the situations and people in our lives now is all that anyone really notices. We have a lot of control over that, in fact.

Today is a clean slate. The opinions others have of me
will be influenced by my kindness, little more.

JULY 8

I spent my whole life doing what I was told.

MARIA REGNIER KRIMMEL

There is no shame in having followed orders. Perhaps our options to do otherwise were limited. It may be that one of the real freedoms of growing old is that we can refuse to follow the orders of anyone we choose, unless our refusal means breaking the law.

Each of us can profit from doing an inventory of our lives. What periods were particularly good for us? Which were fraught with turmoil? Let's recall the many people and circumstances that contributed measurably to our growth, whether painful or not. We might be able to see a pattern in the way situations seemed to unfold, and recognizing that now can help us to plan better for whatever lies ahead. It's absolutely certain that much still lies ahead.

It's not unusual to feel that our lives were seldom our own. Parents, spouses, employers, and even friends wielded a certain amount of control over us. We may still feel a bit under the thumb of others. But it's always possible to change our minds about how we experience someone else's demands. Freedom is a state of mind, in the final analysis.

I am in charge of me today.
Another's requests are only that.

JULY 9

Leaving my work when I was still wanted was good for me.
It's hard getting kicked out,
and that happens to a lot of people.

FRAN COYNE

How your career ended has had its impact. It's terribly unfortunate that many individuals are pushed out the door, often to make way for the younger, more technologically capable worker. But that can't color forever how the rest of one's life appears. There's a great deal to be said for the belief that "everything happens for a right reason and at the right time." That may not be compatible with your philosophy, but it can offer comfort.

Another way to look at our current situations is to acknowledge that we must still have a purpose for living or we'd not be alive. The purpose doesn't need to be of gigantic proportions, in spite of what we may think. Simply being present in the life of a lonely neighbor or a sick grandchild may be God's only purpose for us today. Let's not second-guess the plan for our lives. Let's just show up.

How we left our occupation just isn't as important as the fact that we now have time to devote to other pursuits. Any one of them will be just as valuable to the total scheme of each of our lives as the occupation we had. Hindsight will enlighten us if we wait for it and have faith.

I can grow in the belief that I still have great purpose.
Today's opportunities are divine.

*I don't do what I do just so people will think kindly of me.
I like doing what I do.*

JANICE CLARK

We're lucky if we like everything that we do. But many of us have to develop a willingness to like many of the activities we're involved in. Is that unusual? Probably not. Nor does it matter. Acting as if we enjoy a menial task or an unusual pursuit offers us a different perspective on it. Just looking at it through more willing eyes changes not just how we see it, but how we feel about it. Often we discover that we can enjoy that which we dreaded before.

Because we wanted to be liked, and it's human nature to want that, we often volunteered for committees, for jobs, for assignments of all kinds that we didn't want to do. There's no shame in that. But at long last, we can dare to be more selective about what we'll do.

We are needed. That's why we're still alive. And while not everybody likes us, those currently in our circle of acquaintances need us and we need them. The work that is yet to be done relies on all of us. Pitching in begins to feel good when we have the right attitude.

> I don't have to like everything I need to do today,
> but I'll feel more open to all the tasks
> if I remember they need my input.

JULY 11

What I liked best about my work was the involvement with other people. I miss that.

BUD SHERMAN

Finding activities that involve other people is only as hard as we make it. Unfortunately, it's easy to get stuck in our complacency. While still employed, people came to us, more or less. Now, we may have to seek them out. If we're a little on the shy side or doubt that we have enough to offer a group, we'll too easily pass up an opportunity to get involved. Let's simply decide to jump in with both feet, anyway. We're no different from anyone else. Everybody feels a little fear when first entering a new group. There's nothing to lose but our loneliness! Can that be so bad?

A good way to get over our fear of a new group, is to focus on just one person at a time. Take an interest in what he or she is doing now, or has done in the past. Get that person involved in a discussion about himself or herself, and in no time, you'll forget your own self-consciousness. Interacting with just one person will make it easier to interact with the group a second time. We don't have to know everyone immediately. And we don't have to like everyone, either. Just making contact with one other person will affect how we feel about each new encounter in the future. If we want other people in our lives, we have to do the footwork.

> I can be idle today or surrounded by
> the good cheer of others.
> The choice is mine.

JULY 12

*The first couple of years of my husband's
retirement were hard on me.*

LOUISE JEROME

There is an adjustment for everybody when the work life of a family member changes. Routines are interrupted; expectations go unmet; plans often have to be reformulated. Patience and time will help to clarify the new parameters for each member of the family. But being open with one's feelings and willing to negotiate new routines will alleviate much of the stress.

Few of us were prepared for the dis-ease that often accompanies retirement. We likely anticipated lots of travel, late nights with friends, and satisfying hours of reading or pursuing the hobbies we always wanted to try. There wasn't much that we contemplated that didn't sound appealing. And yet, many of us struggle with depression that we hadn't expected. We struggle with spouses whom we've always loved. We struggle with our own feelings of uselessness, not knowing where to put our attentions first.

Just realizing that there are many stages to the adjustment we're making helps. We will find the peace we seek; it will likely come in stages, too. The good news is that we aren't faced with a deadline. Staying in touch with how we're feeling and seeking understanding from our companions will make all the difference.

How I feel today is important to share with others.
I deserve to be peaceful.

JULY 13

*Keeping busy keeps me from getting edgy and depressed.
I need to be busy.*

PAT JEROME

Depression is a condition that most of us confront sometime in our lives. In the early part of retirement, it's most common. We have gone from being very busy, quite intentional people to being more laid back with few "assignments." The extra un-structured time pushes some of us to question our value to the rest of society. As long as we were avidly working, we had little time to doubt our importance. Are we really worth less now? We wonder.

Clearly, we all know at some level that we haven't lost our worth just because we no longer earn a paycheck. But our psy-che—our emotional balance—may feel jeopardized by the change in our lifestyles. For some, just being busy, too busy perhaps, kept us from considering our self-worth throughout our more productive years. Nothing is keeping us from this con-sideration now. And that's why the doubt creeps in.

Staying busy as a way to avoid our fears regarding our worth isn't the best way to deal with them, though perhaps it's the most common. It's better that we seek a spiritual solution to our con-cerns. It will sustain us longer. But how do we do that? There's only one way. Seek the inner voice who has all answers. We'll be told we matter still. Being alive is our proof.

**Am I being busy as a way of avoiding my fears today?
Let me slow down, God.**

JULY 14

*I kept telling myself, "I can't stay this way.
I've just got to get better."*

VIOLET HENSLEY

It's amazing how much control we actually have over our well-being—physical, mental, and emotional. If we want to feel ill, it doesn't take much concentration to accomplish it. And while it is true that we may not be able to prevent all serious illness, we can take charge of our response to cancer or heart disease or arthritis if it happens to us. This, in turn, can lessen its control over us.

We help or hinder a physical illness. Constant focus on it exaggerates it. The reverse is also quite true. We diminish its power over us if we go about our lives as though we had been healed. In not-so-rare cases, that is exactly what happens. In all cases, we will feel considerably better.

Learning to own our power over how we feel comes quite naturally once we have tried it successfully. Many of us grew up thinking that *things just happened to us.* Discovering that we don't have to accept all conditions as beyond our control is empowering. Taking this understanding a step further and refusing to let a condition take charge of our lives changes how we perceive every aspect of every day.

**I have power over how I feel today.
What I do with it is up to me.**

JULY 15

I believe you can expect to live longer
if you stay active mentally.

TOM HARDING

Tom's philosophy has certainly held true for him, but is every octogenarian's goal to live longer? Maybe not. The quality of one's life is generally far more important to most people. Of course, it might well be said that the quality of one's life will be far better if the mind is actively engaged. Fortunately, we have absolute control over that aspect of our lives. A quality life doesn't require anything but a contented mind.

It's nice to contemplate the remainder of our lives when we have reasonably unlimited control over how we spend our time. Our work lives and the child-rearing years gave us too little freedom to define just what we were going to do and when. Time is the truly special gift of older age.

Let's not deny that in the past we always had control over how we felt about what we were doing; we always had the power to change an opinion or adjust an attitude that in turn could allow us to feel real satisfaction and joy. But most of us didn't take advantage of our power often enough. It was easier to make others responsible for our feelings. Isn't it nice that we've discovered taking charge actually energizes us?

I can pursue whatever appeals to my mind today.
What wonderful freedom!

JULY 16

The first thing I was going to do after I retired was clean my closets. That was six years ago, and I haven't done it yet.

KATE PAUL

Being too busy to do the mundane isn't all that bad, is it? Who would have believed how rich and full our lives could be? This stage of our lives has pleasantly surprised many of us. We didn't know what to expect, perhaps, but we hadn't counted on all the activities that are beckoning to us regularly.

Is retirement like this for everybody? Unfortunately not. There are those among us who suffer from loneliness or worse yet, ill health. We don't really want to count our blessings by making comparisons to them, but it's okay to be grateful for what has come to us. It might even increase our level of gratitude if we reached out to somebody who hasn't been as fortunate. After all, we all deserve to enjoy what time is left in our lives. Whenever one of us can help anyone else, we will have done a worthy service that benefits all of humanity.

If you haven't been blessed with many friends and good health, what might you do today to improve your circumstances? The first step is simply to take notice of someone else. Oftentimes, our own situation looks bad to us because we haven't taken the time to notice our neighbor. Let's begin there, for starters.

I can spend these next twenty-four hours doing something either exciting or mundane. I will appreciate this freedom.

JULY 17

I never dreamed my crafts would be known around the world. I simply did them.

ALICE MERRYMAN

Hindsight probably allows many of us to see how meaningful our seemingly unimportant activities were. Seldom did we imagine the bigger purpose of any single occurrence. But everything fit so neatly, didn't it? This continues to be true. Even when we don't particularly like a situation or when a person gets under our skin, we can decide to believe that there is purpose in the experience. That decision makes our lives so much more peaceful.

There is nothing more important than knowing peace. It may have taken us a while to come to this understanding, but few of us doubt it now. And yet we feel it far less often than we might. Why is that? The answer is simple, and it's the same for all of us: our lack of peace is due to our egos trying to manipulate situations and people who are in our lives. We aren't satisfied with how something is going, and we become intent on changing it. Just as quickly as we make that decision, our peace has escaped us. What might we do instead? Get quiet and wait. Peace will return. The divine is unfolding. Let's let it happen.

My peacefulness is of my own making.
What kind of experience do I want today?

JULY 18

*I think we need to stay challenged as we age, and I do it
by surrounding myself with people who are bright and active.*

JOANN REED

We are greatly influenced by the company we seek. This has always been true, but in our youth, we had access to greater numbers of people than might be the case now. Depending on our living arrangements, we may be rather limited, in fact, regarding who we can choose to befriend or converse with. The interesting truth about our current condition, whatever it is, is that we have "requested" it, albeit at an unconscious level. Our inner spirit always knows what we need. That makes us pretty lucky. All we have to do is show up.

Perhaps you haven't taken a good look at the people in your life of late. Do so today. Does it surprise you that some among the group are hard to get along with? Are there one or two individuals whom you feel particularly jealous of or maybe superior to? Coming to believe that everyone in our lives is there by design profoundly changes how we see our experiences.

They say wisdom comes with age. Probably that's true. However, unless we are willing to learn from our experiences, we'll not gain much wisdom. We've had a host of them now. Do we know all that we need to know even yet? The answer is no.

**Today is my chance to learn something else of importance
from the people around me.**

JULY 19

The one lesson my dad taught me:
If you're going to do anything in life, do it right.

MONTY CRALLEY

Our parents may have had a way of instructing that often bordered on shaming us. No matter what we might remember about it, or them, they meant well. Their own experiences colored how they parented us. This pattern was probably played out in our own parenting, too. We all did the best we could. None of us did a perfect job. But now that we have the time to contemplate the past, we might want to consider forgiving our parents if we still harbor any grudges. Or we might want to make amends to our children or other family members if we are able to see our own failings now.

We made tons of mistakes getting to old age. Some were intentional; most were not. Do we have to redress all of them? Actually, we don't even have to acknowledge any of them. But if we do, we'll feel far better about ourselves and we'll have helped to break the cycle of the poor parenting we might have experienced.

We all have a chance to do something significant in life. This doesn't have to mean inventing a tool or a drug that will help millions of people. It's really quite easy. Smile at a stranger today, for starters. Consider putting aside an old grudge. Apologize for an unkind action.

I can do something really important today.
Am I willing to examine how I treat other people?

JULY 20

The most important ingredient for a long life is having something you really want to do.

EVA WINES

We all have acquaintances who complain bitterly about their lives. They feel forgotten by their children. Their health may be failing. Money is scarce. They see nothing to look forward to. The state of the world disturbs them. They aren't a lot of fun to be around, but perhaps they serve as good reminders of who we don't want to be. Our teachers are everywhere, we are told.

It's important to monitor how we greet each new day. Is it with welcome anticipation or do we drag ourselves out of bed? If it's the latter, we'd better try something new. Boredom is deadly and there's no good reason for any of us to suffer from it. Libraries are overflowing with books we haven't read about ideas we haven't ever considered. Community centers are filled with people seeking the company of people like ourselves. On every block is a man or woman who would love to share the passion they feel for a hobby they have pursued. All we have to do is be willing to make ourselves available for any one of these options.

Living a long life may not be your goal. And that's okay. But living peacefully for whatever amount of time remains is certainly a preference we can all relate to. How are you doing?

What do I want from this next twenty-four hours?
I can have it. What a marvelous gift.

JULY 21

We are free in this country,
but freedom has certain responsibilities.

JIM BURNS

Maybe we had assumed that one gift of our advancing years was freedom, finally, from responsibilities. If so, we might resist Jim's admonition. Another response could be relief: *We aren't worthless; we aren't done yet.* There is still work we can do and contributions we can make, regardless of age.

Let's consider the responsibilities that might need us. Depending on our health and agility, maybe we can volunteer at a day-care center. Young people need our wisdom as much as we need their exuberance. Perhaps we can take an infirm friend to the grocery store on a regular basis. Mentoring a young person who is just beginning a career is an invaluable contribution, not only to him or her but to the future of this society.

Many types of work don't demand that we retire at a certain age. Maybe it's time to seek a new career. The point is this: As long as we have the willingness and the capacity to interact with others, on some level, our services are still needed. Whether it's sweeping a neighbor's walk, planting flowers at church, telling or reading stories to people of all ages, or passing on one's personal history to a grandchild, there's always something important we can do.

My responsibilities haven't ended.
The world needs me.

JULY 22

Volunteering contributes to a higher quality of life
for everyone involved.

JOE CASEY

Does it really matter if others have as good a life as the one we've worked to have? Perhaps we're not certain, and we may have many acquaintances who appear rather self-serving and seem not to suffer for it. Why should we believe that we're all helped by the efforts of even some of us? Maybe we can understand this best by simply beginning with the decision to believe it. Then we can consciously notice how fulfilled some individuals are after they have given their time to people in need. Firsthand observation is pretty hard to refute.

If volunteering hasn't interested you yet, read the listing in the local paper of all the opportunities available. More than likely one will sound appealing. The good news is that no one is tied to a particular choice forever. The list of possibilities is long, and volunteers are always welcome. Exploring a few of them until one feels just right makes sense. Let's not forget that all parties need to benefit from the experience.

Let's revisit, for a moment, the idea that *everyone* benefits from *anyone's* efforts. This is based on the principle that nothing exists in a vacuum. When love or consideration is expressed in one setting, its effects travel everywhere. The sages among us already know this to be true. Let's all come to believe it.

I have something valuable to share with someone else
today — my life, my attention, my love —
and it costs nothing but time.

JULY 23

Writing fascinated me. I loved the drama of words.
Of all the mediums, I loved words the most.

JANICE CLARK

The creative process is always the same, whatever the medium. It has its own momentum, triggered by one's inner spirit. Experiencing how a story unfolds or a project takes shape results in a surprising outcome most often. But most of us aren't writers or artists. So how can Janice's words apply to us?

Looking at our lives as ongoing stories can be very comforting. We have needed the "stories" that have transpired. Our journey would not have been complete without them. The remainder of our lives will flow in this manner, too. It's not that we don't have input. Just as the artist or writer has to put himself or herself in the studio or at a desk, we have to be willing to acknowledge the situations that are occurring all around us. They hold our lessons. The inner spirit has called them to us.

My life is a story unfolding. Today is a chapter that has
naturally resulted from my experiences.

JULY 24

So many things add up to joy.
Just being with someone can do it.

ALPHA ENGLISH

Taking the few minutes necessary to offer a pep talk to an acquaintance will reward us in many ways. First of all, it simply feels good to reach out to someone who is struggling. Second, it's a way of paying back the human community for some help that was offered to us in the past. We have all needed encouragement at some point in our lives. We may not be able to anticipate just when our next need will arise, but we can be sure it will.

Sometimes we have to listen closely to detect another's waning confidence. Many people, particularly men, frequently fear revealing their presumed inadequacies. A sensitive, caring heart can usually "hear" the need, however. And that's our invitation to offer some help based on our own personal experience. Telling a friend he or she shouldn't feel a certain way is never productive, but telling someone what worked for us is helpful. That makes it easy to know what suggestion to offer. Our own experiences provide us with the only wisdom we'll ever really need.

Today someone may need my encouragement.
I'll listen closely for my cue.

JULY 25

*Helping my spouse find his life after retirement
took its toll on my own life.*

ABBY WARMAN

Many men define themselves by the work they do. This may be an unfair generalization; however, women do appear to make the transition from career to leisure more easily. Might that be because women have more easily shared their fears about change with other people, often other women, throughout their lives? Thus, this time of transition is simply another reason for talking over one's feelings with someone else. Many men don't do this so easily, even with their wives. But if they do it at all, it's generally the wife who shoulders the fear. And the burden can get heavy.

This dynamic has grown out of a lifetime of perceiving our worth, along with change, in a particular way. There is no one to blame. Nobody has been doing it wrong. Our mode of perceiving experience developed from how we were raised to think about our lives. The fortunate thing is that we can consider making minor or significant changes in our process even at this age. This means that we can expect a spouse to seek an additional outlet for his frustration, too.

> **I can listen to someone's fears today,
> but I can't change them or take them away.
> My role is limited and that's good.**

JULY 26

Running a business taught me independence.
I'm grateful for that now. Not leaning on my husband
was good for my self-esteem.

JOANN REED

It's not only women who need to develop independence. Many men also grew up dependent on others: often mothers first, followed by wives and secretaries. Finally, every one of us has had to discover that we can handle whatever comes to us. If in our youth we developed a belief in a Higher Power of some kind, it made accepting our independence a bit easier. We understood that we weren't alone even though independent.

Being able to rely on others now, being willing to ask for help when we need it, may be a bigger problem for us presently than learning to handle our problems on our own when we were younger. The aging process has made it necessary to sometimes seek the help of others, however. And that's good. Even if we don't like the feeling of occasional dependence, others need to be needed once in a while. We'll all take a turn at this in the days and years ahead. And we'll be glad for the necessary companionship of others.

How we feel about ourselves now has come from a lifetime of successes and disappointments. Our interactions with others coupled with our willingness to monitor who we were measured against and who we wanted to be have combined to create our current report card. Do we want to improve our scores?

I still have time to adjust my character.
Today will be ripe with opportunities.

JULY 27

All problems work out—
though not always the way you want them to.

JAMES CASEY

We are relieved of our burdens when we have faith that everything works out. We have the benefit of the past to help us right
now if we are filled with worry or fear. While it may seem that we
didn't get all we'd hoped for when we were young, we can generally accept that we did get what we really needed. Most of us
simply didn't have the wisdom to know what was right for us at
the time.

Being impaired physically isn't easy to accept, particularly if
we were active our whole lives. The lesson here is not that all
conditions in our lives are wonderful. That isn't what "working
out" means. Rather, it means that we'll see the "miracle" in our
circumstance when we open our mind to God's explanation.
The physical realm never supersedes the spiritual in importance. The real message for us and our companions lies in the
spiritual realm.

There is purpose in every experience. Problems do work
themselves out. We can come to believe this, too.

Whatever I need will come to me today.
God can be trusted.

When you lose a spouse, you just have to make up your mind to go on. There must be something left for you to do.

MONTY CRALLEY

Losing a life partner is the hardest thing we may have to face in a lifetime. And it will happen to most of us. Perhaps it already has. When we lose a spouse, we may even wish we could die. That's a common phase we may go through. But it's comforting and uplifting to decide that we still have "work" to do, or we'd have died first. Our partner was simply done before us. Looking at it this way changes the tenor of our lives up to now and the time we have yet to live. It's good if we can feel some excitement about the possibilities that lie ahead. They are specific to us, of that we can be sure.

There are some specific things that can help us go on with our lives after a spouse dies. First, we have to stay involved with the circumstances around us, the situations that had interested us previously. Withdrawing from our family or the neighborhood, even for brief periods, isn't in our best interest. Perhaps one of the most important aspects of going on is the wisdom we can now share with someone else who faces this experience after ourselves. Perhaps offering compassion is the main thing left for us to do in this life, and that's mighty important indeed.

I will go on as well as I can today.
I will be open to the people around me.

JULY 29

We all have a place to fill or we wouldn't be here.
That's what I think.

ALICE MERRYMAN

What do you think about your presence in this life, this neighborhood, this family and collection of friends? Do you chalk up your experiences to coincidence or have they been "chosen" lessons wearing your particular name? Believing, as Alice does, can be comforting. It can offer us freedom from grief and resentment if our lives have been filled with turmoil. But beware; this philosophy doesn't mean the turmoil goes away. It only means we could grow from it if we want to.

Obviously, we are still here. According to Alice, this can mean only one thing: We aren't done yet. Our services are still needed by someone. Must we know who? Not really, but we may be able to figure it out by listening intently to the people who reach out to us. Chances are, we'll have ample opportunities to respond to other people today. They may be the reason we're still here, in fact.

This makes one's life pretty exciting, doesn't it? It's like every moment is a mystery and we have a part in solving it. Just knowing we are truly needed can change one's outlook instantly. Maybe we didn't believe this before, but that's okay. Old dogs can learn new tricks.

Am I using my time as well as I can today?

JULY 30

*If you see someone drawing out in Calvary Cemetery,
that will be me.*

THERESA MCCARTHY

Theresa doesn't spend much time worrying over the future. She gathers so much pleasure from her painting, from her trips to buy supplies, from the neighborhood restaurant, that whatever comes next is okay with her. She sees herself painting her way into eternity. What a wonderful sense of self, what a wonderful feeling of satisfaction.

How peacefully do the rest of us look at our future? Some among our crowd are nervous. We can tell by their demeanor, their ability to laugh (or not) at themselves and their many aches and foibles. Are they afraid of dying? Others seem angry and resentful over past mistakes, failings, or failed friendships. They are finding little joy in the moment and they don't seem to be looking forward to the future. Still others seem bent on leaving their marks by overextending themselves on behalf of organizations or other people. Perhaps they fear they haven't done enough to be remembered and time is running out.

Do you fit into any of these categories? There's nothing embarrassing about a "yes" response. But it's not too late to come to believe that we have done enough; we have done our lives to the best of our abilities. We deserve to peacefully move into our future. Let's try to follow Theresa's example.

The peacefulness I feel today is of my own making.

JULY 31

To tell you the truth, I'm ready to die today.
In fact, I'm looking forward to it.

TOM HARDING

Does Tom's anticipation of death disturb you? Is it hard for you to imagine looking forward to this unknown experience?

There are some steps we can take that will lessen our anxiety about death. The easiest one is to share our fears with a member of the clergy. They have spent hours upon hours counseling individuals who shared this fear. Comfort is guaranteed if we seek it. There have also been numerous books written giving firsthand recollections of near-death experiences.

We can also consider all the instances when we were in scary situations and miraculously pulled through. How did that happen? Is it possible some Power greater than ourselves was in charge? Many of us can relate to this idea. If we were in safe hands then, would we be abandoned to a nothingness at the hour of death? It's not likely. Let's make the decision to give faith a try. It surely can't hurt us.

I need not look forward to death to prove that I have faith,
but today will be more satisfying if I can put aside my fears.

AUGUST

AUGUST 1

*Without a sense of humor,
you're old in a hurry.*

JANICE CLARK

We've all been in the company of constant complainers. They drag down the mood of everyone they encounter. Can we be accused of this demeanor on occasion too?

Maybe it seems impossible to wear a happy face all the time. And it's not always easy to laugh at ourselves, particularly when we're feeling anxious and vulnerable. However, becoming willing to see the humor in our many foibles, learning to not take ourselves so seriously, is well worth the effort. The lucky ones among us learned this trait many years ago, and we recognize them instantly. We generally love being around them, too. Laughter *is* good medicine. Whether it's at ourselves or simply at a situation or a clever movie, laughter lightens our mood, thus lightening whatever burden we might be carrying.

When we were young, most of us had fears about financial instability, war, our children, or our careers. Life does have many serious aspects. But we were never required to handle any of them alone. If we relied on the God of our understanding, all of the burdens were more easily accepted. That gave us time to breathe more easily. Laughter was then more frequent. It can be more frequent now, too. It's simply a decision to see every circumstance with a lighter heart.

**It's so much more fun to laugh than to complain.
It's my choice today.**

AUGUST 2

As long as my name isn't in the obituary column,
I'm pretty happy.

THELMA ELLIOTT

Lots of people make jokes about reading the obituary column to make sure they're still alive. We can all laugh at that notion, but the deeper truth in it is that age and illness take many of our friends and acquaintances. When we read about the death of someone we know well or even casually, it gives us reason to pause and be grateful for our continuing lives. We hope it reminds us to appreciate all the men and women who are still among the living too!

Are we taking for granted the presence of those individuals who are important to us? We probably are. After all, we don't really want to dwell on how swiftly life is passing. We don't want to obsess about death, our own or someone else's, every minute of the day. The dilemma is, how can we keep a proper balance between living and acknowledging the reality of dying throughout one's daily journey?

We are familiar with the idea of living only in the present. Many philosophers, theologians, writers of all kinds, even ordinary folks like ourselves, quite continuously express the importance of now, vehemently believing that now is all there is. Those who have internalized this idea find it easier to appreciate whatever is happening minute by minute. How about you?

Each minute of today is a gift.
I want to cherish all 1,440 of them.

AUGUST 3

I think death will be a pleasant experience.
I don't see it as the end of anything.

FRAN COYNE

How we look upon death influences how we experience the rest of life. If we're afraid of dying, it's likely that we have been fearful about many of the opportunities that have come our way throughout our lives. How troubling life has been for many of us. Living with anxiety is so exhausting and so unnecessary.

How do we change our entire perception if we have worried about the experience of death our whole lives? Believers in a hereafter might say "just change your mind." But that's not so easy. We may have to be more specific, more methodical, and work on this new perception a little bit every day. Let's begin with considering all the blessings we have experienced. Whether we look first to our families, our jobs, our friends, or times we were in scary situations and survived, we'll discover that we have much to be grateful for. And how do we explain that? Can chance have intervened that often?

Careful observation of the natural environment can help us, too. We have all watched flowers die only to rebloom the next spring. That's a most graphic demonstration of the continuation of the life cycle. Can this principle really apply only selectively? The wise say no. How about you?

I will seek the peace of knowing that life has no real end.
Today will be just another step in my journey.

AUGUST 4

*You don't have to go to church to be a believer
in God and his presence.*

HELEN CASEY

This is certainly a '90s idea. Most retirees grew up with a far different philosophy, regardless of whether they were "church-going" or not. It was commonly believed that going to church symbolized belief in God. Not going symbolized the opposite. Isn't it freeing to be allowed broader interpretations?

Whether or not we have always maintained a belief in God is far less important than examining how our lives have benefited when we did. The ease with which people survive even harrowing experiences is evidence of what the belief in a Power greater than ourselves can do, while having no faith can make even the tiniest snag in our lives quite frightening.

It's awful to feel alone, suspended over the abyss of uncertainty. Some unfortunates hang there always. Perhaps they mistakenly think they have to jump through the "church-going" hoops to have faith. Maybe we can share our understanding about faith with someone else today.

I am free to believe whatever pleases me about God.
There are no absolute rules.
Today is for my interpretation.

AUGUST 5

God has the main role in my life.
I depend upon him completely for guidance and care.

ALPHA ENGLISH

Someone like Alpha would agree that the luckiest people alive are those who put God first. Why? Because they can escape perpetual anxiety. When God comes first, all turmoil dissipates. What an easy solution to one's problems.

Since this is so obvious to many of us, why do some resist this "dependence"? There are many reasons. Not everyone was raised in a home that relied on God as guide and protector. Some gave up on God when circumstances were difficult. Others grew out of the habit of turning their lives over to the care of God. It matters little why we resist reliance on God. The fact that we do creates the dissatisfaction we may experience regularly.

There is such an easy alternative to any struggle we may be experiencing. It's simply a matter of changing our minds. Do we want to harbor fear and frustration, or might we rather be at peace? Filling our minds with the awareness of the ever-present God, rather than whatever details we find troublesome, changes how we see and feel about everything around us.

I can change any experience today by
allowing God to look at it for me.

AUGUST 6

Because my parents valued honesty, I have tried to pass that value on to my children and grandchildren, too.

JOANN REED

We are constantly revealing our values to the others in our lives. This has always been true. We aren't always proud of what we have passed on, perhaps, but we did our best. Fortunately, we still have time to make adjustments to our value systems, thus passing on to our families and friends the traits that more accurately reflect who we are now. Most of us are changing a little every day. Even when we think we're too old and too set in our ways to change, we do.

Knowing that others look to us and at us for cues about their own behavior should keep us on our toes. We don't want to leave lasting impressions that make us ashamed. Some of us can see in our offspring characteristics that aren't favorable. Might we have been more careful in our parenting? It's not too late to share our observations or to make amends for parenting mistakes. Since we're able to recognize our input in another's behavior, let's acknowledge our responsibility and set a different example now.

It's never too late to become who we'd rather be. At first we may doubt this idea, but making small steps in a new direction will convince us of the possibility. Having more time now means we can explore this idea as much as we'd like.

I may no longer be content with some former values.
Today is a good day to start making some changes.

AUGUST 7

Simplicity and greatness go together.

MONTY CRALLEY

We have probably heard the phrase *Keep It Simple* thousands of times. It's possible we are mystified by it, even yet. So many things in life have seemed complicated: getting an education, starting a new job, advising children and friends. Not many things can be pursued without careful consideration. When we have approached situations carelessly, we have often blundered badly.

Keeping it simple means doing only the next right thing, not a sequence of fourteen things all at once. To keep something simple means to focus on only a tiny bit of the problem at a time. If we employ a little hindsight, we'll quickly recall how many situations began to improve as we attended to just a portion of them.

God never gives us more than we can handle. How many times have we heard that? It means we'll always be shown the way to handle something little by little, *very simply*, in exactly the order we need the information. Don't we see this is how it has always been? Why would it change now?

Today I need to listen.
I don't need to figure out all my problems at once.

Imagination grows by exercise and, contrary to common belief, is more powerful in the mature than in the young.

W. SOMERSET MAUGHAM

Children are uninhibited. They speak their truth quite openly, at least until their elders redefine it for them. From that moment forth, they, as we before them, see through the lenses of others. It took most of us until adulthood to rediscover our own truths. And even now, we aren't always brave enough to speak them.

Perhaps the greatest gift of maturity is freedom to do what we want when we want and having the willingness to dare to believe whatever pleases us. We really don't have to live according to someone else's standards any longer. As long as we don't harm another, we can believe what we want, do what we want, imagine what we want. And the earlier we matured, the spicier our imaginations.

A major benefit of old age is letting our minds wander to far-off places and not having to account for the lost hours. We've earned our freedom. Let's share our joy with one who is still maturing.

I have paid my dues. I am free to wonder or wander.
This day will be as rich and full as I make it.

AUGUST 9

Self-control is one of the greatest skills I've learned.

JIM BURNS

Most of us assume we have mastered self-control by now. And perhaps we have. A good test is to monitor how we respond to a nagging spouse or a disrespectful postman or vile-mouthed teenager. Do instances such as these make us angry or resentful? If so, we aren't exerting adequate self-control. Letting another's behavior, no matter how petty, disturb our inner peace means we aren't in control of ourselves. But we can be. There is still time to learn how, and most of us have all the time we need.

Why is self-control so valuable? Getting agitated feels good sometimes. We may think it's superior to boredom. But in truth, losing control of our emotions means we are always in the control of someone else. That too often means we are on a roller-coaster of ups and downs that exhaust us. Illness can even result. Another benefit of self-control is that we can lessen the turmoil around us, rather than add to it. As we have discussed before, the impact of any action or thought or quiet response is never ending. It's quite analogous to the pebble skipped across the pond. We are making subtle contributions to the world around us whether we are conscious of it or not. Let's be more careful of our input.

I will consider my input in all situations carefully today. What someone else does need not determine my actions.

Couples need to have their separate interests.
From day one in our marriage we didn't rely on each other
for everything. I think that's good.

JOANN REED

The lack of independence some individuals feel in their marriages can become suffocating as time passes. When neither spouse gets involved in activities separate from the marriage, there is too little that's fresh added to the partnership. It becomes like a stew with no seasoning: bland, boring, and in time, perhaps, deadly. Is an inventory of your marriage relationship in order?

For most couples, retirement is a major adjustment. Each person had grown accustomed to a particular routine and change is seldom easy. Depending on the level of dependence that's been customary in the marriage, going in even slightly different directions now can be threatening. But to not do what one's inner voice suggests is even more threatening, ultimately. Each of us must follow our own calling, if we hope to stay vibrant and alive.

Communicating one's needs and dreams is mandatory during this new phase of a couple's life together. That's not always easy, particularly if intimate communication wasn't the standard in the relationship. It's possible though. The first step is simply desire.

Today awaits my attention. What plan calls to me?
Do I feel good about pursuing it?
Maybe I need to talk it over with my partner.

AUGUST 11

*I thought retirement would mean my wife
and I could do some kind of work together.*

BUD SHERMAN

So often retirement doesn't materialize in the way we'd imagined. That doesn't mean our dreams were for naught. They gave us some direction at the time, and that's always their reason for being. We need dreams about the future. They help to shape our thinking on a daily basis. However, being able to give them up when they don't serve us is an important lesson.

It's not possible to know exactly what we'll need at some time in our future. That's always been the case, of course. But because our lives seem simpler now that our careers have ended and the kids are grown, we tend to think we can figure out what should come next with greater ease. Have we forgotten that God is still in charge of what's best for us? Remembering this will comfort us, particularly if we take a moment to recall the many times we tried to force our dreams upon another.

Whether we embark on a second career with our spouses or seek a solitary activity, we need to feel fulfilled in our choices. It's not always easy to measure how content we actually are, but listening to our inner voice will offer some clues. Let's not act too hastily today.

**In my quiet moments I'll hear the words I need to know
how I want to spend these hours today.**

AUGUST 12

*People need a hobby in retirement,
in fact, throughout life.*

JOE CASEY

What is the real value to a hobby? Developing skills that are different from those required at work might be one value. Making friends with like-minded people is valuable. Expanding one's horizons and broadening one's understanding of life's possibilities are of value. But perhaps the greatest value one gets from a hobby is the opportunity to focus on an activity that's outside of oneself.

It's the human condition to be too easily self-absorbed. Introspection is healthy, but many of us think far too much about ourselves. Hobbies can distract us and that's good. Some think that the process of getting outside of ourselves is what ushers forth our inner spirit, our creative voice. However much or little a hobby might do for us, it is always a change of pace. And it's healthy to nurture a change of pace.

If we have never had a hobby, where do we begin? We might try to recall what interested us as children. Did we like to paint in school? Were we good at storytelling or building little cars or other toys? If this process turns up nothing, search out the classes that are offered in community education programs. The point is to choose something, anything, for starters. It's never until we make a move that we can see where we'd rather be.

**A hobby calls to me today.
Perhaps I am not sure what it is, but it's taking form.**

AUGUST 13

I don't see how anybody goes through life.
I'm surprised how my life has evolved.

JANICE CLARK

When any one of us reflects on the whole of our life, we're probably a bit overwhelmed regarding the multitude of experiences, particularly over those that affected us gravely, in either a positive or a negative way. What a good thing it is that we live only one day, one experience at a time. Hindsight convinces us that we'd not be able to handle any more than that.

Most of us have memories that please us greatly. Fond friendships that we still miss, perhaps; key experiences that revealed to us new understandings; careers and homes that fulfilled us in many ways. Really, we couldn't have orchestrated our lives any more perfectly. We're lucky people, indeed, if we can accept that a Supreme Being played a major role in the circumstances that came to call on us. Those that will yet present themselves have been selected for us, too.

We can't pretend that everything that happened in our lives felt good or seemed necessary at the time. We can only choose to believe that this is so. Getting comfortable with this idea eases our anxiety about what the future may bring. What does come is right and on time. Our perception about it may have to change, but never the circumstance.

I can eagerly anticipate what lies ahead today.
Each day that has already passed gave me what I needed,
and nothing about this process has changed.

AUGUST 14

Retirement means projects can run on for days.

JIM BURNS

Are we really enjoying the freedom we now have for doing a little or a lot? We are probably burdened with memories of when there was not time to get every task done. Extra hours at work were often required. The demands of our families often meant we gave up activities that were special to ourselves. Most of us had to give up a lot to live up to others' expectations. We don't have to feel that burden any longer.

Now that we have the time, what are we doing with it? That's terribly important for us to consider, because having time on our hands can wear heavily on us. Are there projects we never attempted, such as building a rock garden or knitting an afghan or writing our memoirs, because time was limited? We have no excuse now. All that's stopping us from exploring any activity or developing any new skill is our resistance to enter uncharted waters. Getting excited about a wholly new avenue of interest can be cultivated with a tiny bit of effort. Time is on our side at last.

What shall I do today?
Nobody is responsible for determining that but me.
I am free to be me, perhaps for the first time.

AUGUST 15

*My work ethic has always been so strong
that I'm uncomfortable not working.*

SANDY WARMAN

What Sandy feels is common to most of us. We grew up in an era that dictated a strong work ethic. When we met people who didn't share it, we generally doubted their worth; we trusted them less than those who shared our values. Perhaps that was okay then, but the reality is that we are free now to celebrate *not working*. We have done our share. If we can't do this with ease, it might be good for us to talk our struggle over with a friend who seems to be having less trouble.

How lucky we are that we have many friends and acquaintances who are experiencing this transition right along with us. None of us wants to struggle alone. Maybe we resist letting someone else know how we feel for a time, but finally, if we're smart, we'll seek the help and wisdom of others who seem to be realizing more peace than is present in us.

Don't we think we deserve time off? Perhaps if we didn't live up to our expectations when we were younger, we have an extra load of guilt about not working now. Or maybe our reasons for how we feel are far different from this. It doesn't matter what they are, really. We have to come to accept that we did enough, we were good enough, and now the time to rest has come.

**I don't really have to do anything I don't want to do today.
I've done quite enough in my lifetime.**

AUGUST 16

I'm finally giving myself permission to be lazy,
and it's real comfortable.

FRAN COYNE

Isn't it a shame that after years of hard work, we can't just do nothing without feeling lazy or worthless? Apparently we all grew up believing that hard work was all that made us worthwhile. Admittedly, we had to work hard as students and as employees if we wanted to make the grade. But from a spiritual perspective, we were of equal value to all other human beings regardless of our performance. Parents, teachers, and bosses didn't always offer that feedback, but it was true nonetheless.

Most days we will continue wanting to make some kind of contribution. Doing nothing feels lonely and boring after a while. We need interaction with others. We need conversation and laughter. We need to keep using our minds and the many skills we've acquired over the years. Being part of the world around us is God's gift to us until we die; however, we don't have to participate in that world every minute of every day. Napping frequently, reading a good book, or skimming magazines is enough activity on some days. No one is keeping score—unless you are.

I may want to lie around and do very little today.
Nobody has to give me permission. Relaxing can be my choice.

*Even though I was a scientist and traveled all over the world,
retirement has been the most exciting part of my life
because of my painting and writing.*

MONTY CRALLEY

Many people dread the latter years of life, certain that they'll not
be busy enough or meaningly fulfilled. That happens to some.
No doubt we have known a number of people who bemoan the
"good old days" when exciting circumstances were happening to
them regularly, or so they say now. Fortunately, we also know
men and women who are absolutely content with the present.
What is different about this group? Which group are we more
like right now?

Deciding which group we belong to on a daily basis keeps us
on our toes and responsible for the outcome of every day. If we
are feeling bored, we need to find a new perspective. We each
need to make the most of our energy and spend it on pursuits
that will give us joy.

I am in charge of what I do all day long.
These can be the good old days, too.

AUGUST 18

My life has just been full of miracles.

JAMES CASEY

How might you describe your life? Would your description compare favorably with Jim's? The key ingredient is attitude, of course. We will see what we will see! What has given Jim such a positive outlook on life? If we don't share it, is it too late for us to change?

We may have developed a rigid and negative attitude by this age. That's one of the unfortunate possibilities that accompanies a life of strife, and none of us was spared stressful times. We need not be controlled by the past in any way, however. The perception we cultivate is done anew every day. If this seems hard to believe, let's try to *intercept* the old way of seeing our experiences. It does become a habit to see the glass half-empty, but no habit is beyond breaking.

That Jim perceived miracles-a-plenty in his life is owing to a decision he made, perhaps as a very young man, to focus on the possibilities in every situation, rather than the improbabilities. We are of one mind or the other. However we learned to "see" when we were maturing may be how we continue to see now. We aren't bound to this perception though. If Jim can see miracles, so can we. It's as simple as that. What's your choice?

My life has been rich and good.
Even when there was pain and strife, it was still rich and good.
I'll savor this thought today.

AUGUST 19

Jim and I both had a generous nature.
That's one of the good things about us.

RUTH CASEY

There are so many ways to be generous. Some may think that it always means the offering of money, but that's not the case. Having a generous spirit far exceeds giving money in importance. But what is a generous spirit? Fortunately, it's not elusive. It's easily developed by all of us. It's nothing more than the willingness to help others out in whatever way is needed. Maybe it's as simple as listening to a friend who is filled with fear. Perhaps it's doing volunteer work at a nursing home or community center. Calling on someone who is ailing because of health problems is a significant gesture.

Knowing that we are always capable of being generous in spirit gives us a good feeling, particularly if we have had to give up many activities because of our age. The need to feel that we still have something of value to offer others in this world doesn't dissipate as we age. In fact, because of our limitations we might need this feeling even more.

We have all heard the adage, "We must give it away if we want to keep it." This is key to our understanding of how every aspect of life has worked. Having a generous spirit and expressing it willingly will comfort us all the days of the rest of our lives.

I have so much to give today.
By being present to another person, I'll be doing my part.

AUGUST 20

People who love animals generally love people, too.

VIOLET HENSLEY

The willingness to love is not easily turned off once it's been turned on. Thus, those who love freely are perhaps the luckiest people alive. Every experience they have offers them an opportunity to share love and acceptance with someone else. And ultimately, all of us reap the benefit of the love expressed by any one of us.

Seldom do we contemplate how important every tiny expression is that we make. Unconsciously, we frown rather than smile; ignore rather than acknowledge; discount rather than honor. All in the flash of an instant, we make a "contribution" to the world at large. It's awesome to acknowledge the responsibility we each have for the positive rhythms of the universe.

Let's not take our responsibility lightly. And when we realize we don't love someone all that easily, let's determine to practice. Generally, it's easy to love children and small animals. They don't intimidate us. Let's hone our skills repeatedly, starting now.

Today is a good day to give love away.
Each person offers me an opportunity.

When I met Harry,
I knew immediately we should be together.

EDITH HUEY BARTHOLOMEW

Listening to our inner voice changes how we see the events in our lives. It won't steer us wrong. Our ability to decipher the message, to not confuse the "advice" that comes from the ego with the wisdom that comes from our inner voice, is what we have to perfect. The ego can sound very wise. It has practiced its art for as many years as we have been alive. But its advice is always meant to keep us hostage to it. We're not well served by the ego.

The wisdom that arises from our inner voice does nothing but serve our better interests. It fosters love in our hearts. It ushers us toward individuals who need us as much as we need them. It makes us willing to forgive the transgressions of others, helping us to know that another's actions always grew out of fear. The inner voice is God's messenger. It speaks ever so softly, but if we are attentive, we will hear it.

Edith seemingly heard the "messenger" when she met Harry in her later life. He showered her with love and devotion. He inspired her to continue her work as a nature photographer. Their companionship changed the world as perceived by each of them. Let's listen to our inner voice and relish the surprise that might be in store for us.

My inner voice will show me the way to proceed today.
It will never lead me astray.

AUGUST 22

*If you think of others
you will do many wonderful things.*

ALPHA ENGLISH

We feel conflicted occasionally because we want to put our wishes first and we feel guilty. It's like walking a tightrope to be comfortable with how much attention we give others while still meeting our own needs. Recognizing that we are pulled in two directions and asking God for guidance will solve the dilemma. We will receive a new perspective should we care to acknowledge it.

How does thinking of others change us? When we get our own ego out of the way, we discover how natural our feelings of love are. They seem to flow unhindered, and we generally feel love in return. When love surrounds us, any task is easier, any dream is more easily realized.

We have all heard friends complain that they're *tired of thinking about others first!* They resent the lost time. The truth is that thinking of others with a good attitude will seem to double the time we have for ourselves. This is one of life's mysteries. Don't doubt it.

> I have twenty-four hours before me.
> Giving attention to others as well as myself
> will lengthen and brighten my day.

AUGUST 23

*Sometimes the worst things that happen to us are
the best things for us. They slow us down and make us think.*

ALICE MERRYMAN

How shortsighted we often are. We think we understand the reasons for what's happening in our lives, but that's seldom the case. Looking back on our past will reveal this, if we're open to seeing the truth. Lost treasures, failed relationships, missed opportunities devastated us when they occurred. Yet often, in only a brief lapse of time, we were able to see the folly in our disappointment. Something better was always in store for us. We simply had to make way for it; our loss opened the door.

The aging process quite often troubles us. Our health is precarious, perhaps. Our financial stability fluctuates; friends move on and loved ones die. How can any of this be good? we wonder. Let's try looking at these changes in another way. Life is change: of our bodies, our minds, our dreams, and our fears. Even a cursory review of our past reveals many changes that we dreaded when they occurred. We don't have to like them, ever, but they do help us become who we need to be. A tragedy makes us more thoughtful, perhaps, or more cautious. The death of a spouse can initiate more independence. The loss of movement due to arthritis can interest us in a new hobby to fill our time. There is always another way to see whatever is changing around us.

I will look at my experiences today from a new angle.

AUGUST 24

*I needed to drop all my activities for a while
in order to determine what I really wanted to do next.*

PAT JEROME

It's important to take an occasional breather from our heavily scheduled lives. Being on the go constantly gives us too little time for an honest assessment of which activities really are priorities. Our calendars fill up, seemingly by themselves. Let's get back in the driver's seat regarding our daily plans. We seldom give our best effort to projects or groups that don't really interest us, so why are we involved with them at all?

Many of us entered retirement with little clarity about the kind of life we want to forge now. We stumbled into activities to ward off boredom or the fear of having nothing to do. There's nothing wrong with having approached it that way. There are no definitive rules about how to retire. Trial and error is the real test. And in that process, we'll decide what fits each one of us; seldom will two people do it exactly alike.

If we are even a tiny bit uncertain about our commitment to the activities we're currently engaged in, it's time to sit a while and seek our inner voice. Time is far too precious to spend it in ways that aren't satisfying. And the depth of our satisfaction is a good measure of whether or not we are fulfilling the real purpose God has for us at this stage of our lives.

**I'll slowly consider what I really want to do today.
Whatever truly feels right is probably the right course to take.**

AUGUST 25

All of my self-worth was based upon the job,
my advancement in my career.

SANDY WARMAN

All too many of us were controlled in just the way Sandy was. And in the early years of retirement, we're often compelled to tell others what we did for a living, before telling them anything else. Feeling the need to establish that we were somebody of substance is typical. In time, perhaps, we'll see this need as sad, or folly and irrelevant. Why did so few of us grow up with the knowledge that we are worthy simply because we are here? If we still falter in our attempt to believe this, there's time to work on it. The good news of retirement is that we have lots of time for whatever we want to do.

If our self-worth is still an issue, perhaps our grandiosity is at fault. Is the opinion we want others to have of us too inflated? We have limitations in these later years that we must accept. We may have to settle for them knowing that we have only so much disposable income, for instance. But not a single one of us is too old to listen to the voices gathered around us, or too tired to respond in a kind way to questions or comments. Wanting others to think well of us isn't a sin, and it's even quite simple to accomplish. It takes little more than genuine respect and the expression of love and concern for one another. If only we had known self-worth was attained so easily in our youth.

It's never too late to change my behavior or my opinions.
Regardless of my age, I can be my better self today.

AUGUST 26

*I neglected many parts of my own development
when my husband retired.*

ABBY WARMAN

Unfortunately, it's all too common for women to do as Abby did. Many of us spent our lives always doing for others rather than ourselves, assuming that our job was to focus on the needs of others first. We got a lot of training along these lines from our own mothers and grandmothers. If we're not all that happy about it now, that's okay. It's also not very fruitful to be angry about it. What's done is done. What remains to be done is another thing.

Nothing is keeping us from taking a look at our own needs presently. Are we giving them all the attention they deserve? Let's consider our physical needs. Are we content with how we look? Should we exercise more? Are we dealing with our emotional needs regularly? Do we seek guidance from a friend or professional if we're troubled? How would we grade ourselves spiritually? Have we made a practice of spiritual guidance for comfort and security? There are a lot of things we can do for ourselves right now. Do we need to get busy?

The good news is that it's never too late to start taking better care of ourselves. If we are overwhelmed by all the seeming neglect of the past, decide to do only one small thing to begin with. We are guaranteed to feel better instantly. Let's vow to not add to the neglect today.

I can make a difference in my life today.

AUGUST 27

I can't think of one thing I was really good at.

RUTH CASEY

If we fail to see our strengths and can't remember our successes, perhaps we need to explore the past in more detail. Looking at old photographs might help. So might asking others who knew us then. Without a doubt, we excelled at many things. Sometimes our humility hinders our recollection; on occasion we simply have low self-esteem. Seeking to know our past better, with the help of friends and close family members, is worth whatever effort we give it. None of us should harbor for long the feeling that we were failures at life.

How is it that some people maintain confidence in themselves while others are faced with such a struggle as Ruth's? We all excelled at something, most of us at hundreds of things. Do we not remember because of embarrassment or shame that we weren't as "good" as our siblings or friends whom we measured ourselves against? Let's seek help from God if we doubt ourselves today or in our past. Let's practice believing that we were as good as we knew how to be. That's the absolute truth!

The past is gone. Regrets do us no good. We had a specific part to play in the lives of those around us, and we played it. The lessons we were "assigned" were handled. Let's look to the present now. That's what counts today.

Have I forgotten my strengths? If I have, today is a perfect day for seeking to remember them, one at a time.

America was very disappointing to me when I first came.

MARIA REGNIER KRIMMEL

We have all experienced the disappointment of unmet expectations. Disappointment is always difficult to accept. Fortunately, with age often comes wisdom, and we realize that the fulfillment of any expectation is tied closely to the attitude that one has cultivated. Those of us who have favorably responded to the many experiences in our lives, defining each of them as an opportunity, know that preconceived expectations can set us up for either disappointment or victory. Few of us prefer the former.

Knowing that what we expect influences what we get should be our shorthand to a more satisfying life. Unfortunately, that isn't always the case. We may have become too accustomed to seeing the glass half-empty to realize how seeing it half-full changes everything about an experience. The good news is that none of us is beyond making a significant change in how we look at life. If the level of our contentment isn't running high, it's worth the effort to monitor how we are assessing our opportunities. That's the key to fulfillment.

**Since I'm in charge of how I judge my experiences today,
I'll determine their value to me.**

I wish I hadn't lost track of the guys I was stationed with.
I kick myself for that.

TOM HARDING

We all have regrets, don't we? Some of us left jobs or spouses or neighborhoods, only to wish we hadn't. Perhaps we closed the door on our family of origin and then felt grief when parents or siblings died. More commonly we regret the instances when our mean-spirited behavior or attitude hurt someone else. We weren't always honest and forthright; we didn't always try to help a friend or co-worker who needed our advice. We simply didn't put our best self forward when the opportunities for doing so presented themselves.

Dwelling on the "shoulds" of past years is so fruitless, though not entirely unexpected of us old-timers. If only we could get comfortable with the reality that we did the best we knew how to do at the time. Many considerations were forced upon us in our younger years; we had many worries we weren't really prepared for; we simply didn't always make the best use of the information we had available. And often we didn't seek the counsel of others when it might have made a difference. But the past is gone. Let's quit digging up the bones of old regrettable experiences. All they do now is cloud our minds when we're trying to respond to today's opportunities.

I won't have anything to regret tomorrow
if I respond to today with my best self.

AUGUST 30

I believe that everyone needs a mentor.

HARRY BARTHOLOMEW

We have all had mentors, many of them; in fact. We might not have labeled them as such, but throughout our lives we have been picking up ideas and mannerisms from many people. From some, we sought to learn specific skills, perhaps on the job or while in school. A few inadvertently became our mentors simply because of our proximity to them. Along the way, we may have chosen some mentors impulsively and to our detriment. The process of mentoring is how most of us learn, ultimately. Have we forgotten that we, too, have served as mentors for many others who have shared our journey?

We obviously are not through living yet. Thus we are not through mentoring either. Every encounter we have with someone, even at our age, is mentoring in action. One moment we're on the learning end; the next perhaps we're acting as teacher. Mentoring has always been a two-way street.

We have never been able to control another's mentoring, but we have always been free to choose or refuse to follow his or her example. What we can control, and this has always been true, is the content of our own mentoring. Are we satisfied that we've done our best?

Today I'll remember that my role as mentor isn't over yet.

AUGUST 31

*Doing things separately from a spouse
is very important in retirement.*

LOUISE JEROME

Not everybody agrees with Louise. We all know couples who seem to be inseparable and they appear to prefer that style of life. But it's important that each of us decides what is best for ourselves. We shouldn't try to follow another's example if it doesn't work for us.

Before retirement, most of us had detailed routines that gave structure, thus security, to our lives. Perhaps we need to explore what we could do differently now that we have extra time at our disposal. If we didn't have much of a life outside of the home, separate from other family members, before retirement, we may not realize we can opt for greater freedom now. In some cases, we may have to compromise and negotiate with our companions about the "separateness" we seek.

It's not always easy to change how we live when we've been stuck in a certain pattern for many years. The change isn't just hard on others; it's also difficult for us. Habits aren't easy to break. Being a homebody with few outside interests clings to us pretty tightly, but if we want to explore new vistas, now is the time. We don't have to do anything forever. We can always revert to our old ways if they're more comfortable.

**Am I doing what I really want to do with my life now?
Or are today's activities decided by habit or by my spouse?**

SEPTEMBER

SEPTEMBER 1

No day is like any other day. Isn't that interesting?
And you never know what the next day will bring,
and that's exciting.

ALPHA ENGLISH

Alpha has not lost her zest for life. Although nearly ninety, she nurtures a young mind and a wise heart. Her attitude influences those around her too, making them fortunate people indeed. We have the capacity to bring only joy to those around us, too. What's the key? Perspective.

The eyes with which we view our circumstances take charge of the day. What may look scary to someone else, such as giving a talk at the book club or playing bridge with a new partner, may actually excite us. Or the reverse may be true. The important lesson is, if others can look ahead with glad anticipation, so can we. They have not been endowed with any qualities that we can't acquire.

Most of us were too busy in our youth to pursue all the activities that interested us. Education, careers, families were the necessary priorities. Now is our time. We'll discover that we have enough time to journey in any direction that calls to us if we have cultivated an eager attitude.

I am embarking on a special mission today.
I pray to look upon the experiences with a glad heart.

SEPTEMBER 2

You can't let adversity get you down.
Keep smiling.

VIOLET HENSLEY

Violet's smiles certainly fit this category. She lights up rooms with her joy and energy, her fiddle playing and storytelling. We don't all smile quite so easily. Why is that? Some naively assume one's easy, individual circumstances determine the willingness to smile. A few hours with a soul like Violet convinces us otherwise. The work we've done, the environment we inhabit, the struggles we've had or have been free of do not determine our happiness, thus the frequency of our smiles. That's good fortune, in fact.

Smiling is first an attitude and then an action. We don't have to be bubbling over with inner happiness to smile. On the contrary, if something is bothering us, we may discover it will not loom so large if we focus our energy on smiling at a friend or even a stranger. Some would label it miraculous how changed a problem seems when we decide to put our energy into smiling at the passersby in our lives.

The separation we feel from others is what often gives rise to our problems, regardless of their details. Giving a smile and getting one in return diminishes our sense of separation. Problems diminish, too.

How do I feel today?
Even a few smiles will lift my spirits.

SEPTEMBER 3

*The most important legacy I've passed on to my children
is loyalty to one another
and the willingness to help someone else.*

HELEN CASEY

How we behave toward others always serves as an example to all who observe us. No doubt some of us wish we'd given more thought to the example we set for our children and friends. Let's not be too hard on ourselves, though. What's past is past. Communicating with our loved ones about our earlier shortcomings gives us freedom from them. It also offers us another opportunity for example-setting.

Valuing loyalty reveals so much about the Spirit that abides in Helen. The first thing it says is that the Spirit in someone else has been valued too, by her. And is there any more important expression than this? That she can see the results in the lives of her children blesses her now, in the same way that her example has blessed them throughout their lives.

Life's lessons are so subtly passed on. Often we're not even aware of our roles as teachers. However, observation of those who grew up closest to us reveals just what we taught. There's still time to alter the legacy if we have changed our minds about what's important.

I will serve as someone's teacher today. That's how life works.
Someone else will show me their way of seeing too.

SEPTEMBER 4

My wife always said, "Believe in something, because if it isn't so, you're not going to know about it anyway."

MONTY CRALLEY

Faith can have such a powerful impact on every aspect of one's life. On so many occasions, we feel alone, frightened, or confused about a decision we need to make. Or perhaps we have friends or family members who are in real trouble because of finances, personal relationships, or health challenges. Trying to solve problems in isolation is very difficult, and it matters not how old we are or how many other situations we have survived over the years.

We don't have to be religious to appreciate the help and comfort that can come from having a belief in some Power that's bigger than ourselves. Many of us understand this and have relied on it for years. Some of us still resist letting anyone help us with anything. If this is your typical stance, consider trying something new. Isn't freedom from shouldering all the burdens of life an appealing idea?

Every day, we are visited by at least one circumstance that gives us pause to worry a moment. Let's not let these moments turn into minutes or hours. Let's have a little faith—that's all that's ever needed.

> Nothing can get me down today if I seek the answer
> I may need from the Source who has it.

SEPTEMBER 5

In my many years as a teacher, I tried to impart to children to "do unto others as you would have them do unto you."

EVA WINES

Passing on wisdom such as this is invaluable. If only one of Eva's students chose to live accordingly, the world was made a better place; Eva's example was powerful. Even as her health was failing, she lived according to her own dictates. In her gentle presence, one felt her peacefulness, and feeling peace from any source is all many of us need to be prepared to pass it on.

Because our lives have changed, because we are out of the main work force, because we have far fewer responsibilities, we sometimes think we aren't needed anymore. It's quite possibly true that we aren't needed for the activities that demanded our attention in the previous decades. But *our work* isn't done. These times we live in might suggest to some of us that our most important work lies ahead, in fact.

Conveying the feeling of peace to someone else, be it stranger or friend, is doing exceedingly important work. For much of our lives we might not have known just what we "taught" others. But we can all know now how it feels to express love and the gift of peace to another. The legacy we can leave behind will make a difference in the world. Let's do our part.

**I need do so little today to make a difference.
Sharing my peace with someone else will do it.**

SEPTEMBER 6

I want to think that when we die,
our presence is still felt by others.

JOANN REED

For some it's comforting to believe that we're never really gone when we die, except bodily. That may not be true, of course. The point is that we each need to cultivate a belief about death that makes us secure while we're still very much alive. We have been involved in discussions with people who insist that there is only one way to interpret death. Our view might be quite foreign to them, thus out of the realm of possibility as they see it. But it's irrelevant, finally. None of us will ever know the "end" until we're in the midst of it. It's best to settle for our own explanation, and then go on with living.

If, like JoAnn, you cherish the idea of remaining present in others' lives, that may give you a clue about the importance of those others right now. If such is the case, can you honestly say that you're treating them with as much love and acceptance as they deserve? Do we ever let others know just how much they really mean to us? Every time we hold back a loving thought or remain quiet when we might have expressed compassion, we're relinquishing our opportunity to be *present* right here and now. Let's not waste these moments of actual togetherness.

I'll take every opportunity to show someone I care today.
I'll not waste my life or my time today.

I got a lot of my value system from the books I read as a child.

RUTH CASEY

Our value systems were honed from a number of sources. Parents, peers, teachers, the church all made significant contributions. But so did all the experiences we had. Everything we did or read or discussed with others had an impact on how our values were formed.

Having a set of values to guide us has been extremely important to how our lives have evolved. We struggled far less with decision making when we knew who we were. Our lives continue to be fraught with the occasional struggle. How fortunate that we have the experience of seeking the inner guidance we need in any circumstance. Our value systems are safely tucked away there.

Getting old sets up many obstacles; we don't need any extra ones. If we are uncertain of how to behave in particular situations, we complicate our lives. If we find ourselves in this predicament on occasion, perhaps it's because we have not sought the wisdom within. It has not departed us. Our values never leave; it's just our use of them that may get rusty.

My values will guide me in handling any problems today.

SEPTEMBER 8

I grew up knowing I had to be a success for others.

SANDY WARMAN

The pressure of performance is daunting and extremely stressful. Some, like Sandy, were controlled by it their whole lives. Perhaps that was your experience, too. Are you free of it now?

The desire to be successful never was a bad thing in and of itself. Teachers encouraged it right along with our parents. Employers reinforced the importance of being successful. But there is and always was a difference between enjoying a job done right and driving ourselves ragged to impress others. Sandy's experience reflects the latter.

Whatever reason we used for seeking success isn't all bad though. If it motivated us to stretch ourselves, it meant we discovered abilities we might not have known we were capable of. The contribution we made to the world around us was affected accordingly and that changed our lives forever. We can come to believe that however we lived our lives was simply as good as we were capable of. No matter what motivated us in the past, we can take charge of what motivates us now. Finally, that's all that really counts today.

Today I'll be aware of the motives behind my efforts.
I don't have to impress anyone.

SEPTEMBER 9

Talking to other women is good therapy for me,
particularly now that I'm not in the business world daily.

JOANN REED

Our need to interact with others, either casually or intimately, generally doesn't abate as we age. Some might say it becomes even more important because we have far fewer responsibilities to occupy our minds. If being with others, whether in conversation, at the card table or just enjoying the shared silence of the moment, is important to us, let's make sure we seek companions for this part of our journey. Being alone is nothing more than a choice. Let's not forget that.

If we're not feeling particularly enthusiastic about this stage of our lives, let's figure out why. Are we lonely? Or bored? Depression isn't uncommon among older folks. It may seem we have lost our way since we aren't following our old routine anymore. A number of us will need to seek the counsel of a professional, in fact. Perhaps we'll need medication or simply the encouragement to get involved in new interests. It's important that we take whatever measures are necessary. Our jobs aren't done or we'd not still be alive. Let's make sure we're able to do them.

Virtually any activity can be good therapy. It really doesn't matter what we choose or how often we switch choices. We'll find what fits us in time. Our assignment is to keep looking.

Whatever I do today can be therapeutic.
Is that what I need?

SEPTEMBER 10

In my lifetime, I helped a lot of people.
That's what I'm proudest of.

JAMES CASEY

Are you aware of the many people you helped throughout your life? It's doubtful that you are. Many of our benevolent acts were performed quite unconsciously. However, our particular line of work might have made helping others an expected occurrence. If so, we have many specific recollections, perhaps even the names and faces of people come quickly to mind. What a good feeling it is to know that others benefited from knowing us.

We can all realize our value in the lives of others. Even when we were drawn toward individuals we didn't particularly like, they needed us; we needed them. We don't have to understand how this worked. It simply was and is a fact of life that we get the opportunities we need for our growth. This is still true, in fact, regardless of our age. We aren't finished yet or we would no longer be passing this way.

It's good to feel proud of our accomplishments. It's better if we also remember the "silent partner" who made our successes possible. We all have acquaintances who boast about themselves. We generally don't relish listening to them for long. Everybody received God's help. Many don't acknowledge that, however. Let's share our understanding of "how it works" with others today. It's a beneficial message to carry.

I did the best I knew how to do.
Even when my accomplishments weren't perfect,
they were okay. Today will be likewise.

SEPTEMBER 11

*Passing on character to my students was what I hoped
most to do—being honest, upright,
and having respect for their fellow man.*

ALICE MERRYMAN

Honesty and integrity are generally character traits that we have valued.

We each decided, when we were much younger no doubt, what character meant to us. We were influenced by our parents and teachers, in the same way that Alice influenced her students. And we, in turn, helped others formulate their definitions by our examples. Living according to our standards lent meaning to our lives. It also offered examples to others.

By this age, our characters are pretty well set. If we have valued honesty in the past, we'll no doubt still value it. If loyalty and integrity mattered before, they will still matter. If generosity gave us good feelings, it still will. There's peace in realizing that we are fully developed men and women. Knowing ourselves means we aren't caught in the uncertainties of our youth. We've earned the right to simply go within when we are deciding how to respond or feel about a changing circumstance in our lives. Our inner character knows who we should be. We can always trust it.

**Others can tell what I value by my actions and
my revelations today. Will I feel proud of them too?**

SEPTEMBER 12

We need to give back,
to plow something back in the ground.

JIM BURNS

It's not uncommon to hear an acquaintance say, "I want to give back." But are we convinced of just how important that is? What does "giving back" really mean? There are many answers. It's about staying involved with the human community, even when we don't have to. It's about choosing the stimulation of others' ideas over the loneliness of self-absorption. It's about offering our wisdom to those who can profit from it.

We are here by design. What we have learned, accomplished, and shared with others were parts of our "assignment." And the proof that we aren't *done yet* is that we're still here. There must be additional lessons for us to learn. The men and women who accompany us on our journey today need us for their lessons, too.

It's comforting to know that we don't have to discern the particulars of what to give back, what to still accomplish, what to yet learn from our experiences. If we are open and trust our inner spirit, we'll do the right thing, whatever that is at this stage of our lives.

Today I will be alert to invitations
to join with others on our mutual journey.

SEPTEMBER 13

*Doing my job to the best of my ability gave my life purpose.
I feel there is no purpose to my life anymore.*

BUD SHERMAN

Many of us share Bud's opinion, unfortunately. Appreciating ourselves and recognizing our worth as human beings apart from the job we held is a learned attitude. Why did only some of us develop this attitude? Generally speaking, the family we grew up in set the stage for our current self-assessment. This doesn't mean we should blame our parents for how we currently feel. It merely explains it. We always had the choice to think and feel differently. We still do, in fact.

Believing that we have no real purpose now that our careers have ended shortchanges us quite dramatically. It also cheats the rest of our companions. Our purpose is far from over. Some would go so far as to say that our *real* purpose was never even reflected in the work we did. It was always loftier, more elusive, quite separate from what we did. Our work was simply our opportunity, the conduit to fulfill the actual purpose assigned to all of us: to love one another.

We'll never be finished with our real purpose. That's the exciting news. It means that whatever we set about doing today can be done more purposefully if we have love in our hearts. Choosing to adopt this attitude promises to change how the rest of life looks to us. How about it?

**My work is not complete. I'll have many
opportunities to express love today.**

SEPTEMBER 14

*I think I was a wonderful mother
but a terrible parent.*

RUTH CASEY

Perhaps you hadn't thought of these two "labels" as separate in meaning. But considering them this way for a moment might be refreshing when you sort through the recollections of your past. Every parent makes mistakes. Every human being, whether a parent or not, has survived a life riddled with errors. And that's okay. We really haven't disappointed God. We may have disappointed our children or our friends, however. Fortunately we still have time to make amends.

Mothering and parenting might not differ for everybody. Setting limits on acceptable behavior might have come quite naturally, as did the ability to give total and unconditional love. However, some may have found it easier to offer compassion than to discipline. The reality is that our children needed both. Let's grant ourselves a reprieve. If we think we failed at one or the other, let's acknowledge it and let it go. We really can't redo the past. We can't reteach or better love our children now. We can share our concerns with our loved ones, but whatever we did is done.

I have some regrets. We all do.
But I won't let them create a shadow over my activities today.
Every day I can make a fresh start.

SEPTEMBER 15

If you don't have any loyalty to what you are doing,
you ought not be doing it.

TOM HARDING

We understand loyalty to friends and family members, but does loyalty to an activity imply the same thing? To be loyal to an activity means to stick with it even when we hit the inherent snags. Let's consider a hobby for instance. Are we so frustrated when we can't track down a particular stamp or seem unable to complete the five thousand-piece puzzle that we consider quitting the activity in disgust? If so, we probably lack the loyalty that Tom alludes to.

Each of us has to consider for ourselves whether or not we value this kind of loyalty when it comes to the "extracurriculars" in our lives. We're not failures if we decide to drop some hobby for another one. Sometimes we can't see that some interest doesn't fit us all that well until we get deep into it. What's more important is that we remain loyal to our values, whatever they are. When some activity loses its appeal, for any reason, and we continue to stay with it out of shame or embarrassment, we're not being loyal to that which is most important ourselves.

Today, I'll ask myself if my hobbies suit my true interests.

*I had no children because I didn't want a child
to feel toward me as I had felt toward my mother.*

MARIA REGNIER KRIMMEL

Many of us had difficult relationships with our parents while growing up. External conditions often made our parents' lives difficult, which in turn affected how they responded to our needs as children. Most of us have some legitimate complaints about our childhoods. Hopefully, we can also say that we know our parents did their best.

It helps if we can acknowledge that we made mistakes too, as parents. And those of us like Maria, who had no children, still were in relationship with many other people, of all ages. How we fulfilled our roles in someone else's life has probably not been forgotten. If we failed in any way, we can only hope we have been forgiven.

Hanging on to the failings of a parent or some other significant person in our lives has distorted how we've responded to many other experiences throughout the rest of our lives. Not being able to react to every situation with a fresh perspective, hanging on to past disappointments, has cheated us of the lives we might have enjoyed. It's not too late to make a change. Is one needed?

**I will make sure I'm not looking at my circumstances today
through yesterday's experiences.**

SEPTEMBER 17

Retirement doesn't mean giving up all activities.
In fact, it's best to hang on to all the activities you have
outside of work, for a while, at least.

SANDY WARMAN

Leaving a career generally offers us more freedom, more un-claimed hours than we'd imagined. Not unlike learning any new skill in our youth, practice at filling the hours in a meaningful way is necessary. It simply takes time to adjust to the newness of this schedule. Remember, it's a process. There is no deadline. We can take as long as necessary in our adjustment to the freer life.

Not giving up all activities is a good beginning. We need some sameness to our lives after we've relinquished a long ca-reer. Making too many changes all at once is not in our best in-terests. Besides, the activities we had chosen had special mean-ing for us. We still need those special connections, perhaps even more now that we are seeing fewer of our former associates.

There is no simple blueprint for what we're adjusting to now. Each of us has to forge our own path. However, a suggestion that might fit for everyone is to stay involved with at least one on-going group or activity for the first year. We need to know we still matter, and we'll get that assurance.

My old interests can still bring me joy.
Today I can make an effort to reach out to
a longtime friend or colleague.

*One of the upsides of retirement is
all the people we have met.*

LOUISE JEROME

Some of us have had the privilege of extensive travel, making many new acquaintances along the way. That might not have been your story. However, new people are really only a house or a street away. New people come into our lives because we seek them out; it matters not where.

Whether or not we value making new friends might depend on our family situation. If we are caring for an ill loved one, we may lack the freedom to spread our wings. Yet, having someone to share our stories with, having access to a fresh perspective on any condition we're facing, is so helpful once we have taken the plunge to make a new friend. Even when we think we don't have the time or the energy it takes to explore a new relationship, we'll soon realize that interaction with someone else lifts our spirits and offers us lots of unexpected energy.

Being involved with others is something we can all do when we age. Maybe we can't continue traveling or playing tennis or competing to our satisfaction at bridge or other games, but we can talk to others. In that process, our lives will reflect new direction.

**I am never too old to seek out a companion to talk to.
My life will be the better for it.**

SEPTEMBER 19

I don't have to pretend to be something I'm not.

FRAN COYNE

What is it that makes us so susceptible to trying to be someone we're not? Psychologists would say it's low self-esteem. We fear we're not *enough* as we are, so we attempt to project a persona that we think will make us more acceptable. It's both exhausting and dishonest. But worse, it prevents us from ever being at peace.

Even though we may have been controlled by this struggle for many years, it's not too late to change our behavior. We have always been just who we needed to be, as we were. This is an idea we simply have to embrace. It may be difficult initially, but let's remember how much we respect someone else's honesty and humility concerning their shortcomings. We're not expected to be perfect. Life's experiences offer us opportunities to improve our perspectives and our behavior. We can honestly "grow into" the person we'd rather be by being aware of our actions, regardless of our age. That's far better than continuing to pretend, and instead of exhausting us, it empowers us. We can use all the energy we can acquire at this age.

Today I will be honest about who I am and how I feel.

*My personal goals throughout my life were too often
connected to the needs of other people.*

PAT JEROME

Pat's realization is not uncommon. Many of us share a similar awareness about our lives. Having had our goals intermingled with the needs of others wasn't wrong, so let's not criticize ourselves for that. However, it's quite appropriate to decide how we want to spend our time separate from everyone else's needs. We aren't, by assignment, the family caretaker. Nor does the success of the greater society or even one small organization rest on our input alone. We can perhaps chalk it up to habit that we began, long ago, to think in these terms.

Taking stock of where we are now and what we are doing may surprise us. How much of any day is bringing us genuine joy and satisfaction? If not most of it, we need to reconsider our priorities. That doesn't mean we should opt to be selfishly motivated, but rather decide to put our personal interests at the top of the list, followed by activities that also benefit others. We'll discover that when we address our needs first, we become more willing to help others. Everybody wins when we live this way.

As I look to this day,
I'll carefully consider what I really want to do.

SEPTEMBER 21

I don't think we're in charge of our lives.
For this I thank God all the time.

JANICE CLARK

To believe that we are in charge of everything that has happened or could happen in our lives is extremely daunting. Certainly, some events we'd like to take credit for: our career successes, for instance, or the achievements our children attained. We worked hard in those areas, didn't we? But since we can't accept only the good outcomes as in our charge, it's better that we let God be in charge of everything. That's not so bad, really. It means we always have the comfort of a companion in every situation, one who's not just along for the ride but one who wants the burden of driving us through the storms as well as the pastoral landscapes.

Most of us still have many years to experience before we journey into our last phase of life. Believing that what lies ahead for us was handpicked for us is pretty exciting. God has a plan for us. There was always a plan for us. Helping it to evolve through our willingness to listen and learn from those who journey with us is the part we need to play. We need not orchestrate anything else. We just need to show up and have faith. Doing the next right thing in every instance assures us of the right outcome. We'll always know what that right thing is if we seek to know it.

It's easier to look ahead at this day if we believe
we're never alone. Our successes are even more fun when
we know we have a "silent" partner.

SEPTEMBER 22

I hope I won't get so I can't walk, but if I do,
I'll be grateful that I can still move.
People who can move have so much to be grateful for.

ALPHA ENGLISH

If more of us were as determined as Alpha to take responsibility for making our lives better, far fewer of us would be harboring anger, depression, or waning confidence. We can all be certain that as we age, our levels of agility and energy will decline, but that doesn't mean we can't still go where we want. It merely means we may have to make an alternate plan for how we get there.

Let's never assume our lives have to change totally. Giving up our dreams, regardless of their nature, may be far more injurious to us than proceeding with even risky undertakings. Getting old doesn't mean giving up. We all know individuals who settled for that, however. And many of them appear to be waiting for their end. What separates us from them? Attitude. A simple change of mind makes all the difference in who we are and who we can yet become.

Let's never forget that doing the "next best thing" will always bring us contentment.

I will have many opportunities to move forward or
sit still today. God, please help me choose the next best thing.

SEPTEMBER 23

My spiritual life has changed a lot in the last ten years.

JAMES A. CASEY

Our spiritual lives should change as we grow in our understanding of this mysterious world and our many experiences. Our perception of God when we were young served us then. Many of us saw God as Santa Claus, the big jolly man who rewarded us for being good. But with maturity came a different viewpoint. God was turned to in more obvious ways, perhaps. When we needed help or comfort or sought a special favor, we said a prayer. There was never anything wrong with that approach, but, too often, God remained distant, too seldom utilized.

With full maturity, most of us have come to realize that God is simply an ever-present friend. God knows our needs. We don't even have to make a formal plea. Quietly listening for his presence is all we really have to do. And our conversations with others make this very simple. We'll always hear what we need to know if we truly listen to the words of a friend. If we let our hearts speak for us, we'll be allowing God to reach others through us, too.

The spiritual life does change as we change. It becomes what we need it to be without any effort on our part. Wanting to have a connection to God is all that's necessary.

**I will be in touch with God today through my
conversations with others.**

*My greatest achievement was my relationship with
the young son of a good friend.*

MARIA REGNIER KRIMMEL

Maria was a world-renowned silversmith. Because she is female, this was considered an even greater achievement, and yet she considered a particular relationship with a youngster to have been more important than having her work owned by famous people and on display in the finest museums. How do we judge the relationships in our lives? Have they mattered as much to us as our careers or our hobbies?

Naturally, we each have to answer that question for ourselves. For some of us, relationships were often difficult, whether at work or in the family. Some of us sought intimacy with others but failed to achieve it due to forces beyond our control. Our experiences are as different as are our personalities. But we're not too old to forge better relationships with others if that's our desire.

How do we determine if it's a relationship that we long for? Monitoring one's feelings and thoughts will offer clues. Are we lonely? Are we feeling sorry for ourselves? Do we seem to be always "waiting" for something or someone else to change our lives? If the answer is yes to any of these questions, let's reach out to someone today. Offering friendship is the only way a relationship can begin. If we want one, we must do our part.

How I spend today will be my decision.
If I want to share it with someone else,
I'd better make the first move.

SEPTEMBER 25

*At my age, I'm not really interested in volunteer work,
but I would like to have more acquaintances.*

THELMA ELLIOTT

Thelma is eighty-six. Making a commitment of time to an organization might not be in her best interests. Nonetheless, seeking more friends is important. Being lonely in old age is never necessary, but how do we find new friends when we're limited by the circumstance of age or transportation? A place to begin is a local newspaper or church. Groups are always seeking new members.

Maybe a new friend is as close as next door. Is there someone on your block whom you haven't met yet? There is no better time than now. Maybe he or she has been hoping for a friend too, but was not as brave about reaching out. One of the characteristics we have going for us is that most of us, at our age, have quit worrying about what others might think of us. If we want a new friend, we'll find one.

We simply can't wait for someone else to change our lives for us. If there is something we want today, let's make plans for getting it. What have we got to lose?

Today is open to a new plan and a new friend.

*We all give out vibrations, and we know within minutes
if we have anything in common with another person.*

MONTY CRALLEY

From the time we were children, we gravitated more easily toward some people than others. Friendships that grow from common interests are important and generally enduring.

Those friendships that have been forged by necessity should not be discounted, however. And we have all had our share of them. Maybe we had to be part of a team in the workplace, spending great amounts of time with individuals who thought and worked very differently from ourselves. If we were able to keep our hearts open, if we were willing to listen to and respect ideas that were different from our own, we likely grew from the experience. It's quite possible that it prepared us for the next stage of our development.

Let's take pride in the times we got beyond our narrow viewpoint and "tried on" the interests of others. What we'll see is that every time we loosened up, we got exposed to someone we needed to know, and this process made us a better person.

**I may have a chance to make a new friend today.
I'll remain open to others regardless of how different
our interests appear to be at first.**

SEPTEMBER 27

You make a lot of mistakes in life,
but you still end up where you're supposed to be.

JAMES CASEY

Jim's philosophy allows for human error. We've made many mistakes during our lifetimes. But what does "ending up where we're supposed to be" mean? To most this implies a belief in a particular destiny for each of us. That may be a comforting thought to many people. We know we'll get done what we're supposed to do.

Does it really matter if we missed some of "God's dancing lessons"? No doubt we learned whatever we needed to learn through some activity. There always were many chances to make our mark. Without a doubt, we made it, too. If you share Jim's vision about life, you'll realize you are still making it. We're never really done, *until we are done.*

Looking at life this way gives us plenty of reason to put our clothes on every morning. Our journey is not complete. The invitations to our destination keep arriving. When looked at this way, life seems exciting and well organized, doesn't it?

I will probably make a mistake or two today.
That's no big deal!

My intense dislike for my mother finally eased up.

MARIA REGNIER KRIMMEL

Intensely disliking any person is debilitating. Far too much energy goes into the feeling which, in turn, adversely affects how we feel in general. When the recipient of our hatred was or is a parent or sibling, we are faced with double the shame about our feelings. At the end of the day, it's not easy to justify mean-spirited feelings. They contribute nothing to the rest of humanity.

When our dislike has been triggered by another's behavior, we tend to think we're not responsible for it. "If they hadn't done what they did, I would have acted better." Hopefully few of us have spent our lives trapped in this mind-set, because it's simply not true. Regardless of what anyone did or said, we were responsible and accountable for our responses. This remains true, of course. Likewise, what we do or say to others, no matter how insensitive, can't be the cause of their responses. No one's behavior gives license for anyone else's response.

If our feelings toward someone aren't peaceful, let's consider how we might change them. That doesn't mean we have to like the other person. It merely means we'd feel better if we sought to let our feelings change. They can't unless we invite them to do so. And miraculously they do, when we ask.

**I may not like everybody I'm with today,
but my behavior can still be respectful.**

SEPTEMBER 29

*I know Edith and I won't live forever,
but we have the attitude, why not?*

HARRY BARTHOLOMEW

Harry and Edith's attitudes are so refreshing. They are guaranteed the joy they deserve by the outlook they have cultivated. Have they done the impossible? Certainly not. Octogenerians everywhere can be just as fulfilled and happy if they decide to see their possibilities rather than the barriers that hinder their dreams. We make whatever world we experience. This was true in our youth; it will be true until the day we die.

If we're experiencing grave health problems or emotional turmoil, we may think it's not possible to feel happy. Many friends, no doubt, serve as examples of this unhappiness. But there is another way to see whatever befalls us. The *miracle* is that no situation is beyond looking quite different if we decide to "change our mind."

Going about one's day with the belief that good is coming at us confirms that good is what we're getting. It's not mysterious. It may only seem that way if we've had a lifetime of practicing the bad in all our experiences. Many years ago Abraham Lincoln said, "We're as happy as we make up our minds to be." Why dispute that? It's so much more sensible to prove that it's true.

**I'm on my way to happiness today.
It's simply the result of my mind's work.**

I've got a long list of things to talk to God about.

FRAN COYNE

What we expect about the afterlife contributes to our level of comfort in this life. If death scares us, if we think punishment awaits us for our every transgression, we'll live in constant dread of the inevitable. This, in turn, will influence how we experience all the situations we still have to live through. Fear becomes all-encompassing, and it distorts every detail of our perception. Living without fear has just as measurable an impact.

The final stage of life can be seen as an opportunity to seek answers to the situations that have troubled us over the years; this can redefine how we think about death. It lends an air of excitement about the final phase. It also reflects a far different understanding about God, God's role, and our part in the *divine* plan. To have a discussion with God, as Fran suggests, implies one considers God a friend, a confidant—surely not someone ready to inflict grave harm on us.

Being able to seek an explanation for all the mysteries of our lives and the lives of our loved ones gives death a significantly different feel. It can become an experience that we anticipate almost eagerly. Is that so bad?

There are experiences in my life that I never understood.
I can now bring these unresolved concerns to God.

OCTOBER

OCTOBER 1

You become more authentically yourself as you get older.

BETTY FRIEDAN

It probably doesn't take much reflection to remember times we lied to the boss about why a project was late. Or to a spouse or parent about where we were. Or made an excuse to an acquaintance about why we couldn't attend a social function. And the times are numerous when we pretended to agree with an adversary rather than risk losing a promotion or a friendship.

But were we really phonies every time we stretched the truth or kept silent rather than disagree? The answer lies within. The question we must address is how did we feel each time we opted to skirt the truth rather than risk the consequences? If it bothered us, even a little bit, it will be easier to explore our authenticity now.

In the long run, nothing was ever gained by our glazing over the facts. Maybe we "saved ourselves" in the moment, but we chipped away at the soul within. We are free, at last, to be ourselves.

I enjoy real freedom now.
The only person I want to impress is me.
Being honest is all it takes.

OCTOBER 2

Growing old is no more than a bad habit
which a busy mind has no time to form.

ANDRE MAUROIS

It's folly to deny that we grow old. Our bodies age; our limbs get stiff. Memories sometimes fail; hearing and vision aren't as acute as in our youth. But *growing old* and *being old* rest in different categories. We've all met the "old" woman who is a mere fifty two. But some of us prefer to emulate the eighty-six-year-young line-dancer at the club. Our states of mind are better gauges of *real* age than our wrinkled bodies.

Having busy minds may indeed mean we'll not grow old, as quoted above. Continuing to learn new skills or joining a discussion group at church can keep us thinking young. But a busy mind may mean something quite different. Some keep their minds busy with constant worry and, thus, age before their time. Obsessive thinking, which certainly busies our minds, can be very unhealthy in fact. Having a quiet mind heals and refreshes us, many spiritual leaders believe. How we busy our minds is what counts.

Taking charge of what I dwell on today determines how young or old I feel. I will use my power thoughtfully.

OCTOBER 3

There's youth, middle age, old age, and old old age.
Now in old old age, I plan to stay off scaffolds thirty feet high.

LOUIS FREUND

Deciding to be cautious is a good decision at any age. But as we age, quite possibly it becomes even more important. A break does not heal as quickly; a fall can lay us up for weeks; misplaced money or possessions might be gone forever. Taking a little extra time for every activity, every thought even, promises us immediate rewards. Of course, this was true in our youth, too. But then, we dared to take risks and generally got away with them.

Being a bit more cautious doesn't take any of the excitement out of life, even though it may seem so at first. We can look at this another way, in fact. We can see being cautious as taking specific control over how we move through our experiences each day. Being more deliberate feels quite good, actually. It frees us from playing catch-up all the time.

There isn't much that we can't attempt on most days. Perhaps moving all the furniture or cutting down a full-grown tree is a bit beyond us, but not the decision to get someone to help us accomplish these, or any task. Working smarter is what getting older is really all about. We are all life graduates.

I will work smart today.
I will take my time and get whatever help I need.
I will also do what I can for myself.

OCTOBER 4

*There are too many things to do and
not enough time to do them all.*

EDITH HUEY

We are never too old to pursue our "heart's pure desire." While our families were growing up, we may have had to postpone a time-consuming hobby, a trip we longed to make, a friendship that beckoned. What a treat to realize this is no longer the case. Whatever we can imagine, we can at last pursue. And there is no better time than the present to begin the pursuit.

We all know women and men who sit idly in front of the television, lamenting the losses in their lives. There's no doubt about it, growing old and staying alive assures us of many losses. But it's a choice whether or not we moan about that inevitability or celebrate the fact that losses also release us to enjoy an even wider range of untapped possibilities. Despite the sadness of losing someone we love, not having to take care of an ailing spouse or parent does free us up.

Make a list of all the dreams you deferred when you were younger. At least a couple of them will still interest you. All it takes is the decision to pick up where you left off so long ago.

**Beginning a new activity can make each day more exciting.
The decision is easy if we believe it.**

O(TOBER 5

*If people I'm with know more than I do, I figure we're on
even ground because I can learn from them.*

TOM HARDING

The interesting thing is that we'll always be with people who
know more about some subject than we do. This has always
been the case. Yet, we probably didn't appreciate this fact when
we were young. We often felt as though we had to "know it all,"
which meant we couldn't allow someone else to enlighten us
when we were in conflict with them. The wisdom that can come
with old age is so comforting.

Being able to admit there's much we don't know relieves us
of a heavy burden and opens the door for our exposure to new
ideas. We are generally surrounded by men and women who
have specific information they are eager to share. Deciding to be
a listener, nothing more, in some settings is so refreshing. It's appreciated, too, because we all like to hold forth on occasion.
Giving others the chance to share their knowledge is our ticket
to education.

Recognizing that we have information not known to others,
too, is important. There will be opportunities for us to share
something of value, thus placing others on even ground with us.

I may know more about one subject today than a friend.
He or she will likely have something to share with me, too.

OCTOBER 6

Once you do creative work,
you cannot not do it.

MARIA REGNIER KRIMMEL

How broadly do you define creativity? Far too many of us are quick to say, "I'm not creative at all." But that's primarily because we have defined it too narrowly. Being accomplished at photography or sketching, painting or writing, the flute or the clarinet are what comprises creative talent, we think. But that's not really so.

Being creative is a given. We all share it. We simply haven't all understood this because of our narrow definition. It helps to regard how uniquely we all perceive our world of experience. We don't doubt that we each see things quite singularly. In fact, we "create" that which we see. In turn, we can recreate that vision through any medium that appeals to us. The main ingredient for our creative success is discipline. Once we have overcome our resistance to the idea that we are gifted, that we are creative in a specific way, we simply have to do it. The doing then becomes its own gift, one we grow compelled to open every day.

I am never too old to believe that I am creative.
I may have to give myself a pep talk,
but then I only have to get busy.

OCTOBER 7

In my heart, I never expected
anything for the help I gave.

JAMES CASEY

Being truly altruistic, as Jim perhaps was, isn't one of life's requirements. Most of us did expect something for our benevolence; likely we still do. And this becomes a problem when our expectations are unmet. Seldom do they match that which we receive. It's so much better if we can give freely of our time, our thoughts, our prayers, our help. Then we'll not be disappointed.

How successful are we in helping others? Has that been a priority in your life? It's never too late to make it one. Jim had so many friends, so many relatives who were both openly and quietly indebted to him. The good feelings they conveyed upon him softened his challenges in life. He had many, many challenges. We all do.

For everyone, life is ebbing away. Regardless of how old or young we feel, we are forever moving toward our end. That's been the process all along, of course. However, in our youth, in our more productive years, we pretended otherwise. Few of us can continue to pretend. And that's as it should be. We've done our part. We're still doing it, certainly, but we can rest a bit. Let's be assured that we have never disappointed God in our offerings to others. And that's what really mattered.

I am not finished giving yet.
What opportunity will I grasp today?

OCTOBER 8

*It greatly humbles me that people have idolized me
and my work as a smithy.*

MARIA REGNIER KRIMMEL

Being idolized by others for some trait or talent we're blessed with is not uncommon. We may even be unaware of the respect others feel for us. We may well hold others in high esteem, too, without having shared our feelings with them. While it's not always necessary to share these special feelings, it's nice to receive compliments. We're delighted to know others have appreciated our contributions. Let's consider the probability that most others feel likewise and express our admiration.

Some of us believe we have no special talent. On the contrary, we have all been blessed with the skill to do something very well. Perhaps we haven't had the inclination to follow through on our calling, but it has been there, nonetheless. Is it too late to pursue a new avenue now? Certainly not. Maria sets a good example, in fact. After she had to give up smithing because of arthritis in her hands, she took up painting and batiking. Let's never assume it's too late to begin a new venture. All that really stands in our way is our unwillingness to be a student.

Is there something I've thought about trying but haven't dared to do yet? Today is a good day to take the plunge.

OCTOBER 9

Edith and I try not to take ourselves too seriously.
We laugh a lot at ourselves.

HARRY BARTHOLOMEW

We'd all benefit if we followed Harry's suggestion. What does it take to shrug one's shoulders and smile rather than nervously frown at all the experiences that seem to hinder us? Really nothing but the willingness to accept that whatever befalls us is no big deal. In the total scheme of one's life, no single misfortune is truly paramount. In fact, if we've cultivated humility, we'll quickly see how irrelevant most of our mistakes are.

Laughing over our many experiences, even those that troubled us at the time they happened, is good medicine in our old age. We can never laugh too much, some would say. Respected physicians have been known to say laughter can change the outcome of an illness. We may not understand just how this works, but we have all experienced how a good laugh changes the way a situation looks to us. Could it be that illness is a product of the mind? Might our physical health actually be in our hands?

We don't need to accept this idea wholly for it to have a positive impact on our lives. And since we're still here, reading these pages, let's do our part to "see" whatever comes at us today as worthy of a smile, if not a belly laugh.

I am as happy as I decide to be today.

OCTOBER 10

Keeping my mind active through good, intellectual discussions is important to me. Talking over golf scores doesn't take us very far.

LOUISE JEROME

Small talk is what engages us much of the time. There's nothing shameful about that. Many of the individuals we're in the company of are strangers to us. Inconsequential discussions seem safer then. Yet, keeping our minds active through thoughtful discussions about the world expands our knowledge and awareness. This exercises our minds in important ways. Just as muscles atrophy when unused, so do minds.

Many people shy away from in-depth discussions. Maybe we frequently do that, too. Oftentimes it's because we feel inadequate to others. Maybe we assume they are better educated. Fears of inadequacy are familiar to most of us. Will we ever learn that we are and always have been all that we've needed to be?

One of the good things about growing old, for some of us at least, is that we've lived long enough to realize that most worries don't materialize;, most situations aren't as serious as we anticipate, and most people are more approachable than they first appear to be. Taking risks to share our thoughts gets easier the more we practice it. Let's not shy away from this today.

**I'll dare to share my opinions today.
A good discussion can energize me.**

OCTOBER 11

Retirement makes it possible to do
what you've never had time to do.

FRAN COYNE

It's an all too common refrain: "If only I had more time." That's one wish that has probably come true for all of us now. But how appreciative are we of the extra hours? Do we squander them, complaining about the imperfect world we inhabit? Let's consider an alternative, if that's the case. Let's take a few moments right now to note the blessings we've experienced over our many decades. Let's recall, too, the good fortunes that have been bestowed on friends and family. Now let's allow ourselves to dream a bit about what we'd like to experience next in our lives.

We'll change our perspectives on the past as well as the present if we do this exercise. Generally, that's all we need to do to realize just how prolific our many opportunities for new experiences really are. It has been said that any worthy, reasonable idea for action that comes to us is not by chance but rather a suggestion from our *divine inner voice*. Whether we believe that or not right now, let's "go along." What can it hurt to follow through on a suggestion that isn't going to infringe on another person? We just may discover that we are finally doing what we've been waiting to do all these many years.

If I'm not sure what I want to do today,
I'll take a moment to fantasize about the possibilities.
One of them will seem right.

OCTOBER 12

Each day is different and has a surprise in it,
like a Cracker Jack box.

ALPHA ENGLISH

It's interesting to ponder the notion of surprise. Not every one of them, in old age, is all that welcome. Hearing bad news about a friend or having a special trip we'd been counting on canceled can leave us dismayed and worried, right along with surprised. Seeking solace from others while cultivating a willingness to accept that all things happen for a reason gives us the armor we need to make the best of every situation and disappointment.

It's an interesting image to think of each day as a box of Cracker Jacks. The moments of our lives have been very tasty. Some were sweet, some were a bit salty, and there were always wholly unexpected moments, the surprises that we were ready for even though we may not have imagined as much. We can look forward to the same daily agenda throughout the remaining years.

Does it help to know that there is a divine plan unfolding in our lives? Many of us find comfort in that. All of us can cultivate that belief.

I am ready for my surprise today!
It is meant for me at this time.

OCTOBER 13

I don't have time to sit on the porch.

VIOLET HENSLEY

Is there really anything wrong with "sitting on the porch"? From Violet's perspective, it would depend on what one's *sitting* was all about. If it was because of boredom or depression, she'd suggest you get busy, get involved with others, get a hobby. If it was because you were watching birds or small children at play, she'd approve. The key is maintaining an active mind. An idle mind sees few pleasures in a day.

Some of us don't know how to begin a hobby. Or maybe we're shy about getting involved with new people. These feelings are more common than we might imagine. Gravitating easily toward others or having the courage to take up a hobby requires persistence, patience, and willingness. We're always our own worst critic in everything we do.

Today is calling. Can I do something new today?
If I need encouragement, I'll call a friend.

OCTOBER 14

Every morning I thank God for this beautiful sky,
for this perfect world.

EVA WINES

Being grateful for the many mysteries of life, those we see but don't understand and those that are hidden from our view, can help us stay grateful all the time. There's not much that happens in the natural world that we can adequately explain; being awed by it all reminds us that we're not in control of the external world. And that, in turn, helps us remember that a Greater Power is making a contribution. Always.

What's so important about gratitude? It seems like such a small gesture. Can it really make a difference in our lives? The answer is yes, of course. It's not that others are changed by it; it doesn't change the circumstances of our lives. But it does quite emphatically change us and how we see the world around us. In that process, everything changes, absolutely everything.

Making the decision to cultivate a grateful attitude every day gives us something extremely important to do all the remaining days of our lives. Even though we can never hope to change others by our actions, we'll note, in time, that some acquaintances seem *mysteriously* different after a while. Might our gratitude have played a role?

What I can't do today is irrelevant. I can think or feel
whatever I want to, and that's a powerful realization.

OCTOBER 15

*We need to help others when they need it,
not just when it's convenient for us!*

HELEN CASEY

Many of us were terrifically busy our whole lives. Careers, children, community involvement, and hobbies filled the hours. There were not many hours left. The pattern our busyness set for us may convince us we still don't have enough time. Perhaps it's appropriate to reconsider this feeling. Is there really any deadline facing us now? If there is, who has set it? It's really quite freeing to step back from our activities and evaluate which are necessary and which are just habits that hinder our availability to others.

At the same time that helping others is important, it's also important that we don't give up our own lives to only help others, unless of course we truly feel peaceful doing so. Taking care of everyone else can be just as habit-forming as selfishness. Neither option does anyone any good. The best guideline to follow when asked for help is to first ask ourselves if we can offer genuine solace or pertinent solutions. Have our own experiences educated us appropriately? If the answer is yes, then let's seek the guidance of our inner wisdom before offering anything.

**I can help me by helping someone else today
if my heart is in it.**

OCTOBER 16

Making other people happy is very important to me.

MONTY CRALLEY

It's very human to pretend we are kinder and more compassionate than we really are when someone needs our help. Many of us have been pretty selfish, in fact, for most of our lives. Do we think it's too late to change?

Let's take an inventory of just the last twenty-four hours. Were we asked for a favor? Did we respond willingly or did we resist, at least in our minds? What about the conversations we engaged in with a spouse, a friend, the store clerk, or mail carrier? Were we respectful listeners, or did we interrupt and discount the other's viewpoint? How many times did we stop to consider doing a nice turn for someone less fortunate than ourselves? Did we even contemplate for a moment calling a friend who has been shut in lately because of illness?

We hope we can feel good about yesterday's actions, but we at least have a chance to feel good tomorrow about today's opportunities.

Regardless of my age, nothing is keeping me from being kind to others. Today is a great opportunity.

OCTOBER 17

I feel best about having helped others believe in themselves.

BUD SHERMAN

Encouragement is one of the greatest gifts we can give one an-other. Chances are we can all remember someone who encouraged us many years ago. Perhaps a teacher or an employer took a special interest in us, and we have never forgotten that person. It's likely we are remembered in much the same way by someone else, too. It's nice to savor these memories, isn't it?

There is nothing stopping us from continuing to make memories for others. We will experience people and situations today that will benefit if we pass on encouragement and praise. We will benefit as well. It feels good to acknowledge another's contributions to the world. It strengthens our own willingness to contribute.

No conversation is without purpose. Even those exchanges that seem meaningless offer us opportunities for bettering someone else's opinion of themselves. What greater offering have we to make than to be loving and helpful to someone traveling this path with us? If we haven't given much attention to this part of our assignment before, let's begin now. The homework will make all of us feel much better.

A few words of encouragement to another is all that's asked of me today. I can handle that.

OCTOBER 18

I never admitted I was afraid people didn't like me,
not even to my wife.

SANDY WARMAN

Perhaps it's not unusual that we kept secrets from our closest allies. Quite likely we feared we'd not survive if they were to reject us. And, in fact, wouldn't they leave if they really knew us? We may still be ashamed of our "secret" shortcomings. But we're greatly diminished by such acts of self-protection. The reality is that we're not protecting ourselves at all but quite the opposite.

Is it too late to learn self-disclosure? Therapists and spiritual leaders say it's never too late to tell another person who we really are. And they would go so far as to say we'll not feel worthy or healed or content with life until we have shared ourselves fully with someone else. But how do we gather the courage if we have kept our secrets this long?

Maybe writing down what we'd like to share with someone else is a place to begin. Seeing what terrifies us in black and white might lessen our fear. We can take this one step at a time. The next decision might be to ask a very old and trusted friend to listen without responding to our words. The act of telling someone, anyone, will change what we think about ourselves. Let's try it.

I have an opportunity today to change my life.
I'll begin by getting a piece of paper and a pen and
writing down my shortcomings.

OCTOBER 19

The most important thing I learned in life was the value of getting along with others.

PAT JEROME

Pat's philosophy sounds so simple and reasonable. Many of us would agree that our relations with others are important, but it has not always been easy to keep our exchanges smooth, to keep uppermost in our minds the notion that respect breeds respect.

Even a cursory glance back at the past will reveal how successfully we got along with others. The major conflicts in our lives, at work or at home, aren't easily forgotten. Nor should they be if we haven't made our appropriate amends.

The important idea here is that our common pattern of behavior in the past is more than likely how we still respond to the people and situations in our lives. If we haven't placed a premium on getting along with others in earlier experiences, we're likely not committed to this principle now. Do we have to be? Certainly not; we have the freedom to be whatever kind of person suits us. However, most of us want peace and joy in our lives. If we aren't feeling much of it, just maybe we need to monitor our responses and reactions to those who journey with us.

My responses and reactions to everyone today are within my control. If I want to feel peaceful, I can.

OCTOBER 20

I tried to pass on my love of books to my children.

RUTH CASEY

We have been passing things on to children or other significant people in our lives for as long as we've lived. We can all feel good about the legacy. But if we are aware of passing on certain traits or conditions that we now feel uncomfortable with or sorry for, it's not too late to address them. Fortunately, it's never too late to say we were wrong or that we're sorry.

We have never been perfect — not at parenthood, not at anything. What we can hope for is that we didn't harm anyone else irreparably while we were "learning" to be human. At our age now, we likely have many recollections of mistakes we made. The good news is that we can decide to believe that we did the very best we were capable of. And that's true, even when we made obvious blunders.

We are helped if we believe that those who have journeyed with us, whether children or friends, have been there by choice. What they have needed to learn in this life could be accomplished in our company. Believing this, as many sage people do, takes the responsibility off us for the outcome of others' lives.

Today I can focus on passing on a positive attitude to others.

OCTOBER 21

If I ever just sat down and propped my feet up,
I'd be miserable. I'd make others around me miserable, too.

ALICE MERRYMAN

Recognizing who we are is extremely important. When we don't understand ourselves very well, which may still be the case for some of us, we're easily disappointed and generally unprepared for the challenges that we're bound to face. Being alive has meant surviving many tough times.

It helped if we believed that every experience played a key role in our personal evolution when difficulties overwhelmed us. Further, we're helped by knowing that what was true in the past remains true. The challenges haven't ended. That's the way life is. But we can take them in stride. Getting on with life, not sitting down to wallow in our misery, is the best way to survive a difficult situation, according to Alice. She's nearly ninety now, so one would have to agree with her.

Each of us has already decided how to interpret our experiences. We have also determined how to spend our waking hours. But are we content with our decisions? If we have any doubts, we can rethink who we are and become who we'd rather be. Just because we're in a latter stage of life doesn't mean we can't make new decisions. Shall we try?

Today is an open book.
How I turn the pages is decided by me only.

OCTOBER 22

When I look back on my life, it seemed to always be in chaos.
I was a meticulous housekeeper because
it was all I could control.

RUTH CASEY

It's far too easy to focus on the trouble spots in our lives. As a result, we simply don't give ourselves the credit we deserve for all of our successes. Humility may be the obvious reason this is true for some. Others honestly fail to see their strengths. How willing are you to look for and acknowledge yours?

It's never too late to take an inventory of our lives. Quite possibly, we weren't ready for an exercise like this before now. Many of us need the shot in the arm an honest inventory would give us. We have been successful human beings, every one of us. It is a worthy assignment to make a list of all the situations or events we're proud of having contributed to.

Looking over our lives this intently will turn up some of our weaker traits as well. And that's good. We need to celebrate our wholeness. Being human means having good traits as well as a few not-so-good ones. Many people could remind us that our roles as teachers may have been more sufficiently handled through our failures than through our successes. We can never be certain just what we are "teaching" someone else. We can only be certain that we are.

I need to watch how well I handle things today.
I deserve to feel good about myself.

OCTOBER 23

There was no job training for parenthood.
We made mistakes.

JAMES CASEY

Most of us grew up and became parents very much like our own parents. Our own parents were terribly busy just trying to make ends meet. It's not that they weren't good parents. They may well have been, but the focus in those years was not on "perfect parenting" but on providing the family with the essentials.

A lot has changed in this regard over the last few decades. Hundreds of books have been written about parenting. Perhaps our children have read a few of them and have expressed their anger at our failures. But we did our best. That's what we need to accept now. In time, they'll accept this, too.

There were many stages of life for which there was no actual training. Being good partners and companions to our spouses was probably the result of many steps forward and a few backward. Being willing to exchange ideas with our partners was probably our best training. In reality, that kind of exchange nurtures every relationship and every experience any of us have. We are not through with our training. As long as we live, we can learn from and teach one another.

I am both a teacher and a student today.
I'll never be too old to learn.

OCTOBER 24

Have you ever tried to befriend someone who snarled at every circumstance in life? Perhaps a neighbor or an acquaintance from church comes to mind. Generally, we dread getting caught in conversation with them because their negativity occasionally rubs off on us. We can't always avoid people like this, even though we'd prefer to. There is a solution to our dilemma: quietly bless them for reminding us that life is much more pleasant when we seek the brighter side.

Only a pained person sees nothing but the darkness. When we are drawn into his or her circle, let's consider it our assignment to offer a brighter side. We often can't change a person's opinions, but we can avoid strengthening those opinions with our assent. We need not argue with him or her. Simply offer another perspective with a smile. In some instances it won't take much more than this to get a friend to see his or her folly, at least once in a while. Every time we offer another view to a troubled friend, we give him or her food for thought and hope for change.

Nothing can "make" me unhappy today.
I can choose my attitude.

OCTOBER 25

Life takes new twists all the time.
Very little works out as we expect.

FRAN COYNE

If most circumstances had worked out the way we expected, our lives would have been far more harrowing. It's so common to expect the worst. Coming to believe that everything worked out in the right way gives us a lot of comfort. If that's not how we feel presently, perhaps we can seek the counsel of a friend who is more convinced that everything has had its purpose and has made its contribution to who we have needed to become.

If we grew up with rigid parents, we came by our own rigidity quite honestly. It's hard to break long-standing patterns of perception and behavior. Learning to be more flexible, to roll with the punches, so to speak, takes concerted effort that is preceded by willingness. It's never too late to learn a new response to the unexpected outcomes that are destined to occur.

We aren't living in a vacuum. Life is and always was about relationships. Learning from one another, realizing the necessity of every person's role in our lives, coming to understand what we have given others, too, is what this life experience has been about. That it hasn't evolved as we'd expected or hoped doesn't preclude the fact that it has evolved exactly right. Let's seek the comfort in that.

Today will undoubtedly offer me some surprises.
I'll remember the goodness in that.

OCTOBER 26

After a year of marriage, my husband retired.
I wasn't ready for this big change.

ABBY WARMAN

So many events happen unexpectedly in our lives. But is it really that big of a deal? Some might say it's a matter of perspective. Regardless of what happens, we can seek the good in it.

Some events are surely bigger than others. Marriage at any age is pretty big. So is a job change or retirement, planned for or spontaneous. We may need the emotional support of others to adapt. That's good, though. The reality is that we need the support of others for most situations in our lives, even though we may not acknowledge as much.

One of the blessings of everyone's life is that support of some kind is always available. If we haven't sought it before, we might not recognize its presence. And too, we may think that support comes wrapped in a particular way. Actually, it's as varied as are the people in our lives. We simply have to seek it. It will come, and with it will come peace and acceptance.

Getting older doesn't mean my life stops changing.
The changes attest to my continued life.
There is good in that.

OCTOBER 27

I was so frantic that I thought I was having a heart attack.
Thank God it was only stress.

SANDY WARMAN

We complicate many aspects of our lives unnecessarily, don't we? How much easier living would be if we assumed that whatever had transpired, no matter how dire or frightful, was exactly what was needed for us to evolve according to the divine plan. Our worries would be over if we could develop this perspective. What is standing in our way?

Many of us simply lack faith that there is a Higher Power in charge and that we're okay, regardless of what's happening. Having a peaceful perspective generally comes from having cultivated a set of spiritual beliefs that gives one strength in times of turmoil. Some grew up in homes where these were dictated. Some among our number grew up with none. Our problem may be that we want to feel hope and peace, but we don't know how to create it at our age. We think we're too old now, that we can't change. Not true!

Changing our minds is all that's ever necessary if we want to change our experiences. Maybe this doesn't seem possible. If we've grown accustomed to thinking that our problems are unique, far more serious than others' problems, we'll be challenged, certainly. But let's look again. Might we be wrong?

I can see my life peacefully or fitfully.
What shall I make of today?

OCTOBER 28

Every time I get worried about something,
I say my prayers more.

JIM BURNS

Whether we grew up in religious families or not, most of us seek help from some Greater Power when we're faced with terrifying situations. Often it's at an unconscious level that we ask for extra help. But the fact that we do elicit strength from some source comforts us, and this enables us to walk through the experience that appears so daunting.

We never outgrow the need for strength and comfort. That's good news. It means we don't have to assume that just because we lived to this ripe old age, we should have all the answers. In fact, some would say that we'll not have all the answers until this phase of living is entirely over. Many of us find that idea comforting. It's too awesome to think that we need to *know all now*, to understand how every detail of living should unfold. It's quite enough to limit our focus on the details of the next twenty-four hours.

Let's be vigilant about our search for guidance and comfort. And let's not forget that we have to listen for the response. If our minds are filled with worrying, there will be no space for the answers to enter.

Praying for solutions or comfort or just a moment of peace
will change my perspective today. When my perspective
changes, so do my experiences.

About the time I wish I were dead, something falls
in my path about which I make a difference.
Then I figure God was saving me for that.

JANICE CLARK

Not everybody has the easy faith that Janice has, but perhaps we could all cultivate it. They say it's never too late to make a friend of God. He's been waiting in the wings all along. But some may question this point, particularly if they have lived this long without attending to their spiritual side. Indeed, it's not a requirement. However, those who have sought the counsel of a Higher Spirit have found comfort in the knowledge that they are never alone. Furthermore, they generally are able to see a pattern to the events of their lives, and they know that all situations have played their part in the total unfolding.

It is pretty exciting to believe that anything that crosses one's path today is by design. One of the plusses of believing in God is knowing that we don't have to handle any situation that occurs without guidance. We never have to have all the answers. We never have to have any of them, in fact. All we have to do is seek them from the only Source that really has them.

If we haven't allowed our lives to be this easy up to now, let's give this process a chance. There's no reason to keep struggling with the circumstances that happen to us. They are there as lessons, nothing more.

I will acknowledge the rightness of
whatever comes my way today.

OCTOBER 30

*My spirituality is becoming
more important to me as I get older.*

JOANN REED

Having a spiritual life is more important to some of us than to others. How we grew up might be a contributing factor. If religion was forced on us, we may have rejected it as soon as we left home. Then, *coming to believe* in a force or power outside of ourselves takes willingness. We may not have that, even yet. But if we sense that others among us are feeling more peace than we're accustomed to feeling, we might seek to know why. Perhaps they have sought and found a spiritual path that comforts them.

One thing that's no doubt true for all of us, regardless of how we grew up, is the wish to feel connected to the world around us, to the people in our lives, to the idea that life has held some purpose. On occasion we lose this feeling. For any number of reasons, we become lonely; our separateness from others is all that we can perceive. Even though the spiritual path tells us that we're never alone, that we're always in a state of oneness with others, we may see only our differences. Let's look again if that's the case.

I will find more joy in today if I seek to be with
rather than separate from others.
I will try to remember that spiritually we are one.

OCTOBER 31

*I think the afterlife will be a lot better
than what we've got in this world.*

TOM HARDING

It comforts people to believe in an afterlife. The idea of nothingness is unsettling. Besides, the anticipation of joining with our dead loved ones gives us hope and peace. In times of turmoil, and we have all experienced lots of that, we need to be able to imagine a time of freedom from all this strife.

Our beliefs about death are important, but so are our beliefs about life. If we aren't particularly happy about this life, we need to do something about our attitude. Just waiting for "the next life," is not very fruitful.

So where do we begin? How do we change negative perceptions that have been honed for years? The steps are simple. A negative perception is nothing more than a bad habit. Monitoring our feelings will be a shorthand to our thoughts. Our feelings and thoughts create our perceptions. Thus, taking charge of the feelings we'll cultivate will make the difference in our present life, and that's the only one we get to have right now.

**Maybe my afterlife will be great,
but what I think and do right now is what counts.**

NOVEMBER

NOVEMBER 1

As we grow old, the beauty steals inward.

RALPH WALDO EMERSON

External appearance is so important to us when we're young. And in this society, most women struggle to maintain their looks well into old age. We learned from grammar school onward that how we looked outside often carried more weight than who we were inside. It's not easy to unlearn an idea so well etched in our minds. But Emerson's wisdom is a place to begin.

What is beauty? No doubt there are as many definitions as people alive. To some it's a rose in bloom or a swan gliding on a placid lake. An elderly woman pushing a loved one in a wheelchair is beautiful. So is an artist's model in quiet repose.

Philosophers have suggested that our actions reveal our beauty. From that perspective, nary a one of us fails to be beautiful if we're thoughtful. We have all been touched by at least one beautiful soul in our lifetime. How many others have we touched with our own?

**I can polish my beauty today by evincing
one kind act after another.**

NOVEMBER 2

*To behave with dignity is nothing less than
to allow others freely to be themselves.*

SOL CHANELES

Being either parents or employers makes setting limits on others' behavior second nature. We did it quite appropriately for many years. However, that's not our job anymore. Even when a spouse or a friend chooses to think or act in ways counter to our best judgment, it's not up to us to correct or criticize them. They are responsible for themselves.

Occasionally we experience inner conflict because our values are not shared by loved ones. No matter our age, we relish agreement among our friends, but this just isn't a perfect world. The perspective we have of any situation reflects our own personal history, and none of us share identical histories. Actually, that's quite fortunate. It makes the tapestries of our lives much more colorful.

There are benefits to growing old. We can dare to say what we really think. We can decline invitations or pursue myriad hobbies, answering to no one for a change. The same is true for our friends and family members.

**I will be proud of my behavior today,
and I'll let others be responsible for themselves.**

NOVEMBER 3

You can't imagine how it will come, but everything we need is here for us, and we have to learn to draw it to us.

JEAN WILL

One of the supreme gifts of growing old is learning to worry less. Only the luckiest among us escaped worrying about our children, our jobs, our spouses when we were younger. We just didn't understand that worry affected nothing except our attitudes and our potential for happiness. How fortunate that time hasn't run out for us. We can develop freedom from worry through a mere decision, made as often as necessary.

From ministers, favorite books, friends' counsel we were told that everything we really needed to fulfill our purpose in this life was available to us. What we had to learn to trust was that the doors to our fulfillment would open when we were ready to pass through them. And they did.

This is still the case. Anything that needs to be handled by us today will beckon. Believing that we are in the right place, right now, makes it so. There is no need for worry. All is well.

I am on God's course for my life.
I'll get what I need today.

NOVEMBER 4

We have to motivate ourselves.
We can't expect others to do it for us.

HELEN CASEY

For much of our lives, we had obligations of various kinds to motivate us. Jobs, children, yard work, and other household tasks, not to mention extracurricular activities, gave our lives meaning and balance. Now our responsibilities are limited. Few if any people are relying on us to provide sustenance of any kind. We probably always said we wanted more freedom and fewer responsibilities, but now that it's here, are we really glad?

Becoming motivated to do something that's not necessary to our survival is difficult. Acquiring the discipline needed to pursue activities that aren't required may even be considered an art. If we weren't interested in hobbies when we were younger, then we probably aren't familiar with how leisure time works. Fortunately, we can learn.

The first step is to daydream about something you always envied in someone else. Perhaps it was his or her command of particular information, or their agility on the tennis court, or joy at playing cards. The envy we had indicates the activity we might pursue, at least initially. We can change activities as often as necessary. We will find one that pleases us to the point of perpetual motivation. Patience pays off.

I have all the time I need to move in new directions now.
My satisfaction with living will grow
if I'm busy having fun today.

NOVEMBER 5

In this life of chaos there is no perfection.
I will struggle always with the hounds of ambition at my feet.

IDA BELLEGARDE

Being hounded by ambition isn't so bad, really, unless we are tired and want to slow down. If that's the case, we feel like we're not measuring up. In actuality, we have done enough already. We have earned this time of rest if that's our wish. And we can ignore "the hounds."

When we reach this age, we fall into many categories. Some of us want to be always busy, involved with others on a regular basis. Others of us want more solitude in our lives. Reflecting on our accomplishments and contemplating additional goals might invite our attention. Considering the restitution we may need to make to others is appropriate at this age, too. There is no right way to grow old. There are as many ways as there are living people.

Taking some time to consider how we honestly want to spend each day is one of the rewards of growing old. We no longer need to fulfill anyone else's expectations. We are free at last.

I am free to do whatever appeals to me today.
Staying quiet or accepting an invitation to
join others are options. It's my choice.

NOVEMBER 6

Underpromise and overperform.
That's my motto.

FRAN COYNE

Fran's motto may be a good one for him. It may feel comfortable to many of us; however, it's not an absolute principle that we all need to live by. Getting trapped by the need to overperform, to overachieve, implied low self-esteem for some. They (or we) may have thought just *being* wasn't ever enough. When that was our personal assessment, quite likely no amount of achievement gave us the security we sought.

Security has never actually come from who we are or what we did with our lives. While it's true that our work may have resulted in a good salary, it took more than money to make us feel secure. That mystified many of us. Perhaps it still does. We always knew someone who earned far less than ourselves who seemed at peace and worry free. Didn't we ever wonder how he or she did it? Are we beginning to get a glimmer of how peace is actually attained now?

One of the gifts of these later years is having the time to contemplate some of life's mysteries. Undoubtedly we all have many recollections of how disaster was averted, how plans went awry, how timely, in retrospect, our meeting of certain people seemed to be. Whatever our motto, there always was a guiding force in our life. All we had to do was show up.

If I worried all my life that I wasn't doing well enough,
it's time to "give it up." Today I'll pray to believe
that God was never displeased.

NOVEMBER 7

Those who are held down, they don't have a plan.
You got to have a plan.

CEDELL DAVIS

Having a plan for doing even the smallest task simplifies it. When we were younger, planning how we were going to build a table or secure a new job was done methodically. It's no different now that we're older. We still have to do the footwork if we want the results. Relying on the memory of past successful planning gives us the courage to pursue whatever dream beckons to us today.

Having dreams, whether they are large or small, gives us reason to get up in the morning. And that's the joy of being alive. Those who quietly wait for the end to come miss opportunities to teach others that life is as full and as rich as are our plans for each day.

We don't need a big or complicated plan for the day or week ahead. A simple list of the steps to take in finishing a painting, making a get-well note for a friend, or calling a relative we miss enlivens us. It's as simple as that.

> Having a plan for today is not complicated.
> I get up. I make a decision, and I move on it.
> Nothing ventured; nothing gained.

I don't see that we have a right to be on this earth unless we are putting something back—beyond our family.

LEE ERICSON

Not everyone would agree that we owe a debt to the universe. The more cynical among us might argue for just the reverse. Perhaps the best way to evaluate this is by looking at what makes us happy. Do we get good feelings out of offering something to those around us, or do we resent it? We won't all agree, and that's good. The universe needs balance. However, our individual behavior at any one point in time can tip the balance. Let's not forget that we have this influence, whether we acknowledge it or not.

What does it mean to put something back? The answer is as complicated or as simple as we choose to make it. Offering friendship to a lonely child might be a way. Volunteering at church or a neighborhood center would count. Helping a friend who is alone and lonely get through a holiday is giving back too. We don't have to donate money or adopt a homeless family. We simply have to be willing to care about others and then to express that love in myriad ways.

I can easily give something back today.
Just offering a smile will brighten someone's morning.

NOVEMBER 9

Making a big salary is not all there is to life.
It's the quality of your life that counts.

MONTY CRALLEY

The definition of quality is elusive. Few of us would describe it in exactly the same way, but we all understand it. Each of us has had to define quality for ourselves over the years, and this definition has possibly changed as we have changed. It's important that we grow and change in our understanding and appreciation of the elements in our lives. And it is those elements that finally make up the quality of our lives.

As we have aged, perhaps we consider the good memories of youth as contributing to the quality of our lives now. Or maybe it's having a good friend who still calls or visits regularly. Having a great collection of books to read and reread or discovering a hobby that fascinates us lends quality to our life. It can be anything, really. The only requirement is that it gives us joy and makes our lives worth living.

The quality of my life today will vary
with where I place my focus.

NOVEMBER 10

My advice to the younger generation is
"get off your duff and go to work."

TOM HARDING

A lot of old-timers express harsh judgment of the younger generation. True, some young people are lazy, expecting the good life to be offered up on a silver platter. But the same can be said of some old people. Not everybody is committed to working as hard as we might have been. Not everyone had a secure home environment and parents who offered support and guidance.

Our impulse may be to complain bitterly about the state of the world, about the crises in our cities, about the irresponsibility of the youth, but our complaints have no good effect. They solve nothing. They only add to the frustration and turmoil. What might we do instead?

There's really a plethora of opportunities just waiting for people like ourselves who have time to spare. Let's consider getting involved with the community around us if we're not happy with the way it's being run. Let's dare to take on an "assignment" as a mentor to a young person who seems to prefer sitting "on his duff." This will have an effect, a good one. Do we dare get involved?

I can be more than an armchair philosopher.
Today I can reach out and make a difference.

NOVEMBER 11

My motto is: don't retire from something,
retire to something.

PAT JEROME

Pat's distinction may initially seem to be a tiny one, but it's really quite a profound difference. It means we are consciously moving from one focus of our lives to another focus; retirement doesn't have to mean stopping all together.

Before retiring, we may have fantasized about the joys of having nothing to do. Being overwhelmed with work, family responsibilities, and social involvements made the prospect of time on our hands quite appealing. It loses its luster quickly, however. Boredom, even depression, becomes common. Then we long for the days when we couldn't keep up with all the activities that needed our attention.

We worked hard to reach this stage of life; surely we're meant to enjoy it. How we define enjoyment is important. But all of us come to understand that joy is found in interaction with others. Let's look to the present with gladness. It's waiting for us.

I am as eager to face this day as I've decided to be.
If I'm wavering at all, I'll take stock of my attitude.

NOVEMBER 12

My greatest feeling comes from knowing
I have had an effect on something.

JANICE CLARK

The reality is that everything we do or think or say has its effect. Of course it follows that our effect may not always be good. However, Janice is referring to the positive impact she has so often had. Her small Arkansas town owes a debt of gratitude many times over for her hard work. Can the rest of us feel so certain of such an effect?

It's valuable to take an occasional inventory of our many involvements with others. Are we proud of how we behaved in all instances? Did the circumstance get a positive boost from our input? We can be certain it got a boost of some kind! We can also be certain that whatever opportunity we had for acting was not coincidental. There are no coincidences. The invitation for us to act, thus affect situations and people, was quite intentional. Have we always acted in the best interests of others?

All of us have memories of when we didn't do the right thing. Fortunately, we can acknowledge our mistakes and try to repair the damage. Even more advantageous is the realization that we can be free of bad memories in the future if we show great concern about every action we take today.

My life has been quite purposeful.
Today's opportunities to act are no different.

NOVEMBER 13

It's been my experience that people need a variety of experiences when they retire.

FRAN COYNE

Retirement generally means forty to sixty "free" hours to fill per week. Most of us eagerly anticipated this phase of our lives, but are we as content as we'd imagined? No doubt some of us are. We've begun detailed projects on our home that we always dreamed of doing. Or we've gotten involved in a neighborhood community center, learned to play golf, taken a fun part-time job, or started an elaborate quilt. However, a few of us are feeling at loose ends. Why is that? More important, what can we do about it?

Being busy with jobs and family meant we didn't need to ponder what we really preferred doing with our lives. The kind of soul-searching we may find ourselves doing now isn't always pain-free. Some of us may grieve our many lost opportunities in the past. Or we'll struggle with the memory of our failings as parents or employees. Perhaps we'll even be haunted by some memories from our own childhood. This gift of time can wear many wrappings. But we can also cultivate our imagination and fantasize ourselves pursuing hobbies or projects we'd never dreamed were possible before. Nothing is stopping us from trying anything that beckons—nothing but our own fears. Let's take a risk today.

Eagerly arising to do something I really want to do today is a choice. Making this choice will determine my level of joy.

NOVEMBER 14

Although I knew all along I would have to retire
from smithing, it came as a shock to me;
I turned my energies to the garden.

MARIA REGNIER KRIMMEL

We all retire from something. Maybe it's a stressful career we give up or a sport that's too taxing. Perhaps we give up our involvement with a civic organization or we decide to hire help around the house. For everyone there is a time for letting some things go. Sometimes by choice, sometimes by necessity, the changes come. This means we have opportunities to put our energies elsewhere. That's worth celebrating even though we may resist it.

If we've been busy all our lives, we'll not doubt the value of hobbies or volunteer activities. Developing a whole new career, part-time perhaps, isn't out of the question. Actually, nothing is out of the question. Where there is a will, there is a way, so it's said.

Even though we may fight giving up a cherished job or a sport we were good at, the very fact that we felt passion for it means we can develop passion for something else. That's the important reason for doing anything, after all. Passion brings out the best in us. That's what any activity needs from us.

Whatever I choose to do today will be far more rewarding
if I grow excited about it. No one has my opportunity today.
Only my name is on it.

NOVEMBER 15

I love my little studio with a passion.
If they ever throw me out, the next day I'm going to die.

TOM HARDING

How passionate are we about the interests in our lives? We might think Tom is exaggerating, but there's something to be said for that level of passion. A person doesn't dread getting up in the morning if he feels that excited about his life. We can all understand, and perhaps even envy, the thrill that Tom feels about his "special space." We could all benefit from just such passion about either a space or an activity. When life has lost its excitement, its joy, the wait for death is long and painful.

Not everybody develops passion so easily. Where does it come from? Those who have it quite possibly have always had it. Perhaps they aren't the only ones to ask. So where do we go for an answer? Let's try exploring the idea with a friend today. He or she may feel real passion for something, or maybe he or she did in the past. It may help both of us rekindle it.

Passion is really nothing more than concentrated effort that nourishes the spirit. What it requires is the willingness to put other endeavors aside to pursue one that really interests you. The more involved one gets, the greater will be our nourishment. Our lives will change accordingly.

Did I look forward to getting up today?
If not, I can do something about that.

NOVEMBER 16

My main regret in life is that I didn't finish college.

JOANN REED

Most of us have regrets. Some are quite serious, in fact. Alcoholism or some other addiction may have interfered in our parenting, our work life, our relationships. Because of our own problems, we may have been emotionally or physically abusive toward people we loved. None of us was as good as we wish we'd been. Hopefully, we can accept who we were and forgive ourselves for our shortcomings. It helps if we have made our amends, our apologies to those whom we harmed.

If one's main regret is in a lesser category, like JoAnn's, consideration should be given to "picking up" where we left off. Many unfinished goals can still be completed. Most of them aren't really age dependent. If we're troubled by an unfinished one, let's explore how to move forward with it. If it no longer captures our attention, however, maybe it's time to develop a new goal, one that matches better who we have become over the years.

The main idea here is to have a goal, to pursue it, to achieve it, and to have fewer regrets over how we have lived our lives. We can't really erase the regrets of our past, but we can vow not to repeat them. Let's make some progress today.

Today I will focus on goals rather than regrets.

NOVEMBER 17

My accomplishments have been simple
and not very important, but I've had an interesting life.

ALICE MERRYMAN

Having an interesting life is what we've all wished for, no doubt. How we defined "interesting" varied, of course. Advanced education appealed to some. Experimenting in the garden or the kitchen or the workshop gained the attention of others. Traveling to foreign countries or writing one's memoirs lent an interesting element to many lives.

Did it matter if our lives seemed interesting to others? Not really, yet each of us benefited from sharing our interests with others because of what our pursuits had taught us. Sharing what we had learned with others always gave them greater meaning. It also helped us remember that we were a necessary link in the human community.

We are still an important link. Aging makes us doubt this perhaps, but look around. Friends still call, strangers still smile at us, children and grandchildren still remember our birthdays. We have added a richness to others' lives. Whether most people appreciated all the fruits of our interests isn't so important; that we continued to find meaning in our own lives is what offered a wonderful example. What better legacy could we leave?

Today I will reflect on the richness of
my experience and relationships.

NOVEMBER 18

All I've ever tried to do is live right.
Death will come and I'm not afraid.

EVA WINES

Most people our age aren't afraid of death, it seems. Is that because we have experienced the death of many loved ones? Or is it because we have come to believe that there must be something beyond this chaotic world? Some among us may have been blessed with a belief in an all-loving God throughout their lives, which relieved them of the burden of fear about their own demise. Whichever category we fall into, we can be grateful that death doesn't frighten us, that we accept it as the next phase of life, nothing more.

We may come into contact with people today who don't share our peacefulness about death. Perhaps they grew up in abusive homes and never "outgrew" the images of a punishing God. Let's consider our contact with others as an opportunity to help discover more peaceful perspectives. It's not our job to change them or try to control their outlook. But if we can point out a new direction by our example, we will have added to the peace of the world. There is really nothing else we can ever do that's more important than this.

Am I willing to do my part today
to foster peace in the lives of others?

NOVEMBER 19

We all have to serve as torch bearers sometime.
I'm glad when the younger senior citizens begin
to get involved with our program.

ALPHA ENGLISH

It makes little difference what kind of activity we're involved in. When there are others present, we hope they do their fair share of work. Although we know people who struggle against letting others make decisions, each of us knows that having responsibility for all details quickly tires us out.

Being glad that others are willing to get involved is a much better way to see any situation. We don't really want to be loners, even when the circumstances get complicated because of others' input. Too much solitude creates too many conversations with ourselves. Generally, we don't see all that clearly when we're isolated from others. It's no coincidence that we have been drawn into the company of others. Let's try assuming that means each of us needs to lead on occasion. Just as often, we need to follow, too.

Being a "torch bearer" is a universal assignment. Passing the torch on to others is just as important. Are we ready to step back and let others take over? Have we done enough yet? Each of us must answer this question. Are we listening?

I can stay fully involved or slow my pace today.
It's up to me.

NOVEMBER 20

I believe there has been a grand plan for my life;
so much has happened that I hadn't counted on.

LOUISE JEROME

What Louise believes might offer great comfort, particularly to a mind that is fraught with fear and uncertainty. But it's not all that important whether or not we believe that God has planned every detail of our lives. In fact, if we have had more than our share of turmoil, we might feel that God has been punishing us. Just coming to believe that we haven't walked through any experience alone is where the comfort lies. This may not be an idea we were taught as youngsters. We may not be convinced of it now. But deciding to suspend our disbelief, for a time, in order to discover the peace within this idea is worth it.

Recalling our past, any portion of it, will no doubt bring to mind outcomes to situations that took us by surprise. We so often thought we knew what was best for us and others. What folly! What relief, too. Trying to *play god* in others' lives is a heavy burden. We may still be caught in this maze, but getting free of it is possible. It may mean we have to change our perspective on the way life *really works*, the role God plays in our lives, but we can open our minds to new ideas. We're older, for sure, but minds can change at any age. Let's settle for an idea that eases our journey.

Today can be as restful as I make it.
What comes to me is right for me.

NOVEMBER 21

*I continue to count my blessings. I try never to forget
that there are many people far worse off than me.*

JAMES CASEY

No matter how grave one's condition, we can always look over
the fence and see someone who suffers more. It's really not appropriate to consider that as good luck; however, it gives us
pause to express some gratitude. It helps if we have cultivated a
spiritual program that guides our thinking. The fortunate
among us truly believe that we are never given more than we can
handle; regardless of our circumstances, we can always carry the
load if we seek the support of God.

Are you as peaceful with your set of beliefs as Jim is with his?
None of us has been spared difficult circumstances over the
years. We have all had losses that disturbed our security; we have
had dreams dashed; we have failed to attain goals that we'd set
our sights on. But life went on. Many good things did happen
for us and for our families. We understand with growing clarity
that life is a process of ebb and flow. As situations change, instead of fearing the unknown, perhaps we can rejoice in the constant movement forward. We are always moving forward.
Always.

**My life is as it should be today.
My attitude decides how I'll feel about it.**

NOVEMBER 22

I think everybody has to experience a certain amount of pain on the way to maturity.

RUTH CASEY

Our lives have been a series of lessons, many of them not particularly easy. It's generally the case that the ones we gained the most from were the hardest or the most tedious. Is pain always a requirement for growth? Hindsight may suggest that, but we need to realize that our willingness to grow or change, coupled with the faith that we were always in safe hands, could have made all of our transitions quite smooth. Nothing ever had to be as hard as some of us made it.

Attitude, along with faith, has always had a powerful impact on our perceptions of life. No two people have ever made identical observations of any situation. Needless to say, we all make a choice about how to interpret the varied circumstances in our life. So-called accidents of nature are seen as quite purposeful to some, while others are defeated by them. Physical ailments are accepted as opportunities for developing another dimension of one's life by those who prefer a positive outlook. Our freedom to interpret each experience as a lucky opportunity or as undeserved devastation has always existed and will never be taken from us. How have we managed that power so far?

Am I content with how my life has evolved?
Where it goes today is in my power.

NOVEMBER 23

I've been alone most of my life.
Even in a crowd, I'm alone.

MARIA REGNIER KRIMMEL

We have made our lives what they have become. Sure, we can point to the privileges or lack of them as contributors to how we developed. And the example set by parents or peers influenced us. But in the final analysis, we each have had the primary responsibility for how we evolved, for who we have become. If we're satisfied with the results, that's wonderful. If we're not so happy about the opportunities that have seemingly come our way, perhaps it's not too late to reinvent ourselves.

Some of us, like Maria, have preferred the solitary life. Depending on our occupation or the talent we honed, that might have fit us best. The only real consideration, then or now, was whether we were living the way we wanted to. If we felt content, we had chosen correctly. If peace eluded us then or now, we might want to reconsider what can be done differently.

It's not an awesome responsibility to accept complete charge of ourselves. It's always been that way, in reality. Many just didn't celebrate the assignment. Some tried to make others responsible for whatever happened. Unfortunately, the blame was often accepted. Let's make sure we know who is in charge now.

I will have the day I want to have today.

NOVEMBER 24

Friendship means more than money.
That's what I want to pass on to people.

VIOLET HENSLEY

When we were young, we seldom valued friendship the way we do now that we're old. We may have believed that if we had enough material "stuff," we'd fill the void within that hinted at our happiness. Only with the passing of the decades do we understand the folly of our thinking.

Most of our acquaintances have made the same mistake, so we're on equal footing. We're lucky for that. It means we can dispense with the materialism of our lives and focus, instead, on good conversation, lots of laughter, and the sharing of dreams about the future. When we change the focus of our lives in this way, we soon realize we have changed our entire lives.

Looking ahead to a time with less disposable income is not nearly so troublesome when we've grown in our appreciation of friendship. It costs us nothing, except our willingness to listen and love a little.

Money may have moved me in the past.
How grateful I am that the hug of a friend satisfies me more.

NOVEMBER 25

Right now I don't envision my future being very satisfying.

BUD SHERMAN

How does your future look? Do you dread getting up in the morning because you have nothing to look forward to? That's not uncommon, particularly early in our transition to the retired life. Fortunately there's a solution if that's your situation, and it's so simple. Decide to join a friend in an activity that captivates him or her. Even if you don't particularly like it at first, make a commitment to this friend and yourself to give it a few tries. Generally speaking, all we have to do is get outside of ourselves and we discover that life is still pretty fulfilling. Remaining stuck in our disinterest only escalates it.

A few among us may never get beyond the boredom, and that's our choice. In time it may turn to depression, and then it's even harder to get motivated about the future. It is a fact, however, that depression cannot overwhelm us forever, providing we want something different for ourselves. Have we made the right choice?

No one really wants to remain stuck in the darkness forever. If we have moved beyond it ourselves, let's take stock of all the people in our lives today. Is there someone close by who is suffering? We can recognize the signs. Maybe it's our turn to offer a helping hand. The gesture will be very satisfying, at least to us.

I can make this day satisfying by my actions.

NOVEMBER 26

I like people who are genuine.
You can perceive when people really are who they profess to be.

ALPHA ENGLISH

At least once in our lives we were guilty of projecting a false front. Maybe we were with someone we envied greatly and wanted to impress them or had to attend an event that frightened us a lot. Perhaps we were simply trying to win somebody's friendship and feared he or she would not like the real us. Going after a job we feared we weren't capable of may also have pushed us to project a self that wasn't the real thing. In any such instance, we expended far more energy with far less comfort than the situation called for. We didn't likely convince anybody anyway. We can all recognize a phony.

One of the quiet pleasures of old age is that we can more comfortably be who we really are. That doesn't mean we won't try to impress someone with our knowledge or willingness to be of service. Nor does it mean we won't seek new friends. We're simply willing to settle, more easily, with who we have become over a lifetime of experiences. Because we have grown to appreciate the differences in our friends, we're more at ease with our own differences. Perhaps it has felt like a long winding road getting to this place of comfort, but isn't it nice to have finally arrived?

I am, with no pretense, exactly who I need to be.
I can rejoice today.

NOVEMBER 27

My dad died young so I think I'm on borrowed time.
I count my blessings.

JIM BURNS

Many worry, particularly as we age, how we will complete our necessary purpose. If we haven't been the purveyors of brilliant research or solved a problem of major proportions, we doubt our significance to the lives of others. At times like these, it's good to remember the tiny acts of kindness others have done for us and how much they meant. That's our indication that someone else mattered in our lives. We have offered just such help many times too and the circle is completed.

It's never how grand our offerings to others are or how specific. What counts is that we were present in the experience, whatever it was, and offered others hope and love. Our lives are less mysterious, more intentional, when perceived this way.

I'm still present today, which means the blessings I deserve and the ones I offer to others are still unfolding.

NOVEMBER 28

My vision for the coming years is to get as old as I can.

MARIE BURNS

Marie's statement gives us reason to chuckle, perhaps, but it's also very thought-provoking and wise. To get as old as we can doesn't happen without some effort. It takes a commitment to fostering good health, which means a further commitment to a nutritious diet, adequate exercise, and the release of our worries about other people and situations we can't control. This last requirement is thought by some as the most important of all. Medical evidence suggests that stress held internally does us grave bodily harm. Circumstances may prevent us from getting all the exercise we need, and our diets may occasionally be under the control of others who care less about nutrition than we do, but no one keeps us worried about uncontrollable situations except ourselves.

If it has been our habit to worry, can we change that now? Or is it too late anyway? Have we already cast the die for whatever health challenges we may experience? There's really no simple answer to these questions. But there are tools for stopping worry. The most accessible one is to replace the troubling thought with one of peace or God or a happy memory. Then keep replacing the worry every time it surfaces. We don't have to be perfect at it, only vigilant. We can be certain that getting free of worry won't initiate poor health, and that's quite worth the effort.

**I can add to my longevity today by how I eat and what I think.
That's rather exciting, isn't it?**

NOVEMBER 29

Life is not over until you breathe your last breath.

DON KENNETT

Knowing that we're *not done yet* gives most people a sense of relief. We still have time to complete a picture or a book or have closure with a friend. One woman told me how glad she was to wake up each day. She knew it meant she still had work to do, that God wasn't finished with her yet. God must not be finished with us either. Here we are, reading these words. Let's share some of our wisdom with someone else today. What we do between now and the last breath is what counts, and our time has not run out. Our purpose has not been completed.

I have so much to offer others if I remember to think of them first. Today is my opportunity to demonstrate this.

NOVEMBER 30

I usually just lived one day at a time.
I never had a sense of where I was going.

RUTH CASEY

Did any of us really know where we were going? We probably spent many hours, days, weeks even, making detailed plans for the people around us. These plans didn't usually suit others so they didn't often materialize. God, however, always had a plan in store for each of us, although, sometimes we were the last to know it.

Is there any reason to think that anything has changed? Not really. We're still *here,* so that means God is still in charge of whatever should transpire today. Our part is to be willing to listen to God's direction and to follow it. We don't have to know where our steps are leading us. Just like Ruth, we can simply move forward, trusting that we will end up where we need to be.

We may have complicated our lives for too many years. That's not unusual. Busy people tend to do that. What we needed to do, where we needed to go, was always under the direction of God. It still is. Let's rejoice that our part is doable.

Living one day at a time works best.
I'll give up thoughts of all else today.

DECEMBER

DECEMBER 1

I retired at sixty eight not because I had to, but because I didn't want to be too old to have fun in retirement.

CATHERINE PAUL

Looking forward to this stage of one's life makes it more exciting, doesn't it? We have all known men and women who dreaded "being turned out to pasture." Maybe that was because they didn't know how to relax and do something only for the sheer joy of it. The work ethic was strong for most of us. We grew up in times where hard work was not only expected, but in most instances, demanded. To not be productive was guilt-inducing. How many of us feel guilty these days?

Catherine has chosen to focus on fun rather than productivity. There are no rules for retirement. If one prefers to keep working at something, whether making a job of a hobby or finding part-time work, it's okay. The point is that we need to make retirement something satisfying. We are all going to experience it, after all, so we'd benefit most if we found joy in it.

If having too much freedom is difficult, if you need more focus, or if specific expectations from others makes you more comfortable, then seek to plan your days to meet those needs. Making retirement fun, however one defines fun, is the challenge now. Let's meet the challenge!

**Am I looking forward to this day?
Do I need to make some changes in my plans?**

DECEMBER 2

I know a woman who chose going back to work over divorce after she and her husband retired.

JOANN REED

What we experience in retirement often doesn't measure up to our expectations. Maybe we planned wonderful trips, lots of long-awaited-for uninterrupted time with a spouse, or the pursuit of a joint hobby. When we got our dream, we realized that too much togetherness made us irritable. Many are baffled by this occurrence. They doubt their ability to love one another. In extreme cases, they begin to doubt whether they ever loved each other. If you are in a situation similar to this, relax. Love isn't measured by the number of hours we can tolerate one another.

There are many options in between the extremes of total togetherness and the separation that occurs if one returns to work, or worse, leaves a marriage. That's not to say one shouldn't opt for a job if that appeals to you. But no one should have to seek work as a means of escaping a spouse. It's more likely that we need to honestly communicate how we're feeling at not having enough hours to one's self. Being alone sometimes or spending the day in the company of others doesn't mean we love a spouse less. If this is difficult to believe, perhaps we need to seek the counsel of a professional to see us through this transition. We deserve happiness. Let's make sure we find it.

**Today I will do what I must
to be happy in my relationships.**

DECEMBER 3

The days never feel boring to me. I get up, have breakfast,
put on my makeup every morning of the world.
One morning recently I didn't put it on and I felt just lost.

THELMA ELLIOTT

The things that give meaning to our lives can be very small and
not particularly important to someone else. That matters little,
really. What's more important is that each of us discovers how to
get joyfully involved in the twenty-four hours that lie before us.
Having a reason, any reason, to get out of bed is the first step.
The day then begins to take its own shape.

Being thankful that we woke up another time gives some of
us a jump-start in the morning. Looking forward to a morning
walk or meditation, perhaps reading a few spiritual passages or
checking in with God in prayer, sets the tone for the remainder
of the day. Having a routine has grown in importance, no doubt.
Routines give structure to our lives. Some of us need this more
than others. All of us seek to feel secure; however we find it is
quite all right. That's one of the freedoms we've earned by living
to old age.

If we aren't looking forward to the day ahead or beyond, let's
consider the need to expand our friendships, to explore ideas
with family members or our doctor. Delving in to a new hobby
can excite the soul. Let's take a good look at our lives and change
whatever needs changing.

I need not feel lost today, regardless of my circumstances.
If I do, I'll ask others to help me find a solution.

DECEMBER 4

When I started smithing, it was like lightning hit me.
I had to do it.

MARIA REGNIER KRIMMEL

Maria's passion for her art was compelling. To experience that feeling and not follow through would have been a slow death for her. That level of passion for any activity is enviable, in most respects. But like any element in one's life, it can get out of balance. Passion can be equated with enthusiasm. We want it, we need it, but we have to occasionally step back and take stock of all dimensions of our lives. Are we ignoring areas that deserve more attention?

Maybe this isn't a real concern for us any longer. Most of us have ended our primary careers, whether as professionals or as homemakers for the family. We have more time now, so we needn't worry so much about the balance in our lives. Too much attention to any single area, whether a job or a hobby, left too little time for the many other activities that also deserved some attention when we were busier. Too narrow of a focus worked against us.

One of the benefits of growing old is that we have fewer things to focus on. We can go overboard, in fact, and no one is seriously harmed. Passion for an activity is something we all deserve to feel if we have thus far escaped it. Aren't we lucky that we still have this to look forward to?

Today awaits me. Enthusiasm is mine to manufacture.
Do I want it?

DECEMBER 5

I heard a story once about an old man who washed his old boat every day. When asked why, he said because he got joy out of it. I like that story. That's why I do what I do, too.

ALICE MERRYMAN

Experiencing joy from what we do is the best reward of all, isn't it? We might appreciate the monetary results, if there are some, and we are pleasantly touched by compliments from others. But the experience of getting outside of ourselves, getting fully absorbed by whatever the activity is, and feeling joyfully one with it, is the best reason for pursuing any activity. There is some activity that will do that for each of us. Have you found yours yet?

Alice was too busy working on the farm with her husband and raising their children to search for outside interests when she was younger. But as the changes began, changes like those that are inevitable for all of us, she promptly saw that she needed to find meaningful interests. Painting, caning chairs, and making dolls from corn shucks filled her days. She didn't know that she'd be good at any of these things, that she'd gain notoriety, but indeed she did. Her work is in the Smithsonian, she met presidents, she was on the *Today Show*. But what has meant the most to her is knowing real joy. She feels that every day, every time she picks up a paint brush or a corn shuck. What an example she is for us and all who know her.

This day will make me joyful if I do what brings me joy. Do I know what that is?

DECEMBER 6

If worrying had made me better at motherhood and
everything else, I'd have been more successful.

JOANN REED

We can all relate to JoAnn's comment, no doubt. Worrying was—or worse yet, still is—second nature to many of us. Whether it was over our children, financial struggles, or our spouses' ill health, we seldom simply trusted that the right outcome would occur. Hindsight enlightened us, but it came too late, of course.

Are we still worrying too much? It may have become such an ingrained habit that we're no longer even aware of it. Perhaps it wouldn't really matter except for the fact that worry has a negative impact on our health. It can trigger multiple minor aches and pains. But far worse, some even believe it can cause cancer and heart disease because of the stress it places on our body's organs.

There certainly isn't any legitimate payoff for worrying. Some may think it makes them more cautious in all their dealings or more concerned about the important people in their lives, but in reality, worry generally just clouds our minds and prevents us from seeing situations as they really are. Let's take a breather from worry. God has everything under control.

I can spend this day doing whatever I want.
Surely worry doesn't honestly appeal to me. Today I will
remember that worrying never empowers solutions.

DECEMBER 7

I had an easy life growing up.
I was not serious, and I'm trying to make up for it now.

TOM HARDING

How we define an easy life may differ because everything is relative. Some of us were raised in prosperous homes, which might have meant we weren't required to seek work or do chores around the house. But that kind of privilege didn't guarantee an easy life. Wealth doesn't eliminate the possibility for abuse of many forms.

To some, the easy life simply means there was little stress, few problems to contend with. Parents were supportive; school work came easy; friends really cared about us. Maybe we feel lucky if that's how our lives evolved, or maybe we are like Tom and feel now that we need to make up for our lives of privilege. Let's seek the counsel of others if that's the case. It's okay to have had the easy route. That doesn't mean we have to pay for it now.

The important element is that we spend the present however we really want to. If we want to be more serious, that's acceptable. If we want to be lazy, that's okay too. If we want to have a positive impact on someone else's life, perhaps someone who had a harder life than we experienced, that's admirable, but not necessary. No one is grading us.

Today I'm free.
The past isn't of concern unless I make it so.

DECEMBER 8

The hardest part of aging is my lack of energy.
Fortunately, my mind doesn't tire as quickly as my body.

HELEN CASEY

It's simply a fact of aging that we have less stamina. But that's not disastrous unless we make it so. Some, in fact, interpret it as fortunate because it encourages a fresh approach to how we spend our leisure time. The book club we always wanted to join at the library doesn't require physical energy. Nor does composing our memoirs for our grandchildren. Making a small booklet of favorite family recipes is a wonderful way to spend some time. Our children's children will treasure it.

Did a particular figure in history fascinate you? What better way to spend some time than becoming an expert on his or her life? Sharing a particular skill or talent with anyone else takes little energy. And the exchange of information energizes us.

We don't have to be physically active to feel alive and involved. Having an active mind takes nothing more than the willingness to keep it open to new ideas.

I am not just my body. In fact, it's not the part of me
that ever really *moves me* to tackle new challenges.

DECEMBER 9

*I think God expects us to have difficulties in order for us
to gain in courage and in faith and in determination.*

JEAN WILL

It has been true throughout our lives that we grew the most
when we successfully faced the difficult situations that are the
norm for the human family. It's not that God wants us to
stumble, but it is good for us to grow and change, to expand our
understanding of life, and to develop a fresh attitude toward
even ordinary events.

Maybe we lost a job, were passed over for a promotion or
two, experienced the sadness of a child choosing a dangerous
pathway. In every circumstance, the God of our understanding
was and always will be available to give us strength, even hope
that all *is* well. In spite of appearances, all is well.

Sometimes we can only be convinced to look to a spiritual
source for comfort when we are overwhelmed by feelings of inadequacy. It is never too late to learn that we'll never feel adequate in every situation if we take God as our partner daily.

**What I want now, what I always wanted, in fact, is peace and
security. It's available to me if I rely on the help of God.**

DECEMBER 10

Perfection is neither possible nor necessary.

MARIA REGNIER KRIMMEL

Not everybody would agree with the whole of Maria's statement. Teachers and parents, bosses and spouses too often demanded perfection, or so we thought. The frequency with which we failed to measure up left us feeling inadequate. Is it too late now to change our thoughts on perfection? Certainly not, but if we sense resistance to this idea, it might help to ask our friends what their views are. If they seem more willing to accept the less-than-perfect, perhaps we can follow their examples and modulate our overly critical voice.

The demand for perfection makes virtually every aspect of one's life daunting. Wanting to please ourselves as well as others is admirable, but if we think no pleasure is possible unless nary an error has been made, we significantly diminish our chances for happiness. Even a cursory glance back at our past will be enlightening. Did we experience real joy in our lives? Are our memories pleasant, or do we feel shame about our imagined failures?

We must know someone who expresses mostly contentment with his or her life. We no doubt know another who reflects frequent sadness. Let's explore their differences. Who are we most like? Should we reconsider how we'll experience the tomorrows we have left?

Doing the best I'm able to do is good enough.
I will embrace this idea today.

DECEMBER 11

If I hadn't had macular degeneration, I'd never
have painted; I'd never have written a book.
You can always turn a negative into a positive.

MONTY CRALLEY

The population is divided into two groups: those who whine over everything, and those who smile and seek the good. It's obvious which group Monty is in. With exceedingly limited vision, forced to use a large magnifying glass to even see what he is painting, he stands at the easel nearly every day. His joy comes from *the doing.*

Is Monty gifted in ways different from ourselves? It's not likely. He has made a decision, a simple one in fact, to spend his time creating that which brings joy to him. Even though many might think one needs excellent vision to paint or write, Monty proves otherwise. All he really needs is desire. That's all we need, too. We don't need to write books or paint, but we do need to find an activity that stirs some passion within.

None of us got to old age without a few creaks and ailments. That's just the way it is. But none of them, no matter how debilitating, can keep us from finding something we can get excited about. It's an attitude problem if we're not in agreement with this idea. We can't change our condition, perhaps, but we can change our attitude. Maybe that's the best thing to get excited about right now.

I am my own worst enemy if I always have
an excuse for not doing something.
Today will be different.

DECEMBER 12

No matter what your problem is, if you look around,
you'll always find someone who is worse off.

VIOLET HENSLEY

It isn't helpful to compare our lives to others. When we begin feeling sorry for ourselves, we can gather some gratitude and gain a clearer perspective on life by noticing that we're surrounded by people who also have less than perfect lives. That's the human condition, after all.

There is an opportunity here. Taking notice of someone else's struggle gives us an avenue for action. Helping to ease the path of another man or woman eases our own, too. We may not understand how this works. In fact, that doesn't even matter. We can trust that this is so and the frequency with which we practice "our opportunity" lightens our own steps along the pathway of life.

Getting old doesn't mean getting dull or bored or depressed or mean spirited. It can mean all of those things, however, if we don't stay engaged with the human community that is present for us to take notice of.

Today awaits my involvement.
Helping another person can enhance my day.

DECEMBER 13

Retiring before you have something to do is a big mistake.
I made it!

BUD SHERMAN

Many people reading this book may have made a similar mistake. We didn't always know we'd be retiring when we did. Too frequently, companies let older employees go before they have gotten prepared for the inevitable. Retirement is a difficult adjustment even when someone is prepared. But when it comes suddenly, as it has for some of us, we're completely thrown off balance.

We can't change what has happened, though. No matter how wrong it may seem, the transition has occurred. However we got to this stage of our lives isn't even relevant now. It's what we do from this point on that counts. We might need a major shift in our perception to move forward; fortunately, that's not really as difficult to accomplish as it sounds. Mainly, we need to make a decision to give up our old attitudes and then be willing to look again at our situations, seeking to see only the opportunities that await us now.

If we're accustomed to feeling negative about our lives, we'll have to work a bit harder to cultivate our willingness to look at them again. It's not an accident that life has unfolded in this way. And our work is not done. Some among us have come to realize that their most important contributions have only just begun. Might the same be true for us?

Am I ready for involvement today?
Do I need an adjustment in my attitude?

DECEMBER 14

*To people who think they are going to retire to golf or fish,
I say, "Bull." What are they going to do in the meantime?*

TOM HARDING

Retirement takes on many hues, as many as there are people engaged in it. It's possible that some individuals can be content in the pursuit of golf on a daily basis, even though Tom wasn't so inclined. Not everybody has the need to feel productive until they die. Those who don't might consider Tom's way of looking at retirement as foolish, in fact. They figure they have worked long enough.

There is no right or wrong perspective on how retirement should look. It varies with the individual. One's personality defines it. So do the many relationships current in one's life. Whether one had hobbies in the past or was involved in extracurricular activities may influence the choices one makes in this stage of life.

There is no single, right way to experience retirement. The best we can hope for is that we find joy in it, that we are able to spread a little joy around in the lives of others, that we can grow in our appreciation of the role God has played in our lives. Regardless of whether we choose golf or painting, we can know peace.

**My goal today is to feel peace.
The activity is simply a channel.**

DECEMBER 15

I kind of floated through life.
I never really planned ahead. I never had a role model.

SANDY WARMAN

If we haven't lived up to the expectations we assume others had of us, we may comfortably point to our lack of goals. It might help us more, however, to explore and recount all the past experiences that brought pleasure to ourselves or others. It's far too easy to express disappointment in ourselves. We did the best we could with the information we had.

If it seems we floated through life aimlessly, let's consider that that's exactly the experience we were meant to have. We can't possibly know what others may have learned from observing us. And we aren't here, even today, for just ourselves. We're part of everyone's learning curve. Role models are facts of life. Are some really better than others? We can't know that. One's destiny determines which role models surface. We got what we needed. We still do.

I have done okay. No matter what my life represents,
it has been purposeful.

DECEMBER 16

After years of being in business together, my husband and I have had to learn to stay out of each other's way now.

JOANN REED

It's fortunate if couples can communicate their feelings; however, many men and women get resentful or sullen instead. Are you letting undiscussed issues hinder your retirement years?

Honest, open, and occasionally risky communication with one's spouse is important. Nonetheless, some couples decide to forego the communication, opting to live separate lives. If that satisfies both parties, so be it. But there are other options. One is to verbally express the desire for intimate discussions. They might not happen instantly, but they won't happen if neither partner makes the first move. Writing a letter to one's spouse, sharing hopes and dreams about this matter, is an option, too. Getting a counselor involved is another idea. Going to whatever lengths are necessary, if a different kind of relationship is desired, is worth it.

Knowing the kind of relationship I want with my spouse is the first step to getting it today.

DECEMBER 17

*In a small town, you can end up being
everybody's confessor.*

PAT JEROME

Some people seem to attract "confessions." Being willing to listen is the first prerequisite. Showing compassion for someone's problems is another. There's nothing inherently wrong with this, but it can be stressful if too many people tell us their troubles. Oftentimes, all a person needs is a friendly soul to bounce some opinions or feelings off. Keeping our involvement "clean," not getting involved in the solutions sought, is generally safe. But vigilance is always necessary.

Establishing our boundaries with others is important when we are in retirement. Simply having more time to ourselves doesn't mean we should squander it away, colluding with the many who seek our attention. There is a fine line between caring about the concerns of others and letting those concerns become our own. Unfortunately, many who come to us want more than a listener.

Being needed is important to most of us. Feeling useful is high on our list of wants. But let's be slow to react to the requests from others to do more than hear their concerns. There are many ways to feel useful. Let's consciously determine which way it will be.

**I'll not have to listen to everyone today.
I'm in charge of where I place my attention.**

DECEMBER 18

I find people rather resent having to give credit to anybody but themselves.

JANICE CLARK

Every one of us is favorably affected by a compliment from a peer. Strangers' compliments count, too. Whether we need acknowledgment or not isn't the point. It's simply nice to have our efforts appreciated. Since we feel this way, let's not forget that others share this quality. Do we reciprocate when the opportunity arises?

What is it about a compliment that matters so much? Obviously, it means someone has noticed us. Not only has our effort been seen, but it has been considered of value. This helps us remember that we, too, are of value. It's not unusual to ponder one's value and purpose. Perhaps as we age, we spend even more time in contemplation about the meaning of our lives.

If we fail to believe that every life is filled with purpose, there is no better time than the present to correct that perception. We have had a mission. We may have missed the cues for right action on occasion, but another opportunity has always and will always present itself. Whether we get the credit we may deserve for fulfilling a particular aspect of our mission doesn't mean it has gone unnoticed. And patting ourselves on the back may be the reminder we need to pat someone else on the back, too.

I'll look for an action by another to compliment today.

DECEMBER 19

People who think too much about themselves
miss many wonderful opportunities to help others.

ALPHA ENGLISH

Self-absorption is not an unusual trait. In fact, it's likely that we have to fight against it daily. That's due to the strength of our egos. They want our undivided attention and they insist on making all our decisions. Putting others' needs first is never our egos' inclination. We are more than our egos, however, and discovering this "other, higher self" has perhaps been the most important lesson in our lives.

Opening up to our higher selves makes it possible to acknowledge the others in our life. Listening to our higher selves will change who we can become. We have all experienced this transformation many times throughout our lives. What we realize is that no matter how many times we have listened, we don't listen all that naturally, even yet. The ego's demands diminish little over time. Vigilance regarding which voice we listen to is our assignment. Self-absorption doesn't reward us. Being available to others makes us rich beyond our wildest dreams.

My prosperity lies in my offerings of help to others today.

DECEMBER 20

Right now I'm content with my freedom,
but if I get bored, I have a list of things I'd like to pursue.
Writing is at the top of the list.

JOANN REED

It's not so important what we do but that we have a plan. Retirement can give us too much extra time if we have no dreams. JoAnn sets a good example. She has begun writing children's stories with the promise of publication. She is filled with joy, and that's the best reason for doing something. Whether she publishes or not isn't nearly as important in the long run. Being filled with enthusiasm about one's life is what counts.

Are you feeling enthusiastic? Hopefully you can answer in the affirmative, but it's not the end of the world if you're feeling sluggish and without direction. The first step to feeling better is to seek the counsel of friends who appear to be having fun. Find out what's different in their expectations about the future. Do they have an idea about what they want to do each day before going to bed? Have they sought the help of their *inner guide* while preparing their list? Have they developed a spiritual perspective that we perhaps lack? Many things may well be different in how we approach life. But if we like what we see happening for them, let's consider imitation.

If I'm truly content today, all is well. If I'm wavering a bit,
I'll willingly talk over my dreams with someone else.

DECEMBER 21

The working of someone's mind is what
most fascinates me in life.

MARIA REGNIER KRIMMEL

Having an interest in how others think has the potential of making every encounter intriguing. We can speculate about people's up-bringings, about their political or spiritual viewpoints. We can appreciate their education and their openness to differing opinions, or feel dismayed at their rigidity. There's little that's more important in one's life than the attention we are willing to give others. We may not have placed much value on our many personal encounters, but they were not without purpose in our lives. Being able to appreciate them now offers us a worthy gift.

Most of us have experienced some distinct disappointments in our lives. Jobs weren't as fulfilling as we'd expected. Children disappointed us, perhaps. Marriages were filled with strife. For many, few dreams ever materialized. We can lament this collection of memories for the rest of our lives, or we can opt to make whatever time we have left more meaningful. The easiest way to do this is to focus more intently on the individual conversations that engage us today. They are not simply coincidence. They contain the messages for the better lives that we desire. Listen up!

Unless I put myself in the path of other people,
I'll not get "the word" today. Do I really want it?

DECEMBER 22

My philosophy has always been that
when things didn't work out as I planned,
I knew I'd done my best.

JAMES CASEY

Our best is all we can ever do. We have memories of times we didn't do our best, but they shouldn't overshadow our successes. We aren't always at peak performance, and that's okay. We still may be doing our best under difficult circumstances. What does doing our best really mean? Perhaps we have a distorted definition, and that's why we frequently feel like failures.

Doing our best involves the following factors:
- giving our genuine attention to the task
- getting input from others on how to do the job
- asking God for insight
- following through on what we agreed to do
- managing our expectations of how well a project turns out

Plans often go awry. That's how life works. We know this well. But this doesn't make it necessarily any easier to accept when conditions are beyond our control. Let's settle for effort. That we can always offer up.

My effort today is what really counts.
I do have control over that.

DECEMBER 23

Getting a kind note from a student I had fifty or more years ago is one of the unexpected pleasures of my life.

ALPHA ENGLISH

Alpha certainly made her mark in the world. The love she exudes at eighty five is reminiscent of the love she undoubtedly showered on students throughout her career. No one can encounter her without feeling her warmth. Each of us sends out signals to others about who we really are, just as was true for Alpha. Are we content with the messages we're conveying? What kind of feedback are we getting?

We have been educating others about who we are our entire lives. The kinds of friends we made, the number of friends we kept, the people who seek to be with us even now are the indicators that reveal the kind of mark we made on the world. Perhaps the good news is that we're not done yet. If we'd like another chance at making our mark, we can begin immediately. Our first opportunity arises when another person has approached us. Let's follow Alpha's example and reap the rewards.

Tomorrow's pleasures likely will result from today's efforts. Am I ready to put my best self forward?

DECEMBER 24

Pat and I were friends first,
before we were anything else to each other.
We're still good friends and that's important to me.

LOUISE JEROME

Being friends with one's life companion is extremely advantageous. Unfortunately, we didn't all get to enjoy that blessing. Many reasons prevent a couple from having the perfect marriage; however, most of us worked to make the best of our situations. And that was good practice for us. Our many years of living have offered us many imperfect situations that we had to survive, and each success made the next hurdle more manageable.

One of the real treats of this latter stage of life is that we have hours and hours of helpful hindsight a mere thought away. Most of us will find great joy in recalling the memories of when we put forth some extra effort to make a circumstance better. Maybe it's our nature to enjoy doing battle with a challenge of any kind and coming out enriched, undaunted by it. Whatever might have been true for our relationships in the past need no longer define how they are today. That makes us fortunate people.

I will work on making all my relationships
into real friendships today.

DECEMBER 25

Maybe the best thing I did for my children
was be there every day. I was always there.

RUTH CASEY

It's good to consider what we gave to the people in our lives. Even though Ruth passes over her daily presence with her children pretty lightly, it was of great value to them. The consistency and security that comes from being able to count on someone every day should not be underestimated.

Many of us grew up in homes where parents were often absent. Work, ill health, irresponsibility, perhaps a disease such as alcoholism hindered their ability to be present when they should have been. We might still suffer from the repercussions of their problems. What can we do if that's the case? One thing we might consider is coming to believe that whatever our particular circumstances were, they were exactly the "education" we needed for the kind of work we were destined to do here. That attitude takes the sting away if we're still smarting over our upbringings.

Maybe we doubt that we did the best we could in many areas of our lives. In fact, perhaps we could have been more caring or more interested. But we need not feel ashamed about the past. We still have the present to feel good about. Let's make sure the list of regrets grows no longer today.

I will live the best life I can today.
Making that decision feels really good.

DECEMBER 26

I've always believed that if you couldn't be happy in your own life, you'd not find happiness with anyone else.

MONTY CRALLEY

Looking to others for our happiness is such a natural, though unhealthy outlook. If at our age we're still struggling with this, it's likely that we think we'll never change. And the older we are, the harder some things may be to change. For instance, our routines—when we go to bed and when we arise, how we get dressed, the way we prepare for the day, the style of clothes we prefer, and the foods we like—may all be hard to give up. Habits can be broken, however. It's rather fun to test this idea on occasion, too. It's healthy to get out of the rut of sameness.

Realistically, the habit of letting another person decide our happiness may be more difficult to give up than giving up unhealthy eating habits, particularly if we have let a spouse or a friend have that kind of control over us for many years. But it's important to make the effort.

We experienced the loss of happiness many times over the years. How many times was it because of someone else's action? Let's be in charge of ourselves, finally. It's never too late.

**My level of happiness is up to me today.
I'll remember this when someone irritates me.**

DECEMBER 27

A quote I relate to is: "The well of providence is deep,
but the bucket we bring to it is small." My buckets,
though small, have always been satisfying to me.

JIM BURNS

A life well-lived is all any of us hope for. How elaborately we define "well-lived" is the key idea. Not much is asked of us, really. We don't have to be rocket scientists or heads of corporations. We need not give birth to the future president or be an Olympic athlete or write a best-seller. The well of providence requests merely that we "carry our load," however much that seems to be at any moment. And how can we be certain of what that is? By quieting our minds so we can hear what the next best thing to do is. It will always present itself.

We may have felt consternation over whether we have lived meaningful enough lives, or contributed something of enough significance to society. The very fact that we feel concerned would suggest that we have contributed a lot. Let's decide to live out our remaining years with enthusiasm and willingness to continue doing our best. If we continue to lower our buckets into the well of all knowledge, we'll move along appropriately. What could be better?

> What I do today is up to me.
> How I feel at the end of it is also up to me.

DECEMBER 28

I'm at peace with God,
so I'm ready "to go" anytime.

TOM HARDING

Many of us feel at peace with God and yet may not be looking forward to death. That's not a requirement. Liking our current experience is really far more sensible since that's the one we're living right now. Staying in the present and getting the most from it is really what God hopes for us anyway. The time will come, when the time is right, to move into the next stage.

Actually, not everybody is at peace with God, and that may be something we want to address. What does it mean, for starters? In general, if we're at peace, it means that we don't fear retribution for our past transgressions. We all made mistakes. We'll make even more of them before we're through; however, we are willing to acknowledge them and make our amends. But even more, we are willing to seek God's guidance frequently, allowing us to choose behavior that won't require an amend.

Just seeking to know God better will nurture the peace we long for and deserve. It will make the present much more fulfilling, and it will guarantee a peaceful journey *onward*.

Being at peace with God may take some work today.
I'll begin with prayer.

DECEMBER 29

I think my death will be a terrific and beautiful thing.

JAMES CASEY

What a marvelous outlook Jim had. And as a matter of fact, his death was beautiful. His eight children, all grown, and his wife were gathered around his bed reciting the rosary as he took his last breath. He wouldn't have asked for more, even if he could have. But the real beauty here is the attitude that Jim had cultivated his whole life, which he modeled until death. Some people just seek "the silver lining." Jim set a wonderful example of that. What do the rest of us look for?

No matter what our current age, we can change the way we look at the circumstances surrounding us if our perspective on them keeps us unhappy. Unhappiness is a choice. We can seek to be happy even when our lives are filled with chaos, even when our financial needs are great, even when our health is deteriorating, even when we feel totally alone. No negative thought has to consume our minds. It does so only with our consent. Do we really have to hang on to thoughts that hurt us so?

Jim wasn't given a tool that was denied to the rest of us. Whatever any one of us can do, we can all do. Let's remember this the next time we begin to moan about our lives.

**I will take stock of my perception today.
What might I see for a change?**

DECEMBER 30

I will live on if I produce anything of value.

IDA BELLEGARDE

Defining what value means is our stumbling block. Objectivity isn't easy. It's so very human of us to either overvalue or undervalue every action in our lives. The reports we wrote, are they of value? What about the songs we performed or the photographs we took? Do they count as valuable? Will we live on through them?

It may be wiser to simply live each day as lovingly as possible and know that we are honoring others as valuable to us in the process. That acknowledgment of them will live on well after us. And that's our goal, isn't it?

We complicate our lives by trying to measure up to someone else's standards or expectations. It's not wrong to want acclaim or respect, but if we're not treating all others well, in every aspect of our lives, then we're not living valued lives. Living on in the minds of others is not that difficult. Having an honored place in their minds is attainable, too.

I can give something of value today by my actions.
Being remembered as good is in my power.

DECEMBER 31

The older I am, the more I realize there is nothing to fear.
Everything is simply part of the journey.

FRAN COYNE

Being spiritually at peace isn't automatic. Perhaps we have worked on our relationships with a god of our understanding for many years. Our personal relationship with a Greater Power needs our commitment and constant cultivation. We're fortunate, indeed, if we have already acquired a peaceful understanding of the role God plays in our lives. If that hasn't happened yet, how fortunate that we have the time now to devote to doing the footwork.

Fear has many definitions; it wears many garments. But the bottom line for most of us is that we lack faith that we have a Companion in our life struggles. It's not easy to believe in something we can't see, and most of us have nothing more than anecdotal evidence that we were being watched over during dangerous moments in our lives. Fortunately, it's never too late to make the decision to believe that all is well, and coming to accept that every experience has been absolutely right for our journeys gives such comfort. We all had circumstances we hated; we all have memories that make us ashamed or full of grief. It is possible to let go of the wish that these experiences had been different; we can accept them as necessary to who we are now. Taking this new perspective can offer us a freedom we'd not have expected.

Today offers me only what I'm supposed to experience.
I am ready.

INDEX